湖南师范大学外国语言文学学科

学学半丛书

◎本书为国家社科基金一般项目"基于虚拟仿真现实技术的口译练习语料库建设（16BYY022）"的成果之一。

◎本书获得湖南师范大学世界一流建设学科——外国语言文学学科出版基金资助。

U0729154

新技术视域下的远程口译研究

蒋莉华 著

湖南师范大学出版社

·长沙·

图书在版编目（CIP）数据

新技术视域下的远程口译研究 / 蒋莉华著.—长沙：湖南师范大学出版社，2020.9

ISBN 978-7-5648-3916-1

Ⅰ.①新… Ⅱ.①蒋… Ⅲ.①口译—研究 Ⅳ.①H059

中国版本图书馆 CIP 数据核字（2020）第 156465 号

新技术视域下的远程口译研究

Xin Jishu Shiyu Xia de Yuancheng Kouyi Yanjiu

蒋莉华 著

◇组稿编辑：李 阳
◇责任编辑：吴晋先 李 阳
◇责任校对：李 航
◇出版发行：湖南师范大学出版社
 地址/长沙市岳麓区 邮编/410081
 电话/0731-88873071 0731-88872256
 网址/https：//press.hunnu.edu.cn
◇经销：新华书店
◇印刷：长沙雅佳印刷有限公司
◇开本：710 mm×1000 mm 1/16
◇印张：13.25
◇字数：250 千字
◇版次：2020 年 9 月第 1 版
◇印次：2020 年 9 月第 1 次印刷
◇书号：ISBN 978-7-5648-3916-1
◇定价：58.00 元

凡购本书，如有缺页、倒页、脱页，由本社发行部调换。
本社购书热线：0731-88872256 88873071
投稿热线：0731-88872256 **微信：**ly13975805626 **QQ：**1349748847

前　言

新兴技术的介入，无论是早期的电话和综合业务数字网（ISDN），还是之后的宽带网络，乃至最新的5G网络，无不深刻改变了人与人之间的交流方式。在各种数字电子技术手段的支持下，人们可以利用实时电话或视频通话召开远程会议，或使用实时流媒体平台与观众交流，人与人之间交流方式的全方位变革方兴未艾。与此同时，随着全球化进程的加快和经济交流密度的加强，语言服务商们迫切需要提高工作效率，以适应口译市场的不断扩大。在此背景下，能够打破地域和时间限制的远程口译形式应运而生。

各国政府和企业一直尝试以数字电信作为提供口译服务的一种方式，以满足不同情况下不断增长的跨语言交流需求。相比其他即时通信类应用，视频会议使得沟通更加直接有效，并且随着其价值得到用户认同，渗透率也逐步提升。根据 Frost & Sullivan 公司数据，2012—2019 年，全球视频会议的市场规模从 319 亿美元增长至 550 亿美元，而从 2017 年以来，全球视频会议的复合年均增长率（CAGR）预计达到 8.3%。Zoom 是目前领先的移动视频会议工具。据统计，Zoom 在 2013 年共拥有客户 4500 家，到 2017 年已达 70 万家，视频会议市场的火热可见一斑。数据显示，近年来，我国视频会议市场的规模逐年扩大，2009 年行业市场规模达 51.7 亿元，较 2008 年的 42.3 亿元增长 22.22%；2010 年市场规模达 66.3 亿元，同比增长 28.24%。目前我国政府使用视频会议的用户比例达到了

30%左右，金融、能源、通信、交通、医疗、教育等重点行业机构的使用比例也不断提高，政府视频会议网络覆盖至乡镇，这对带动视频会议市场的快速发展起到极大的促进作用。市场规模的不断扩大和适用范围的不断扩展，让远程口译越来越受重视。

自2019年年底以来，新冠疫情迅速蔓延，疫情蔓延范围之广、传播速度之快，堪为数十年所仅见。在疫情防控背景下，远程办公需求的不断增加，培养了大众的远程视频会议习惯，提高了视频会议的认可度。面对疫情的防控难度，远程视频会议系统发挥了很大的优势，不仅能远程办公部署工作，还能远程医疗，为患者、家属、医院三方带来帮助。远程医疗解决方案已经有许多成功的应用，可以实现远程会诊、手术观摩、医疗教学、内部会议、医疗应急等功能，有效解决了地区医疗资源的不平衡问题。

在国外，远程口译的实践和研究经过数十年的发展，基本建立了一整套包含行业手册、教育培训、学术科研等在内的完整体系，其中远程法庭口译、医疗口译和手语翻译俨然成为跨越语言障碍、提供社会必要服务不可或缺的组成部分，整个行业进入成熟阶段，学界的研究也随之不断深入和细密。例如，国外学者早已发现，在远程会议口译中，由于口译员的解释、协调、同客户的情感交流等行为很难通过远程会议的形式实现，口译员在心理上不可避免地产生疏远感。为了使产出的目标语符合规范，促进远程观（听）众之间的交际，口译员主动采取了相关策略，例如对源语进行一定的增减、解释、主动协调远程会议口译中的对话速度、进行有效的话轮转换等。与之相比，目前中国学者的研究仍然停留在对电话口译的介绍和案例分析阶段，对远程口译的研究也局限于简单的技术层面，缺乏对全领域的系统认识。因此，中国学界迫切需要一本全面介绍远程口译的入门性专著。

正是基于上述认识，本书从远程口译的基本概念出发，梳理远程口译的历史发展进程，并从科研的角度探讨该领域的研究途径、研究选题和教学特点，为广大口译研究者提供全面翔实的学科背景资料，并为口译培训和测试提供借鉴。事实也证明，将传统的口译研究方法和现代技术结合起来，多方面考察和研究该新兴口译形式中口译员的行为和策略，对扩展研究者对口译员角色的认知极为有利。

本书将由浅至深地对整个远程口译实践及其相关研究进行系统的介绍和剖析。全书共分六章。第一章"远程口译的基本概念"旨在厘清远程口译研究中的一些基本概念，包括远程口译的定义、主要分类以及与现场口译之间的异同。第二章"远程口译的历史沿革"从学科的角度阐述远程口译研究迄今为止的发展历程，主要涵盖远程口译的历史、职业化、学术化进程，以及在此基础上兴起的远程口译研究。第三章"远程口译研究途径和理论范式"重点考察远程口译研究的学科视角、核心理念、方法论、理论范式和模型。第四章"远程口译研究热点"主要从远程口译产品和口译员表现的角度出发，介绍远程口译研究中常见的、备受关注的研究热点，包括口译员素质与能力、口译员角色、口译质量、口译策略、多模态信息等。第五章"远程口译教学"介绍了具有代表性的远程口译教育机构和语言服务机构的教育教学，考察了远程口译教学的课程设置和教学内容，以期对国内的远程口译教学起到借鉴和参考的作用。第六章"远程口译实践与研究趋势"展望在当今科学技术突飞猛进的大环境下，远程口译研究可能的发展方向，包括学科交叉融合和口译学科研究的技术转向。附录以双语庭审为特例，介绍了远程口译现场技术设置、口译形式、人员培训等，为立法人员、法律从业人员、法庭口译员和远程口译技术员提供了详尽的实操手册。

本书的撰写，期望能为远程口译从业人员提供可供参考的实践案例和技术指导，为企业选取能适应远程会议的口译员给予咨询，也可作为学习远程口译研究入门课程的学生的基本阅读材料，为国内的远程口译研究和人才培养贡献绵薄之力。

本书在编写过程中得到了湖南师范大学出版社的大力支持，再次表示衷心的感谢。由于自身水平所限，本书难免疏漏，恳切地期望广大同行和读者批评指正。

蒋莉华

于湖南师范大学外国语学院

目　录

第一章
远程口译的基本概念

进入 21 世纪，人类生活与互联网的关联日益紧密。数字电信彻底改变了人们在全球范围内的沟通方式。与此同时，新科技在翻译活动中也得到越来越多的运用。无论是电视电话会议的日益增多，图像传输方法的不断更新，因特网、宽带网、手机同电脑的深度结合与发展，笔记本电脑的普及，还是网上数据查询的便捷化等，都在潜移默化中改变了口译工作的环境和条件。为了满足不同情况下人们对跨语言交流不断增长的需求，各地政府和企业一直尝试使用数字电信作为新的口译服务手段，形式也从最初的远程电话口译服务，到现在的视频口译服务。口译学界也开始研究基于音频、视频手段的口译服务，特别是基于互联网平台的远程视频口译服务。

口译员采用电话、视频和网络会议等新通信技术，逐步形成了新型口译服务方式。在科技日新月异的时代，口译行业的发展面临着人工智能和远程口译技术发展等新形势的挑战。广义上的远程口译是指在远程通信设备（电话或网络等）的辅助下，口译员开展的非现场口译工作。狭义上的远程口译通常指客户在不同地点雇佣口译员，主要参与者则分布在不同地点的虚拟会议中。虽然各种形式的远程口译可行性在译界颇有争议，但在过去的二十年里，远程口译越来越频繁地出现，引起学者们越来越多的关注。目前，远程口译中出现的各种问题已经得到了初步研究。

按技术形式来分，远程口译主要包含电话口译、视频口译两大类；从口译方式来分，又可分为同声传译、交替传译；从领域来分，有法庭口译、医疗口译、公共事业服务口译等常见形式。与传统口译相比，远程口译具有"非现场性""及时性""成本低"等特征。随着现代通信技术的不断进步，远程口译的音质、画质也得到不断改善。技术质量的提高和成本的下降与口译员薪酬水平的不断提升为远程口译的发展开辟了广阔的市场空间。以下章节将从定义、分类和特点三个方面对远程口译进行全面的介绍。

第一节 远程口译的定义

随着 5G 时代的到来，实时远程通信获得了强有力的技术平台，新型口译服务方式随之诞生。一方面，电话和互联网通信让沟通的方式变得更加灵活，新兴的技术让两个或两个以上地点的参与者能够远程举办电话会议；另一方面，视频会议已逐渐成为实时语言和视觉交互的工具，为两个或多个地点之间的互动提供了技术支持。

目前远程口译的定义在学界尚未形成统一的观点。一般而言，远程口译是指口译员不在会议现场，无法直接观察会议发言人和听众，只能通过转播现场信号的视频和音频系统接受信息并开展工作的口译活动。有学者认为，"远程口译［……］指口译员不出现在会议室，而是通过屏幕和耳机进行口译工作"（Mouzourakis，2006：46）。基于视频媒介的口语翻译被称为视频会议口译（videoconference interpreting，简称 VCI），口译员位于两个地点的任意一方，或以远距离口译（distance interpreting）的方式进行，即所有的口译活动参与者在一个地点，而口译员在另一个单独分开的地点。远程会议口译的主要形式是同声传译。由此可见，与通常的会议口译不同，远程会议口译的最大特点是需要借助先进的视频与音频传输技术，辅助口译员完成口译任务。学界已经研究了通过视频技术手段连接在不同地点的说话者和口译员的工作方式（Braun，2004，2007），但实践中仍不多见。Braun & Taylor（2012）提出了"基于视频媒介的口译"（video-mediated interpreting，简称 VMI），作为涵盖视频会议口译现象的普遍概念。在手语口译领域，典型的视频会议口译（VCI）指的都是远程视频口译，即说话者和口译员位于三个不同地点，参与者在两个不同的地方，口译员通过远程连通（video rely services，简称 VRS）提供服务。VRS 的一个显著特点是口译员通过视频连通聋人，通过电话连通其他口译活动参与者（Alley，2012）。

电话口译和视频会议口译有一定区别。两者都是指利用通信技术获取另一个地点、城市或国家的口译员的服务。在此设置中，电话或视频会议用于将口译员连接到位于同一地点的会议主要参与者。通过电话进行远程口译通常称为电话口译（telephone interpreting 或 over-the-phone interpreting）。通过视频会议进行的远程口译通常也可简称为远程口译，在手语翻译领域称为视频远程口译（video remote interpreting）。远程口译可分为同声传译、交替传译或是对话口译三种方式。如果口译员身处单独地点，则使用三方电话或视频会议，这类型的口译称为远程会议口译（teleconference interpreting）。

虽然 Paneth 在 1957 年第一次提出"远程口译"概念时指出，它"能非常简单明了地使用口译员"，"很容易进一步发展"（Paneth，1957/2002：39），然而远程口译和电话会议口译的发展引发了从业者和口译学者的激烈争论，并指出其可行性和工作条件中存在的问题，以及远程口译服务的效率和口译的可持续性均值得深究。

第二节　远程口译的分类

远程口译是一种新型的口译形式，具有口译的根本特点，即把源语表达的信息转换成译语传达给一人或多人，本质上是跨语言、跨文化的交际行为，要求口译员具有基本的口译技能（如听辨能力、记忆力、笔记能力等），高标准的口译质量，并遵循同样的职业伦理规范。但由于远程口译的具体工作场合、参与方等方面存在差异，导致口译模式、交际语境等方面出现了一定的差异，因此学界对远程口译的分类存在分歧。以下章节将从不同的分类角度对远程口译进行详细说明。

一、按媒介分类

从 70 年代开始，光纤网络技术和大容量通信交换系统得到广泛应用，在技术上和硬件上为大规模、高效率提供电话口译服务带来了可能。目前，电话口译以其快捷、全天候、多语种等优势，在社会上尤其是医疗、事故营救等领域得到广泛应用，发展势头强劲。进入 21 世纪，随着数字技术和网络的普及，远程视频口译，如电视会议口译、网络视频口译等，也得到越来越多的采用和关注。按媒介下分的远程口译类别如图 1-1 所示，以下章节将重点介绍电话口译和远程视频会议口译的定义和特点。

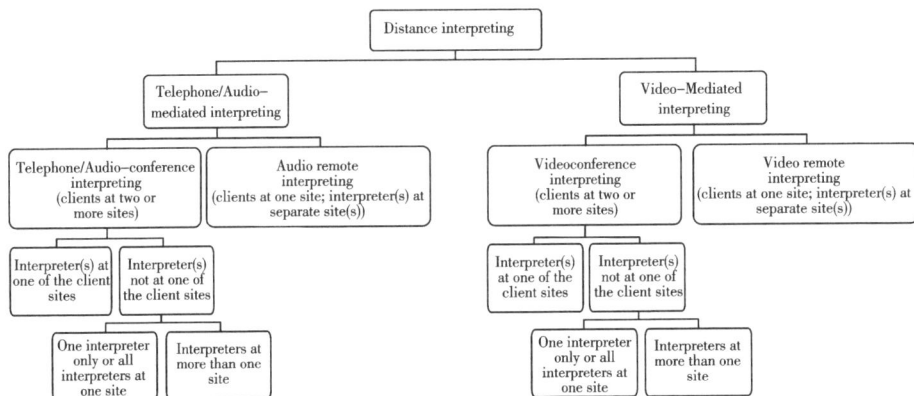

图 1-1　远程口译分类

（来源：http://wp. videoconference-interpreting. net/? page_id＝8 ）

（一）电话口译

电话口译是指口译员在电话端或与其中一名对话者位于同一地点的口译形式（Lee，2007：231）。电话口译只需要普通的电话线和电话，包括无绳电话、移动或双接收电话、扩音电话和扬声器（Lee，2007：237；Kelly，2008：31）。电话口译通常情况下采取交替传译的方式，但新设备下也可使用同声传译（O'hagan，1996：77）。

Oviatt 等人将电话中的对话与现场口译进行了比较。他们认为，电话口译中的口译员非常积极地参与整个对话交际，使用第一人称明确指代自己，第三人称指代对话者，从而避免了误解的产生（1990：1-3）。对医学上使用电话进行远程同声传译的首次研究是由 Hornberger 等人（1996）进行的。他们的早期研究将远程同声传译与现场交替口译进行了比较，结果显示，远程同声传译的信息比现场的交替口译要更加完整准确，并在一定程度上加强了医患之间的沟通（1996：845）。Wadensjö 将警方采访的电话口译与现场访谈口译进行比较后发现，电话口译中的口译员通过各种方式进行了更多的协调，从而确保参与各方之间的理解（1999：254）。高亮（Leong Ko）的研究表明，如果使用高品质设备，口译员能够应付电话中的录音口译，并处理疲惫和注意力不够集中等问题（2006：331f.）。

（二）远程视频会议口译

举行视频会议时，使用由数据接收设备组成的视频会议系统技术（摄像机、麦克风等）、数据处理设备（高速计算机与视频会议卡）和数据复制设备（屏幕、扬声器等），可以开展跨国会议和不同地点的远程口译。

视频会议中口译可以采取以下形式：

1. 视频会议口译（Videoconference interpreting）

视频会议口译指的是双语诉讼程序发生在两个不同地点，通过视频连通后需要翻译促进沟通的一种口译形式。例如，沟通的一方是某个国家的法庭，另一方是另一个国家的远程证人；或在法院之间联系；警方拘留所（例如第一次听证会）或法院与监狱之间的联系（例如还押延期听证会）等。

当诉讼程序涉及双语，需要翻译服务时，视频会议在必要的情况下需要整合翻译的不同方法，因此产生了两种不同方式的视频会议口译。如图1-2所示，第一种方式，口译员可以与主场的参与者在一起，例如法庭（视频会议口译A场景）；另一种方式，口译员可以与监护室、监狱或法院的其他发言人位于同一地点（视频会议口译B场景），如图1-3所示。

图1-2　视频会议口译（A）：口译者在主场（Sabine，2012：33）

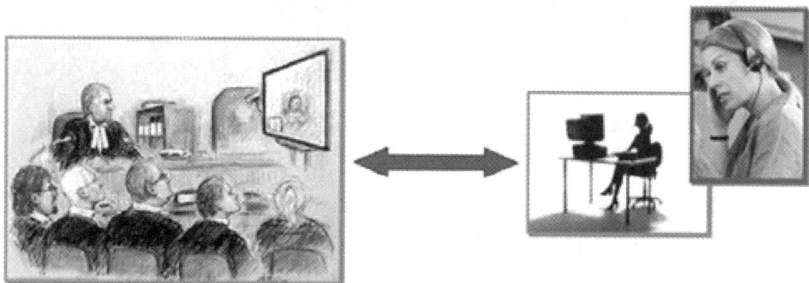

图1-3　视频会议口译（B）：口译者跟其他发言人一起（Sabine，2012：33）

2. 远程口译（Remote interpreting）

远程口译是指诉讼程序发生在同一地点（例如法庭），口译员通过远程视频连通进行口译（例如另一个法院或口译中心）。

图 1-4　远程口译：口译者在不同地点（Sabine，2012：33）

法庭诉讼中远程口译使用视频会议技术的唯一目的是将法庭口译员与诉讼现场连通起来，而视频会议口译则是使用视频连通，不同地点的参与者来进行远程法律诉讼，因此两种口译形式具有不同的动机。远程口译对司法界来说具有很大的吸引力，因为可以迅速及时地找到合格的法律口译员，同时节省口译员的旅行费用，减少口译员的等待时间。

3. 视频会议口译＋远程口译（Videoconference interpreting＋Remote interpreting）

两种形式可以组合在一起。这种情况一般发生在不同地点的诉讼中，口译员位于另一个不同的位置，如图 1-5 所示。

图 1-5　视频会议口译和远程口译相结合（Sabine，2012：34）

自 1976 年以来，联合国和欧盟机构对远程视频会议进行了研究，发现音质问题和远程工作所带来的疏离感，让口译员丢失了部分口译信息。因此，"会议使用新技术的守则"要求提供高质量的图像和声音传输，并将国际会议的工作时间限制为每天两小时以内（AIIC，2000）。

二、按领域分类

按领域来分，远程口译可存在于国际机构（侧重于在多语言环境中的会议口译）、法律机构、医疗和其他机构。

（一）国际机构

国际机构已经进行了一段时间的远程口译实验。早期研究侧重技术因素，涉及口译质量和一系列生理和心理变量。Moser-Mercer（2003）描述了国际电联对会议口译员所开展的传统口译和远程口译实验，取样其口译表现进行研究。欧洲议会 2004 年的研究（Roziner & Shlesinger，2010）涉及 36 名口译员。他们使用多种语对，在两周内对传统口译和远程口译的表现进行了抽样调查。除了调查口译员的表现外，这两项研究还调查了口译员对远程口译的情绪反应，并对压力指标和工作环境的各个方面进行了测量。研究的性能分析显示，作为现场和远程口译之间的主要差异之一，口译员在远程口译中的表现比现场表现的反应速度快，但远程口译中的口译员更容易疲劳，远程口译中的压力激素值比传统的面对面口译偏高，但是整体而言这种差异并不明显（Moser-Mercer，2003：12）。参与欧洲议会调查研究的口译员认为，远程口译比现场口译更有压力，但研究表明，在客观的压力测量中没有发现这种差异（Roziner & Shlesinger，2010）。总体而言，这些研究发现了客观结果与主观感知之间的差异。Roziner 和 Shlesinger 从而得出结论："尽管口译员自身对他们在远程口译中的表现非常不满意，然而根据不同的判断结果，与现场口译的比率相比，质量几乎没有下降。"（2010：242）

2010 年，欧洲委员会口译服务处（SCIC）采用了一种更为技术化的方法。弗劳恩霍夫研究所（Frauhofer Gesellschaft）为 SCIC 开展了一项研究，目的是确定现场和远程同声传译所需的数字视频和音频源的最低质量标准，共有 36 名会议口译员参加了测试。口译员没有执行任何实际的口译任务，仅评估了不同的音频和视频质量。该研究中未包括所谓的"人为因素"，而这些因素在其他研究中被证明非常重要。调查结果为视频和音频传输提供了全面的技术建议清单（Causo，2012）。至于使用研究中推荐的设备是否能改善口译员在口译任务期间对远程口译的主观感受还有待进一步研究。

整体而言，国际机构中远程口译的使用率较高，口译员的专业性强，具有应对远程设备较为成熟的方法。

(二) 法律机构

法院和其他法律机构已将视频会议作为提高诉讼程序效率的手段，减少因被拘留者的押解而引起的安全问题，并支持跨境司法合作。20 世纪 90 年代，许多英语国家在法庭、监狱、拘留中心和警察局设置了视频会议设施，以创建"虚拟法庭"，在法庭和监狱之间建立联系（Braun & Taylor，2012b）。

进入 21 世纪，视频会议技术在全球法律诉讼中开始普及。以荷兰为例，使用基于互联网设备的视频会议自 2007 年以来一直用于审前听证会（van den Hoogen & van Rotterdam，2012）。所有配备视频会议设施的法庭都拥有完全相同的设备和布局，以方便相关人员的工作。其他司法管辖区目前也采取了类似的做法。Fowler（2007）指出，口译员在庭审中的位置、话筒及视频图像的可见性等问题都会影响口译质量。她认为，这些问题的出现主要是由于缺乏远程口译的相关规定，导致口译过程不断重复，且常常出现意义误解。

Ellis（2004）对移民程序中的视频会议口译进行了可行性研究。调查结果基于对 14 名移民律师的访谈和 25 名移民法官、16 名难民保护官员及 17 名口译员的问卷调查。律师们对视频会议的适用性持怀疑态度，而其他三类群体则持积极态度。研究中发现，由于口译员与难民并不在同一地点，他们的个人联系较弱，因而无论是沟通协调还是口译员向难民提供文件视译服务都存在一定困难，也无法使用耳语同传。法官认为交替传译的效果较差，特别是在他们提交最终意见书时尤为明显。通过视频连通进行的听证会也往往持续时间更长，比面对面听证会更加让人疲惫。口译员担心体态语和情绪没有得到有效传达，这样可能会破坏难民证词的可信度。口译员还认为，视频会议通信中出现更多的重复和重叠语音，这些技术问题不仅难以解决，也妨碍了口译的准确性。英国两家慈善机构通过视频连通进行的移民保释听证会研究也得出了类似的结论。3 名口译员和所有其他参与者认为，他们很难跟踪法庭进程，也无法在法庭上看到和听到其他交流信息。

总干事移民服务会议（GDISC）是欧洲移民问题合作的非正式团体。它于 2007 年创建了"口译员"项目。这是一项欧洲范围内的倡议，主张通过远程口译为庇护面谈提供口译服务，克服无法找到翻译人员的问题，这对稀有语言尤为重要（GDISC，2007）。在此过程中，通晓移民案件中工作者语言的口译员与案件工作人员、申请人在同一地点，通晓申请人语言的口译员则位于另一地点。

Braun 教授领衔的欧洲 AVIDICUS 项目进行了迄今为止有关刑事诉讼中基于视频会议口译的最全面的研究。AVIDICUS 第一阶段项目（2008—2011）评估了刑事诉讼中视频会议和远程口译的可行性和质量（Braun & Taylor，2012c）。在调查欧洲 200 名法律口译员的基础上，该项目确定了视频会议中最迫切待解决的问题和视频会议中常用的口译形式，并通过一系列实验研究比较了传统口译和远程视频口译的质量。对数据的定量分析显示，视频会议口译中出现的问题明显增多，这表明口译员面临的困难更大，更易于疲劳，认知负荷也更高。研究结果还表明，通过培训可以实现视频会议口译的改进（如避免重叠语音及使用更好的设备），但沟通行为和交流问题会改变法律沟通的进程，因此需要进一步地研究（Braun & Taylor，2012c；Braun，2013）。基于这些发现，AVIDICUS 第一阶段项目制定了刑事诉讼中远程视频会议的口译准则，并为口译员和法律从业者设计和试行了培训模块（参见附录）。

AVIDICUS 项目还包括了对法律诉讼中的远程口译进行的研究。该领域的远程口译实践可追溯到 20 世纪 70 年代，当时澳大利亚引入了电话远程口译。接着是 20 世纪 80 年代的美国远程口译。美国法院的电话口译项目始于 1989 年，但从未进行过系统分析。随着时间的推移和技术的迭代，通过电话进行的远程口译逐渐被远程视频口译所取代。

基于视频会议的远程口译的一个显著实例是在佛罗里达州的第九巡回法庭（the Ninth Judicial Circuit），它于 2007 年引入了口译员中心。口译员中心位于其中一个法院，并为整个第九巡回法庭的司法机构提供服务，方式包含远程交替传译和同声传译。整体而言，法庭场景中的远程口译实践与研究较为成熟，为其他场景提供了有效借鉴。

（三）医疗机构

医疗环境中的口译方式虽然比法律环境更为多样，但主要还是通过电话来实现。目前移动视频会议设备的出现正逐渐改变这种状况（Locatis et al.，2011）。自 20 世纪 70 年代以来，医疗保健领域对电话口译的需求稳步增长。迄今为止，研究者已经进行了许多关于用户满意度的调查，然而对口译员表现、质量和互动的实证研究仍然缺乏。

在回顾这些研究时，Azarmina 和 Wallace 总结说："这些研究的结果表明，对于患者、医生和口译员来说，远程口译是可以接受的。"（2005：144）尽管在所提及的研究中缺乏对口译员表现的正式评估，但"远程口译与现场口译相比，能达到基本意思准确"（2005：144）。他们同时也发现，口译员更喜欢进行面对面的现场口译，Locatis 等人（2010）调查了 200 多名患者，其中包括 24 名医务工作者和 7 名口译员。结果显示，大多数医务工作者和口译员对现场口译、电话口译和视频口译这 3 种模式的偏好基本相似。患者发现 3 种模式之间没有明显差异，但基本会倾向于用一种模式。52 位口译员回应了 Price 等人的调查（2012）。他们在临床情境中发现，这 3 种方法都能满足传递信息的要求，但在人际关系的沟通方面存在明显差异，因此口译员更青睐面对面的口译。

比利时卫生部目前所进行的远程视频口译研究考虑到了口译中的互动和跨文化协调的特点，并对此提出了建议。根据在比利时 4 家医院进行试点的初步结果，该研究着重强调人员培训、设备使用和相关流程规定的重要性（Verrept，2011）。2019 年底暴发的新冠疫情也助推了远程视频会议口译在各国医疗信息交流、就诊等各方面的应用。整体而言，相比前两种远程口译场景，医疗场景一般更多使用远程电话口译的形式。

（四）其他机构

在商业环境中使用远程和电话会议口译的记录不多，但是一些报告和口译服务提供商的网站显示，这里的口译解决方案多为定制，以满足商业客户的特定要求。他们会将电话和视频会议结合起来使用，进行电话会议与口译（Kurz，2002；Selhi，2004）。

20 世纪 90 年代末，德国的 ViKiS 项目研究了将同声传译整合到视频会议的可能性。与国际机构所进行的研究相似之处在于，该项目是在当时使用日益频繁的 ISDN 视频会议的基础上开发的。这种类型视频会议使得中小型企业能够负担得起视频会议通信成本。项目设计了一个解决方案：使用 ViKiS 设置将口译员汇总到视频会议中。Braun（2004，2007）在分析了口译员对新工作条件的适应性后指出，所有参与者都认为，此种形式下的沟通远比面对面口译要疲劳，和其他参与者建立融洽的关系也更困难。由于 ISDN 视频会议的局限性，特别是低音质及一些难以克服的听力理解问题，口译质量难以保障。口译员需要面对的另一个问题是如何进行远距离互动。由于口译员必须承担主导角色，他们要比传统的对话口译更需要频繁地协调各种问题。远程口译中的口译员有不同的适应阶段。第一阶段是发现问题和提高认识，使用临时策略解决问题。随着经验的增加，工作重心转向避免问题出现和提前预防策略（Braun，2004，2007）。

第三节　远程口译的特点

远程口译是一种新兴的口译形式，口译员通过电话或视频媒介提供口译服务，帮助有语言障碍的各方实现顺利交际。姚斌（2011）将远程口译的特征描述为以下几个方面：

第一，参与人员所处的位置不同。口译工作的要素人员（包括口译员与有沟通需求的双方）经常不在同一场所。有时候是发言人远程，口译员与观众在现场，比如远程国际会议；有时候是需沟通的双方在现场，而口译员远程进行翻译（如医院医患双方见面、法庭庭审）；有时候是三方均不在同一场所（如外国人给公共机构打热线电话，接线员、咨询者、口译员分别处于不同位置）。

第二，非语言信息缺失。相关人员间的交流缺乏肢体语言等副语言工具来辅助理解，口译员无法通过非语言元素获得完整的交流信息，也无法与发言者或观众进行直接交流来干涉语流、纠正及反馈信息。在一些翻译准确性要求高的场合，发言者会有示范动作、证据举证等（如在法庭庭审中出示证据物、医院诊治时候医生的肢体）等动作。这些具有重要的语篇意义，但由于口译员无法看到全景现场的非言语动作，理解产生障碍，从而影响翻译的准确性。

第三，技术投入成本固定。对于医院、法庭、公共机构热线来说，一次性投入设备投资，保持基本维护并对工作人员进行设备使用培训，就可以持续享受及时的远程口译服务。对于偶发性的会议来说，需要技术人员到现场负责音效、影像和传输效果等。由于口译过程中高度依赖通信设备，通信信号的稳定（如电话信号、网络视频信号、摄像设备质量）是远程口译所强调的内容。电话口译受到手机信号强弱、地理位置、话费等因素的制约，使得其他通信模式（如网络视频等）更受青睐。在近几年的远程会议上，远程口译视频设备的技术指标要求达到 ISO2603 标准，卫星传播的图像必须声音与影像完全同步。很多欧洲国家要求按照 ITU 的 H323 标准配备互联网设备。

第四，专业性人才集中。由于远程口译减少了差旅时间，口译员的有效工作时间明显增多。很多专业领域的口译工作（如医疗口译、法庭口译）需要口译员在掌握过硬口译技能的基础上精确把握该领域的背景知识与专业词汇。在这些领域中，口译输出的准确性具有极为重要的意义。此类口译岗位显然非普通口译员所能胜任，而远程口译入门门槛较高（取得除普通口译证书外的专业领域资质证书），增加了专业型人才集中使用，从而提高专业领域口译的准确性。

第五，及时性。远程口译的"及时性"特点弥补了传统口译"耗时费钱"的缺点。欧洲的公共事业服务（医院、出租车、水电煤气电话缴费热线、报警热线等）经常会配备在线的口译员，通过电话、网络视频或其他远程口译设备提供及时便捷的口译服务。当医院出现外国患者时，医生如果无法与患者进行有效的语言沟通，可以马上连线专业口译员，搭建医患沟通平台。相比传统的面对面口译，远程口译效率更高，大大缩短了病人候诊和就医时间。

在远程口译场景中，口译员与交际各方不在同一现场，因此需要借助电话或视频进行三方或多方通话。下面将从口译成本和效率两个方面比较传统口译与远程口译。

首先是成本对比。

从目标对象来说，现在的口译用户不仅限于商务客户，更多的是日常生活需要翻译的散户，例如：看病就医、问路、饮食、娱乐、订票、购物等。如果口译员到现场翻译，在时间和费用上都不划算。传统的口译有最低时间限制，至少要求两小时，如果不到两小时，也需要顾客补上相关费用。而远程口译则没有保底消费，客户根据实际翻译时间支付费用。另外，传统的口译是面对面翻译，这就产生了交通费，时间长的还需考虑食宿费。而远程口译则完全不会产生此类费用，口译成本大幅减少。客户特别是散户会将远程口译作为首选。

其次是效率对比。

从时间上讲，远程口译可以提供一年 365 天每天 24 小时的全天候服务，其服务可以在口译员接通电话/视频的那刻开始。可以说，使用远程口译具有成本效益。其高时效性也是传统口译无法比拟的，特别是紧急情况下（如孕妇生产，急救等），这种快速反应的特点可以减缓险情，甚至拯救生命。而传统的口译则需要客户提前预约，签订合同，翻译公司再预约合适的人员，这中间要经过多个程序。

从空间上讲，电话口译无须面对面，所以哪怕是在深山野岭，只要存在有效信号，口译服务都可以到位，空间的概念完全弱化。而传统的口译，在口译员接到任务后，要安排路线，综合考虑交通、路况等因素，并亲临现场。

从心理上讲，尽管口译员受过专业训练，但紧张感还是很难克服，特别是那些相对内向的口译员。而通过远程口译，口译员可在很大程度上克服心理障碍。

另外，由于口译内容的敏感性，有些客户不愿透露自己的真实身份，远程口译也成了这部分客户的理想口译类型。

从手续上讲，传统的口译需要经过繁琐的手续，而电话口译则是一次性的。例如，客户可以事先与远程口译公司签订合约，遇到语言障碍拨打签约公司的电话，便能马上接通口译员，获得所需的语言服务，系统会自动计费，费用从客人账户中扣除。临时需要电话口译服务的客户可以在电话口译公司的网页上填写申请单和信用卡信息，或者拨打免费电话直接输入信用卡信息，也能立即连通口译员。

远程口译最大的特点就是无须面对面。不过尽管在经济成本和效率成本上都比传统口译更胜一筹，远程口译也存在一些不容易忽视的问题。

第一，非言语信息缺失。

远程口译中的一方或者多方不在同一地点，造成了口译中一种重要信息——非言语信息——的缺失。众所周知，沟通的过程包括语言沟通和非语言沟通，而非语言沟通包括讲话人的肢体语言、眼神交流和话轮交替。远程口译员无法接收这些信息，自然不能将其传达给另一方，这无疑会限制交际效果，加大交际难度。

远程口译是以高科技为依托，将通信服务与口译服务相组合的创新产品。在此基础上，还可引入可视电话和网络视频。可视电话的一个重要意义是，可以为聋人提供手语翻译服务，让他们通过视频电话进行交流，从而开辟远程口译市场的全新领域和新的利润增长点。鉴于远程口译员无法在现场对话各方进行话轮调解，抢话和冷场在电话口译中也时有发生，因此，口译员要采取积极主动的策略防止这种现象。如果出现重叠，口译员应及时停止，让说话人把话讲完；有时说话人反应更迅速，会马上停止重叠，口译员可以就此继续翻译；如果遇到间隔，口译员应及时调整，把间隔时间最小化，保证交际顺畅。

全美翻译教育中心联盟（National Consortium of Interpreter Education Centers）在 2010 年视频工作小组口译研究中表明，视频质量、音频质量、连通稳定性和技术援助的可用性、培训充分度，以及硬件/软件的使用便捷性等条件都可能会影响口译的功效。

Keating 和 Mirus（2003）通过研究发现了远程口译的多种策略，确保以有效视觉信息进行清晰的沟通。这些策略包括，减少标志空间以满足相机的空间限制；调整手掌方向，放慢速度并强调个别标志。此项工作与远程口译中的设备设置有关，表明视频口译服务的消费者可能意识到需要进行的调整并适当地改变他们的通信方法以促进交互。

第二，缺乏口译准备时间。

远程口译虽然没有传统口译亲临现场的心理压力，但却要面对零准备的挑战。远程口译员在工作时间内随时随地都可能接到任务，任务范围之广，不可预测。另外，远程口译的对象差别巨大，不似传统口译，参与者的知识背景结构基本相同。这就要求口译员有更为丰富的知识储备，并接受远程口译的技能培训，比如记笔记。与正式的传统会议口译笔记不同，电话口译的笔记可以根据谈话人说话的内容，采用综述法，而非面面俱到。

第三，缺乏对远程口译员的信任。

远程口译公司对其口译员都有严格的职业准则要求，包括翻译准确、对客户信息保密、服务态度公正等。但由于口译员没有和客户进行面对面的交流，所谓眼见为实，客户并未能完全建立起对口译员的信任，特别是在谈及一些非常重要的信息（如信用卡号、密码等隐私信息）时。在如何快速建立信任的问题上，一方面，翻译公司要严格把关，确保每位在岗人员都具备合格的口译资格；另一方面，口译员要谨遵职业道德规范，特别是保密原则和公正原则。

第二章
远程口译的历史沿革

第一节　远程口译的历史

1973 年，澳大利亚移民局成为世界上第一家提供电话口译服务（Telephone Interpreting Service，简称 TIS）的机构。而在美国和大多数西欧国家，这类服务到 20 世纪八九十年代才开始出现（Mikkelson，2003）。目前，电话口译服务多为大型私人运营商的业务。他们充当了客户和口译员之间的代理商。此外，一些大型医院也拥有自己的内部电话口译员（Angelelli，2004）。当下电话口译的主要形式是交替传译。

虽然一部分电话口译服务正在被视频会议口译服务所取代，但电话口译仍然是一个不断增长的市场。2011 年，全球电话口译服务市场估值为 9.9148 亿美元，而 2007 年为 7 亿美元。Ozolins（2011）观察到，由于线路质量和机密性原因，电话口译服务几乎完全依赖固定电话而非移动电话或基于互联网的链接。因此，虽然"电话革命"从根本上改变了全球商务沟通，电话会议口译的需求不断增加，但远程口译扩展的驱动力并不是电话本身，而是通话费率尤其是长途费率的下降。

电话口译市场增长的另一个重要原因是大众的需求。通过分析 1000 多个电话口译实例，Rosenberg（2007）发现，远程电话口译的需求主要跟人群迁移和相关的语言政策有关，并被广泛运用于医疗环境。商业世界中的三方电话交谈，口译更为常见。Rosenberg 认为，电话谈话中的口译比电话远程口译问题更少，因为三方电话链接使主要参与者和口译员具有"平等"的参与感。在详细分析和比较电话口译对话、不使用口译的电话交谈，以及面对面对话后（Wadensjö，1999），研究者发现了许多交流沟通上的问题，这说明口译员需要更大的精力来协调对话。Wadensjö 认为，电话口译的困难更多地来自情境因素和缺乏共享的语境，而不是电话沟通本身存在的困难（2007：75）。

虽然这些研究涉及交替传译，但 Rosenberg 等人（1996）通过比较电话连线中的同声传译模式与医患谈话中的现场交替传译，发现远程同声传译比现场交替传译更加准确。参与该研究的口译员更喜欢现场交替传译，而远程同声传译对医生和患者更为有益，也更为医生和患者所欢迎。

Ko（2006）和 Lee（2007）研究了电话口译员的工作条件。他们认为，电话口译中普遍存在的高度不满主要源于工作条件（例如低报酬），而不是使用技术本身。随着电话口译的普及，该模式已经实现了技术改进。Rosenberg（2007）早就认为在医生和病人等客户之间传递手机的做法是不恰当的，因此现在的用户越来越多地使用电话免提形式或双耳机电话。

Kelly（2008）全面概述了电话口译的实用性。她列举了一些电话口译的优势，特别是由于种族或残疾原因不方便使用面对面口译时，电话口译具有的独特优势。她提倡采用特定的电话口译协议和电话口译培训。但正如 Ozolins（2011）所指出的，Kelly 主要描述的是美国的发展状况、市场规模和"西班牙语作为大规模少数语种民族语言的特殊情况"（2008：43），这些因素增加了电话口译的复杂性，许多国家不具备此类技术和设备的使用条件，因而采用电话口译的可能性不大，因而她的研究不具有普遍性。

电话口译的发展与获得公共服务密切相关。它在医疗保健口译中的应用尤为广泛。相比之下，视频会议口译的发展最初是受联合国和欧盟等国际机构在提供这种口译服务时所获得的利益驱动的。最早的实验由联合国教科文组织于 1976 年进行，用于测试 Symphonie 卫星的使用状况。该实验将教科文组织巴黎总部与内罗毕的一个会议中心联系起来，过程涉及三种方法：远程电话口译（remote interpreting by telephone），视频链接远程口译（remote interpreting by video link）和巴黎与内罗毕之间的视频会议口译（interpreting in a videoconference）。其中口译员位于巴黎（UNESCO，1976）。联合国在 20 世纪 70 年代和 80 年代后期还组织了类似的实验（Luccarelli，2011；Mouzourakis，1996）。尽管关于这些早期测试的报告并没有明确区分远程会议和电话会议，但研究表明远程口译具有挑战性，因此视频会议口译更为可行。在 1976 年由联合国教科文组织进行的史上首次远程口译实验中，通过卫星传输的会议信号已经能达到电视信号的影像和声音质量水平。之后的 1978 年，联合国又在纽约和布宜诺斯艾利斯之间进行过一次类似的实验。两次实验的初步结论是：口译员开展远程口译的前提是，能够获得发言人的图像，如果只有声音没有图像，口译员无法工作，因此如需在今后的国际会议中采用远程口译，至少应该保证口译员能够从转播现场实况的大屏幕上看到平常在现场同传箱里看到的场景（不过这一点当时的技术还不能满足）（EP Report，2001：6）。

然而，国际机构感兴趣的是远程视频口译。通过综合业务数字网（ISDN）即数字电话线进行视频会议的做法，在 20 世纪 90 年代开始实施，并对远程口译的可行性进行了一系列研究和论证。口译由各类机构组织开展，如 1993 年的欧洲电信标准协会（ETSI）（Böcker & Anderson，1993），1995、1997 和 2000 年的欧洲委员会，1999 年和 2001 年的联合国，国际电信联盟（ITU）与 1999 年的 Écoledetraduction et d'interprétation（ETI）（Moser-Mercer，2003），2001 年的欧洲理事会及 2001 年和 2004 年的欧洲议会合作。

从 20 世纪 90 年代开始，远程视频口译越来越普及。欧盟扩张后成员国之间的交通不便，会议地点口译室的短缺，都使远程视频口译备受青睐（Mouzourakis，2003）。

在法律和医疗环境中采用远程视频会议口译的原因有很多，其中最主要的是合格口译员的缺乏和众多口译任务调度时间的缩短。此外，许多法律和医疗任务持续时间短，让口译员赶赴现场的做法显然不经济。Braun 和 Taylor（2012a）调查了 200 名法律口译员，发现他们对远程视频会议的口译态度各异，许多口译员认为引入视频会议口译只是为了削减成本，但也有很多口译员认为视频会议技术可以改善客户获得的口译服务质量并提升司法公正。调查还发现，口译员对视频会议的态度与他们工作所在国的情况（如设备质量和工作条件）存在联系。这些观察结果与 Ko（2006）和 Lee（2007）关于电话口译的研究相似。

互联网能提供比 ISDN 的系统更好的视频和音频质量，并同相机、麦克风等外围设备一起，为视频会议口译提供更好的技术支持。与此同时，基于网络或云手段的视频会议产生了各种声音和图像质量问题，同时由于在平板电脑和移动设备上使用远程口译服务（特别是在医疗环境中）的情况增多，关于远程口译可行性的新讨论也开始出现。

姚斌（2011）通过研究发现，20 世纪 70 年代以来，对远程口译的研究和探索一直没有中断，但在 90 年代以前，人们最重视的问题依然是技术的可行性，而对口译员在远程状态下的工作条件和自身感受的关注远远不够。随着技术的不断更新变化，远程会议口译早期实验阶段所面临的各种技术问题逐渐得到解决。人们开始意识到，技术问题总能在未来得到解决，而远程的交流方式对口译员所造成的心理和生理压力却并不总能通过技术手段消除。我们知道,在任何口译形式中,技术只是保障口译成功的要素之一,口译员才是决定口译成败的关键。从 90 年代中期开始,实验研究的关注重点转向远程口译能否在口译员中得到有效实施。在技术不断进步的背景下,经过 10 多年的探索,大规模远程会议口译开展的条件逐渐形成。故而在 20 世纪 90 年代,联合国、欧盟等国际组织展开了多次大规模远程实验。在这些实验中,远程会议口译的优势与弊端得到充分彰显和讨论。更重要的是,人们在讨论远程音视频信号传输技术的同时,开始关注从事远程口译的口译员自身,并探讨口译员在新的工作环境和技术条件下面临着怎样的挑战,需要何种应对策略。

1992 年,欧洲电信标准协会(European Telecommunications Standards Institute)的项目组开展了一系列远程口译实验;1995 年、1997 年和 2000 年的欧洲委员会进行了一系列的相关实验;1999 年国际电信联盟(ITU)与日内瓦大学口笔译学院(ETI)联合进行了受控实验;2000 年、2001 年和 2005 年欧洲议会也进行了实验。此外,联合国也加入了实验的行列,分别于 1999 年和 2001 年在日内瓦进行了实验。可以看出,欧盟机构对于远程会议口译实验研究最为热衷,尤其是进入新世纪以后。欧盟的热情背后有着深刻的历史和文化动因。欧盟是世界上提供会议口译服务最频繁、涵盖服务语言最多样、招收会议口译员人数最多的国际组织之一。新世纪以来,欧盟的东扩意味着需要提供更多语言组合的会议传译服务,而欧盟机构原有的配备同传工作室的会议场所已经不能满足日益增长的会议和语言服务需求,急需寻找一种能够缓解同传工作室压力的替代方式。因此,经过多次实验和探索的远程会议口译就成为欧盟机构的选择。

欧盟希望更多地采用远程口译的另一原因是环保。在清洁能源和低碳减排等方面,欧盟一直走在世界前列,其会议口译服务也不例外。如果是现场口译,口译员必须抵达会场,而这必然会增加口译员乘坐飞机或其他交通工具出行的频率,从而间接增加碳排放。因此从节能环保的角度考虑,远程口译更为理想。

此外,一个不言自明的考虑是节约成本。采用远程方式可以节省口译员的交通和住宿成本。尽管目前远程会议口译技术还不完善,需要比较高的技术设备投入,但考虑到网络和远程传输技术的快速发展,在可以预见的未来,技术成本会迅速下降,而由远程方式所节约的成本将会远远大于技术成本。

如前所述,20 世纪 90 年代中期以后,欧洲对远程会议口译的探索如火如荼。1999 年 4 月,国际电信联盟(ITU)和日内瓦大学口笔译学院(ETI)

联合开展了一项为期 3 天的远程口译受控实验。该实验的出发点是"通过受控实验的方式探索远程口译技术的可行性及其对口译员心理或生理的影响"（Moser-Mercer，2003：2）。从实验的合作双方来看，ITU 的目标简单而直接，主要是为了节约未来会议的开支和利用自身在电信方面的先进技术为成员国谋福利。而参与联合实验的 ETI 则更多关注口译员的工作条件和自身感受。

在新冠疫情期间，许多传统的国际会议都转战线上，为了共同抗疫，各国专家也纷纷通过远程视频会议进行沟通交流，因此国际上对于远程视频会议口译的需求也大幅增加，这极大地促进了远程视频会议口译的发展，也带来了新的挑战。

据数字产业创新研究中心对 75 个国内企业的调查数据显示，受疫情影响，69％的企业出现了办公不便，51.7％的企业出现了人员管控问题，同时有相当比例的企业因疫情造成了订单减少，生产经营停顿、现金流困难等现象。67％的会议展览服务供应商调整既定会务规划和人员配置，增强企业风险抵御能力，正如 2003 年非典，成了中国电商腾飞发展的契机，疫情也推动了会议服务行业数字化转型。

新冠疫情之前，远程同传（非现场同声传译）技术仅被视为解决在线多方视频会议语言沟通障碍的最优解决方案。令人略感欣慰的是，经此一"疫"，视频会议及同声传译提供商们开始意识到数字化技术是会议会展中翻译服务市场增强风险抵御能力的依靠。在拓宽未来同声传译视频会议道路的同时具有无可替代的重要性。

第二节　远程口译研究的兴起和发展

人类在技术上的进步不仅刺激了远程口译的出现，而且还扩大了口译员把技能付诸实践的范围。自 20 世纪 90 年代起，电信和数字处理系统的融合对口译的职业实践，尤其是在多语种会议场合的实践，产生了巨大的影响，带来了极大的科研需求。

一、远程口译研究的学术基础

由于电子音响传输系统的使用让话语可以在同一时刻远距离传输到各处的接收者，多语种会议场合的口译因此发生了巨大的变化。20 世纪 70 年代后期，在同传设备中控制信号质量的国际标准确立后不久，联合国有关机构对电话口译中的声音和图像关系进行了第一次实验，从而验证了远程口译所面临的最根本的挑战。此后，连接电视会议的信号质量问题重新引起了研究者对传输质量和技术改良的兴趣（Mousourakis，1996）。除技术问题之外，会议口译员主要还出于心理上的原因抵触电话口译或远程口译，因为在这种"非现场的"电视会议口译中，他们无法直接看到发言者和听众。在针对会议口译员所进行的远程口译任务调查中，由于口译员缺乏积极性而产生眼睛疲劳、体力不支、神经紧张，以及被隔离感等问题最为常见。除了与职业生态相关的研究外，Braun 和 Kohn（2001）利用语言描述手段研究该主题，分析了德语和英语之间模拟电视会议中的语篇资料。研究者认识到低质量传输引起的一系列问题，并找到了口译员自身有效的监控和顺应策略，指出电视口译具有的发展潜力（Niska，1999；Stoll，2000）。

在电话口译中使用单一听觉信号的远程口译，早在 20 世纪 50 年代就得到过人们的推介（Paneth，1967/2002）。电话口译多用于对话交际，虽然经常由于缺乏非语言视觉线索而让人感受到局限，但依然在欧美国家为广大民众所接受。随着电视电话的使用，电话口译也开始服务于失聪人士（Niska，1999）。Wadensjö（1999）探索了电话口译的科研前景。她通过分析远程电话口译语境材料（说俄语的妇女和瑞典警察）指出，口译现场参与者的视听共事可以促进双方的谈话节奏，在较短的时间内增加谈话内容。而另一项研究表明，在美国加州进行的医疗语境下的远程同声传译比现场的交替传译效果更好（Niska，1999：112）。由此可见，远程口译研究主要基于认知心理学和话语分析。

二、远程口译研究的开端、巩固与融合

了解远程口译研究领域，必须回顾电信和技术的发展对口语和手语群体交流方式的影响。技术促进了人们之间的相互连接和沟通，也让各群体在文化交流中发现了彼此的差异。在过去的一百多年里，尽管电话一度被推荐为实时通信工具，但是聋人仍然无法受益。近年来，企业活动和公共服务越来越依赖电话，特别是通过呼叫中心或服务热线，将其作为与客户交谈的一种手段。电话也被用于提供医疗、法律和商业环境中的口译服务（Azarmina & Wallace，2005；Gracia-García，2002；Locatis et al.，2010；Mikkelson，2003；Ozolins，2012；Rosenberg，2007），但主要是为正常人提供的服务，通过手语进行交流的聋人通常依靠家人、朋友或手语口译员以促进电话沟通。北美、澳大利亚和欧洲的聋人一直请求立法，通过提供电话和网络沟通来消

除不平等，例如提供视频口译服务（Turner et al.，2017）。美国联邦通信委员会（Federal Communications Commission, FCC）将其定义为一种标准电话服务，负责确保"通过有线或无线方式进行通信，让听力或语言障碍的群体以某种方式与正常人享受同样的服务"（FCC，2016）。该技术广泛应用至今，可通过一系列服务让聋人独立地接触（或接近）服务者（包括企业和各类服务）。

口译是一项高度复杂的认知任务（Gile，2009；Moser-Mercer，2000），口译员工作环境的改变可能会对他们的表现和处理信息的方式产生影响。口译员在远程工作时的主要问题包括：缺乏存在感，认知超负荷，口译策略的调整，需要掌握远程口译中的知识和技能过多等。在使用音频和视频技术时，口译服务中讨论最多的是交际活动参与者的存在感和参与度问题（Short et al.，1976），这在某种程度上属于主观的经验。与交际活动主要参与者共同出现的口译员可以利用物理地域特征、参与者的姿势、目光凝视程度及面部表情，理解源消息中的意图和语气的理解并进行认知处理，从而掌握上下文信息（Setton，1999）。口译员如果与其他参与者共处一地，他们通常可以借鉴语境化线索推断很多互动的性质和对话者之间的人际关系（Dickinson，2014）。相比之下，远距离有可能破坏口译员的存在感并将其置于不利地位（Moser-Mercer，2005）。当口译员与口译活动主要参与者分开时，一些语境化线索变得难以掌握。在远程视频翻译呼叫中心工作的手语翻译中，聋人与对话者的视频连接通道很多情况下只有一条，对话者则通过电话连接，这对口译员来说是非常恶劣的工作条件（Napier et al.，2018：21）。即便口译员可以看到所有远程参与者的图像，但这些图像只能给予部分有关远程参与者的语境信息（Braun，2004，2007；Napier，2012a，2012b，2013），因此会减少口译员平等参与交际的机会，也不能保证与交际各方在现场看到和听到的内容一致（Braun，2004，2007，2013，2014，2017；Braun et al.，2018；Moser-Mercer，2003；Mouzourakis，2006；Napier，2012a；Napier et al.，2018；Roziner & Shlesinger，2010；Warnicke，2018）。

缺乏存在感或感知减少是否对口译员的能力产生影响仍有争议。通过对现场口译的观察证明，缺乏相关的上下文信息会迫使口译员采用猜测手段并在认知处理和自我监控方面投入更多的精力（Chernov，2004），这种情况也存在于远程口译中（Braun，2004，2007）。远程口译具有很高的认知负荷，因此一些研究开始关注口译员的疲劳（Braun，2013；Moser-Mercer，2003）。在一些情境下，疲劳可能会增加翻译错误的风险，特别是法律环境中。有鉴于此，法律翻译的结果所产生的影响尤其值得研究者关注（Braun & Taylor，

2012a）。Moser-Mercer（2003，2005）进一步断言，口译员在远程口译中会承受更多的心理压力，这些人为因素极大地影响了远程口译服务质量。与此相反，一些研究认为缺乏存在感恰是远程口译的优势所在。部分医学口译员认为，脱离医院环境可以消除干扰和压力，让他们更加专注于口译任务（Gracia-García，2002）。在远程视频链接的口译（Brunson，2018）中，口译员的积极看法与其他因素的相互作用需要进一步研究，尤其是口译表现的质量和整个远程沟通活动的关系。

在会议口译领域，此类研究已经取得了一些成果。由欧洲议会所进行的大规模研究，主要将远程视频口译条件下的口译员的表现与现场会议口译相比。Roziner 和 Shlesinger（2010）通过研究详细报道了口译质量、观众反馈、演讲者的知名度，以及人体工程学因素（包括热舒适、通风、照明和声学）。该研究的参与者为 36 名口译员志愿者，包括 17 名工作人员和 12 名自由口译员，性别男女对半，平均年龄为 45.7 岁。研究小组包括：统计员，翻译员，2 名人体工程师，1 名生理学家，2 名物理环境研究专家，1 名职业医生，1 名眼科医生和几位研究助理。该研究分两个阶段进行，通过特定手段观察人体工程学条件并控制一系列变量，记录每位参与者在现场和远程视频口译状态下的工作状况。除此之外，研究小组还进行了问卷调查，确定由环境条件引起的 19 种可能的身体问题，通过采用取样装置对荷尔蒙皮质醇取样来评估眼睛的疲劳度，并要求参与者进行主观压力评定（例如经验丰富与否、是否疲倦等），进而制定评估压力感知的五分评定量表。

人体工程学因素包括照明和眩光视频会议设置，会直接影响现场和远程视频条件下口译员的不适评级。口译员在"关掉麦克风时"能够放松，但也会遇到各种其他困难，并经常需要保持对现场的观察，并持续跟踪信息。这被证明是由距离而产生的躯体症状和压力感。Roziner 和 Shlesinger（2010）注意到更多的口译员表示，在远程口译中存在注意力问题（27%），但通过测试与压力相关的生物学证据（即唾液的皮质醇分析），分析每天收集的样本，这些差异并未得到证实。欧洲议会研究的第二阶段是评估口译每种方式的表现质量。在之前的远程同声会议口译研究中，口译员认为，与现场口译相比，他们对自己表现的满意度低于远程视频口译（Moser-Mercer，2003）。

此外，该团队在欧洲议会研究中收集了 20 个 3 分钟的口译摘录以供分析，语料库包括 570 个口译片段，分发给 45 名评委（专家口译员），在错误、单词选择和一般性能评估等方面对摘录进行评分（按 5 分制）。结果显示，远程视频口译的成绩评级较低。欧洲议会的研究表明，口译员认为远程视频口

译比现场口译的压力大得多，其表现也比现场要低劣。口译员对他们在远程
视频口译中的表现整体评价较低（Braun & Taylor，2012b；Kurz，2000）。
这表明，远程会议中的环境因素起了重要作用。由于需要实时观看眩光屏幕，
口译员在口译过程中的孤立感最终也会影响其注意力的集中。

　　这与使用交替传译的形式进行的法律视频口译形成了鲜明对比。由
Braun 及其同事在欧洲刑事司法系统视频口译项目（AVIDICUS）中进行的
研究（Braun，2013，2017；Braun & Taylor，2012c）证明了这点。根据对欧
洲 200 个法律口译员和 30 个司法部门机构的调查结果，确定了法律情景下的
远程视频口译最紧迫的问题和最优化的口译方式（Braun & Taylor，2012b）。
该项目的合作伙伴进行了一系列实验，以比较现场口译和远程视频会议中的
翻译质量。这些研究涉及 3 个国家的 15 名口译员。他们模拟现场法律程序和不
同情境的视频会议口译中的工作。数据集中体现的问题表明，视频会议口译情
境下，与法律相关的问题容易被放大，例如引渡的准确性和完整性（Balogh &
Hertog，2012；Braun & Taylor，2012a；Miler-Cassino & Rybinska，2012）。

　　Braun 和 Taylor 进行了进一步的统计分析，涉及 15 名翻译中的 8 名，他
们发现远程视频口译中的口译频率明显高于现场口译。研究结果也证实了这
一点，例如视频会议环境中的词汇激活问题（Braun，2013）。分析还表明，
远程口译中出现的许多问题都是相关的。例如，重叠语音之后通常会有遗漏
（Braun，2013）。

　　另外两项研究实验也值得特别关注。1999 年国际电联开展的一项研究
（Moser-Mercer，2003）涉及 12 名会议口译员，其中 6 人的工作语对为英语
到法语。研究者在传统和远程口译环境中对口译员进行几天的采样，随后侧
重分析错误信息。另一项研究在 2004 年由欧洲议会口译服务处开始进行
（Mertes-Hoffman，2005；Roziner & Shlesinger，2010），包括 36 名口译员的
语言组合。研究在两周时间内针对口译员在传统和远程口译中的表现进行取
样。除了调查口译员的表现外，这两项研究还调查了其他主观因素，如口译
员对远程口译的情绪反应和测量得出的客观指数（如心率和血压等压力指
标）、口译员的皮质醇水平及工作环境的各个方面（温度、照明等）。根据国
际电联的研究报告，"口译员在实验期间反复进行的心理自我评估表明，他们
认为在远程工作条件下压力更大"（Moser-Mercer，2003：11）。另外，国际
电联的实验发现，参与远程口译的压力激素值比传统的现场口译高（Moser-
Mercer，2003：12）。欧洲议会的研究得出的结论也承认"远程口译被认为比
现场的压力更大，高强度的工作和高度的紧张感几乎仍然存在于与远程口译

相关的各种活动中［……］这些主观压力等级与客观的压力测量值之间存在着尖锐的不可调和的矛盾"（Roziner & Shlesinger，2010：235）。尽管自我评级中的数据还不充分，但国际电联的研究已经可以辨别出口译员之间的不适感。Roziner 和 Shlesinger 证实了这一观点："在大多数基于主观绩效衡量标准的研究中，口译员评估自己的表现时认为远程口译不如现场口译"（2010：238）。

从以上研究可以看出，学者们对远程会议口译的早期探索一直没有中断，前期主要关注的是技术的可行性，而对口译员在远程状态下的工作条件和自身感受涉足较少。与此同时，欧洲议会不断推行和资助各种举措，改善视频会议技术，并为远程会议口译制定了技术的最低标准，相关规范详述了视听环境的标准，包括灯光、座位安排、持续时长等各个方面。随着技术不断进步，经过 10 多年的探索，对远程视频会议口译开展大规模实验的条件逐渐具备。到了 90 年代，联合国、欧盟等国际组织展开了不少大规模的实验，充分讨论了远程会议口译的优势与弊端。尤为重要的是，在讨论远程音频和视频信号传输技术的同时，学界开始关注从事远距离口译的口译员自身，并探讨口译员在此新的工作环境和技术条件下所面临的挑战，以及需要应对的策略。从 90 年代中期开始，实验的关注重点转向口译员的表现。

同传统的口译研究一样，对于远程视频口译质量的研究也包括从口译员和客户的"主观"感知到"客观"表现的衡量。研究者展开了对口译员表现质量影响的许多研究（Braun & Taylor，2011；Moser-Mercer，2005；Mouzourakis，2006；Roziner & Shlesinger，2010）。欧洲议会进行了大规模研究，用于比较口译员在远程视频会议口译情境和现场同传情境的不同表现。该研究涵盖了口译员的整体表现、观众反馈、演讲者和听众的"显身性"（visibility），以及各种人体工程学因素（包括冷热舒适度、通风性、灯光和音响效果）等各个方面。研究结果表明，与现场口译相比，远程视频口译员认为自己所面临的压力要大得多，整体表现差于现场口译（Skinner et al.，2018）。在医疗卫生领域，研究者也对远程视频口译员的口译质量有所研究。他们通过比较现场交替传译和远程同声传译视频会议口译发现，后者译文的准确度更高。在医疗卫生领域，尽管相关研究在过去十年中得到了长足发展，但对口译员的表现、准确性等方面的研究仍然不足。

相比而言，国内学者则主要围绕远程口译的历史特点和对教学的启发而展开（肖晓燕，2009；姚斌，2011；詹成，2012；刘春伟、魏立，2017），更多关注传统现场口译和远程口译之间的不同，以及开设远程口译课程的必要性，对于此种口译中的整体质量和口译员表现较少涉及。

第三章
远程口译的研究途径和理论范式

第一节　远程口译的研究途径

上一章我们主要探讨了远程口译研究的职业化、学术化和学科化的过程和三者之间互为基础、互相促进的关系。在此基础上，本章将讨论远程口译研究过程中的学科视角，贯穿远程口译研究始终的核心理念，三者之间的关系，以及应用于远程口译的方法论。

一、远程口译研究的学科视角

口译理论和实践家 Daniel Gile 曾经指出，当下笔译和口译研究范式最大的改变莫过于承认"翻译研究"（Translation Studies）为跨学科研究。口译研究中的跨学科性在于大量借鉴其他学科中的理论和方法，例如神经语言学、认知语言学、语料库语言学、符号学、社会学等（Gile，2004：16）。口译研究在成为一门学科的过程中，大量借鉴其他更加成熟的学科概念和方法（Pöchhacker，2004：47）。因此，要了解远程口译研究中的核心理论及其框架，就要首先了解其主要借鉴和使用了哪些学科视角来进行观察和研究。

谈到口译的学科视角，首先要提到的是口译研究的"母学科"翻译研究。然而纯粹采用翻译研究的理论和方法途径进行的口译研究非常有限，直到 90 年代末，翻译研究的一些基本观点和理念才逐渐被引入口译研究中，进入认识论和方法论层面。Pöchhacker（2004）将此归结为三类原因：一是翻译研究者很多时候将其研究范围局限于笔译，认为不需要将其研究方法和模型应用于口译。即使有少数学者想尝试从理论上对口译进行分析，但由于口译活动转瞬即逝，与固定的书面语言相比，研究起来更加不便，因此放弃了此种尝试。二是口译研究者自身的狭隘性，尤其是主流的会议口译研究团体具有职业封闭传统和自我保护意识，使得口译研究者对一些可能相关的笔译研究成果兴趣不大，例如笔译中的"对等"（equivalence）多年以来一直是翻译学话语研究的中心词，而众多的口译研究者却依旧使用"准确性"（accuracy）等概念，并不加质疑地假定原语和目标语对等。三是笔译研究群体团结并不紧密，翻译研究本身也是"一系列异常庞杂且松散的范式"（Ibid 49）。因此，迄今为止，口译研究更多地受到其他学科研究途径而非笔译或者翻译学研究的影响。远程口译研究也是如此。

口译学者针对远程口译交际和互动的特点，用语言学、认知心理学等相关学科的理论和思维方式、研究方法对远程口译领域进行了多方面的探讨。其中，语言学领域的主要研究途径为话语分析（Braun，2014）。另外，随着当代口译研究中跨学科研究的趋势不断加强，从社会学角度研究口译成为目前国际口译研究的热点。

（一）语言学视角

语言学具有多个分支和交叉学科。在五六十年代口译研究起步之时，口译学者主要借鉴语言学理论和方法对原语和译语中的语音、词汇和语法进行研究。在随后的几十年内，当代语言学又衍生出了许多分支学科，如语篇语言学、对比语言学等，这些下属学科不再局限于研究语言本身，而是把视野扩展到语境和语言的交际功能，以不同的方式为口译研究，尤其是远程口译研究，提供了理论依据和研究模式。

话语分析在其诞生后数十年的发展历程中显示出了独有的蓬勃生命力。话语分析是近年来社会语言学研究较多的一个领域，也是语言学中一个色彩纷呈的研究领域。某种意义上，它是对语言运用的各个方面的研究。人类学家、社会学家、心理学家、哲学家和语言学家分别从不同的侧面切入，试图揭示出话语结构的特征和内在运行规律。对"话语"这个复杂术语的定义往往与诸如"语言"、"交际"、"社会"和"文化"等密切相关。话语分析的出现是人类对语言的认识不断深入的必然结果，体现了语言研究从形式到功能、从静态到动态、从词句分析到话语篇章分析、从语言内部到语言外部、从单一领域到跨学科领域的过渡。由于口译过程体现了话语的显著特点，也成为语言学视角中研究口译的主要路径。

在从理论角度探讨话语之前，我们可以首先从日常生活用语的角度来看看话语的含义。1984 年版的朗文英语词典是这样解释"话语"（discourse）的：话语就是会话，尤其指正式的会话，即在讲话或是作品中将思想观点正式而有序地表达出来，也可以用布道等形式表达出来的一段或是一组连贯的讲话或作品。从这个方面来说，"话语"指的是某种形式的语言运用，公众讲话，或者更笼统地说就是口语或是说话的方式。话语这个术语在媒体和一些社会科学中也广泛使用。"话语"在这里指的不仅是那些带有新思潮的思想家或政客们所使用的语言，还指他们所要宣传的思想和哲学。"话语"实际是在社会互动中为了达成某个目标而说的话。研究"话语"时不仅要把话语当作一个物体，还要将其视为一种处理语言的方式。

话语分析研究者们不满足于对话语的表面描述。Potter 认为话语分析必须在社会实践当中，从语篇和对话两个角度来研究话语。也就是说，语言不单单是描述的工具和交际的媒介，还是一种社会实践和行为处世的方式。这一观点给传统观点带来三大主要转变：（1）从强调对话（话语）和行为之间的区别转变为把对话当作一种行为；（2）从把对话（话语）当作内（外）事件或标志转变为强调对话是指感兴趣的事件；（3）从把行为中出现的多变性看作缺陷转变为承认人们行为之间所存在的多变性。

英国应用语言学家、交际语言教学法创始者之一 Widdow（1979）则从会话功能角度定义话语分析。他认为，话语分析是指对用于交际以完成社会行为的句子的研究。因此，话语可大致定义为句子的使用；其研究目标是自然的会话，既包括书面的又包括口头的；分析的单位可以是句子、句群或是段落。从这一点来讲，话语可以视为一种交际行为，话语的功能只有在社会场合中才能完全发挥出来。

在剑桥语言学丛书中的《话语分析》（*Discourse Analysis*）中，著者Brown 和 Yule（1983）认为，话语分析是对使用中的语言的分析。换言之，话语分析不能仅局限于对语言形式的描述，还要涉及语言功能，即人们使用语言的目的。一般来说，话语分析是指说话者或作者在某个语境中把语言作为交际工具，用来表达意思、实现意图的一个动态的过程。简而言之，话语分析的目标就是考察人类怎样用语言进行交际。他们的观点与著名的美国社会语言学家 Labov 异曲同工。Labov 认为，话语分析就是要制定规则"把所做与所说或所说与所做联系起来"（1969：54）。这种话语分析的关键是将一个语段确定为某种交际行为需要哪些先决条件，只有满足一定条件，话语才可以看作是某种特定的交际行为。

由此可见，所有对话语分析的定义无外乎两个层次：话语是一种结构，话语是一种过程。第一个层次强调话语的组成单位，是对超句单位结构的静态描写，主要揭示各种话语模式中的内部联系和各种句子成分的话语模式；

第二个层次是对交际过程中意义传递的动态分析，是任何形式的语言使用，是一个使用语言来完成的某种目标或行为，强调研究语言的功能是用于达成生活的目标或行为。总的来说，话语分析是对超出句子界限的语言单位的研究，包括研究语言中存在的意义、行为和系统。

首先，话语是一种结构。

回溯现代语言学的发展历程，话语分析学科实际建立在口头交际的基础研究之上。现代语言学一方面强调要研究处于特定情况下的口头话语，并探寻语言、重音、语调、音量等怎样影响话语的声音系统；另一方面，许多非言语行为，比如手势、面部表情、身体位置、身体距离、鼓掌、大笑等，都是研究的对象。研究中有关话语中的视听及身势问题的讨论也形成了话语研究的两种不同模式：语篇和会话。有关书面语篇的研究在过去几十年中有了长足的发展，然而对口头会话研究的重视却仍待发掘。由于口译所具有的言语和非言语特征，话语分析的研究路径近十几年来一直受到研究者青睐。

话语分析专家十分注重研究话语中各种句子的抽象形式，例如词序、词组和分句顺序及可以在句法中研究的各种句子特征。词序的不同和语言形式的差异都使话语表现得多样化。把传统的句法学运用到话语分析当中，不仅可以解释一些过去难以解释的语言问题，也丰富了话语分析的研究途径。

伦敦学派的代表人物 J. R. Firth 早在 20 世纪 30 年代就指出了语境对意义的制约作用。他鼓励语言学家研究会话，从而更好地理解语言本质和规律。因此许多针对话语的分析都采用了语义分析的视角。在涉及语义分析时，话语分析的重心是语段间的意义连续问题，也就是研究话语中所有句子的意义如何融合到一起。这种研究认为，话语由连续的句子所构成，话语的意义是所有句子融合所表达出来的整体意义。实际上话语分析的对象是言语，这个分析单位大于句子或从句的语言单位，并且这些语言序列是连贯的。

研究话语的另一个重要视角是从文体的角度来研究不同形式的话语。某种话语对某些确定词汇的使用在很大程度上取决于话语的类型，整个话语中各语段之间的关系或是说话者（或写作者）的立场与观点。文体所阐释的话语都是以特定的语境为依据的。在不同的语境中，同样的语言特征会产生不同的文体效果，不同的语言特征也可能产生相同的文体效果。从文体的角度讨论话语就是要强调具体运用的话语必须适合特定场合的要求。文体分析认为，尽管话语千差万别，但是许多话语中存在着某些共同的东西（意义、话题、事件等），文体分析所要探讨的就是不同的话语如何表达同样的思想。

结构话语分析派重视的对语言成分的研究，旨在阐述话语结构的规律及各语言组成成分之间的关系。过程话语分析派则研究的是一个动态的话语过程，旨在展示谈话双方在语境因素作用下理解话语含义的交际过程。

其次，话语是一个过程。

当话语研究不断深入时，会遇到一些传统结构主义句法学和语义学所无法解释的语言现象，这些语言现象必须在社会学的领域中才能得到解释。这就表明，话语分析的范围不仅仅局限于音段音位、词缀、句法、语义等范畴，同时还包括来自不同社会和文化环境的人在相互交流时所使用的语言。

Schiffrin（1994）在《话语分析模式》一书中提出，分析话语的几种主要模式是言语行为理论、交际社会语言学理论、话语文化学、语用学理论、会话分析理论和变异分析理论。她同时阐述了各种不同分析模式的侧重点。言语行为理论模式强调通过说话所实现的交际行为。关于语言意义的言语行为理论认为，一切话语不仅表达命题内容，还表达某种实施行为。交际社会语言学认为，实际交际中语言表达的性质可以被解释为谈话人之间话语框架的交换过程。强调语言研究的对象不再局限于传统的句法词汇范畴，而是遍布语言手段的各个方面。交际民族志学则把语言和交际看成一种文化行为。实际上交际民族志学是人类学的一个分支，注重研究跟语言交际相关的民俗文化方面的因素。语用学理论除了规定语用学的形式和范畴、相互关系及使其形式化的最适宜方法，还强调制定经验的自然语言的规则。这些规则使说话者能够将自然语言的法则和适当的语境联系起来。会话分析理论把交谈看作是一种有结构规律可循的社会活动。它同言语行为理论一样，把语言和语言的运用作为社会交际行为的一种形式来研究。变异理论注重语言变体形式的选择与社会因素之间关联性的研究。从 Schiffrin 对话语分析不同研究模式的阐释可以看出，话语分析是众多学科诸如语言哲学、社会语言学、人类学语言学、心理语言学、语用学等的研究对象，它是语言学中一个蓬勃发展的交叉学科。在话语分析的发展过程中，各种研究途径都不同程度地借助了当代语言学的理论成果。

话语分析不仅仅停留在话语中的结构、内部语义及句法表现的层次，话语分析研究的是说话者如何使用话语以完成社会活动，强调话语的交际功能，揭示人类如何理解彼此的话语。荷兰学者 van Dijk（1997）提出"话语行为包括相关的语境及各种策略，诸如发出语音、使用手势、形成语义、使用各种言语行为，以及进行行为互动的话轮转换，形成印象、协商、说服或显示某些种族偏见"。

由此可以看出，话语分析是语言学里的一个跨学科的领域。话语分析学家由于学术背景不同，采用的理论与方法各异，因而会对话语和话语分析采用不同的研究角度和模式。哲学语言学家研究构建的句子之间的语义关系及与语言理解有关的问题，从实验心理学发展出来的一些方法来研究构建的语篇或书面句子序列的理解问题。社会语言家和人类语言学家则主要研究体现在话语中的社会相互作用的结构，特别强调社会语境的特征。因此，由于话语分析的跨学科性质，它研究语言的使用、人的思想和行为互动之间的关系。

从以上有关话语、话语分析的内涵及研究内容的讨论来看，当我们试图给具有复杂特性的话语明确定义时，还可能出现另一个难题：各个不同学科的学者研究话语时没有指定所分析的话语的具体语境，因此难免出现界定不明的情况。

不同学科从不同角度来赋予"话语"和"话语分析"这两个术语的含义及其包括的范围（比如口头语、书面语、超出句子的语言使用，等等）。话语分析这个学科研究的是由抽象的句子结构和组成方式所构成的社会生活。围绕这项主要任务，话语分析最主要的研究方法是记录、转写并分析日常会话语料。另一种方法可以称作人类学的方法，强调研究观察和记录下来的交际行为模式。这便从更广泛的角度观察语言的使用，即把话语作为一种生活和行为方式进行分析，认为话语实践是人作为一个特殊文化成员的知识和行为的一部分。

综上所述，从话语分析学科的发展历程来看，在话语行为的分析方面存在两种不同的研究倾向。一种倾向是从文化背景和谈话的交往目标来分析人们怎样处理话语行为。像 Gumperz、Schiffrin、Tannen 等人的研究都属于这一类。著名人类学家 Gumperz（1983）认为，对话中的发言者不断地推测其他说话者的意图，同时又迅速分析这些意图来作出恰当的反馈。Gumperz 同时提出，话语研究理论必须考虑语言知识和社会文化知识两个方面，这是因为谈话者参与会话行为的必备知识由于人们受不同社会文化情境的影响，会以不同的方式接收会话中所传递的全部或部分信息，并且基于他们在文化背景上的差异，对交际过程中的话语和行为进行不同的阐释。Gumperz 的学生 Tannen 进一步将这种交际社会语言学的研究方法发展到了话语分析层面。Tannen 的分析方法主要有以下特点：（1）记录自然出现的对话；（2）找出交际中出现障碍或困难的片段；（3）找出能够解释这些困难表达意义的一些句型结构的差别；（4）将所有的记录或记录的片段回放给会话参与者听，取得他们自发的阐释和反应，同时也取得他们对研究者阐释的反馈；（5）将交际会话的某些部分放给与说话人同一文化群体的其他人听，以便确定阐释的多种模式。Tannen 的研究方法通过精确的界定把话语分析的核心放在自然出现的对话上，并且这些对话中包含了社会和文化因素。

另一种对话语行为分析的倾向是试图发现支配谈话的话轮、结束语及偏误修正等显性规则。这种研究更加强调所进行的谈话活动，而不是对话的参与者，并试图构建抽象谈话模型，以表明谈话是一种系统的话轮交换而不管是谁在谈话或在谈论什么。

学者们从话语分析的角度研究远程口译发现，与传统的现场口译相比，由于缺乏副语言辅助理解语境，认知加工过程更复杂，远程口译员进入角色状态相对更慢（Sabine，2015：5），这导致口译员在翻译过程中出现了明显的"增词扩容"趋势。Braun 在远程和现场口译的对比研究中提到，实证研究结果表明，现场与远程口译的显著差异之一是大量的增词与增容（Sabine，2017：175），即比起现场口译来，远程口译员的表达会更冗长，增添成分较多。口译的质量准则有明文规定，口译员不得任意删减、增加或者改变原文信息。英国特许语言学家协会准则的 6.4 条款就明确规定："译员应真实翻译，忠于原文，不可以增加、省略或者改变任何内容"（Baraldi，2012：112）。找到增词扩容现象的问题根源与解决方案，是远程口译课程体系建设过程中的重要问题。

（二）心理学视角

在对口译研究产生影响的各主要学科、分支学科和交叉学科中，最引人注目的是心理学，其认识论和方法论的研究路径更多地运用在会议口译（同声传译）研究中。同其他发展的学科一样，心理学也经历了重大的"方向调整"和"范式转换"，这些转变进而影响到口译的心理学研究，包括：对"黑匣子"内部的认知机制的兴趣取代了过去对条件反射层面"语言行为"的研究兴趣；更加重视策略性话语过程研究，而不是针对词汇和语法处理技能的心理语言学；更加针对真实世界中的技能领域进行研究，而不是对建构性实验任务进行分析。口译研究与心理学的很多分支领域相联系，包括认知心理学、教育心理学、心理语言学和神经心理学。

口译认知心理学这一概念在国内外同行中的产生并非偶然，它是口译学与认知心理学等跨学科研究的必然产物。口译教育、口译操作和口译产品的完成离不开认知心理，良好的认知心理有助于口译产品的顺利实现；相反，不良的认知心理会阻碍口译产品的产生。20 世纪 50 年代，在西方国家开始出现口译研究者；60 年代兴起的实验心理学研究促进了口译研究；70 年代形成的以"释意理论"为标志的"巴黎学派"曾长期占据西方口译研究的主导地位；80 年代以意大利 Trieste 口译大会为转折点，口译研究出现了前所未有的发展，主要体现为主题研究的多样化和研究方向的重新定位，同时跨学科研究如口译的神经语言学和神经生理学研究、口译与认知心理学研究、口译语篇学研究等也开始兴起；80 年代至 90 年代，口译的学科地位基本确立，由此建构了口译研究的多模态。然而，早期的口译研究主要是职业口译员的经验总结和口译技巧研究，并主要以教学应用为目的。一些心理学家也纷纷涉足口译研究，他们大多采用实验法和观察法研究同传中的时间间隔、注意力分配、停顿、记忆等问题。一些学者如 Gile、Lambert、Mackintosh、Moser-Mercer、Spielberger、Cassady 和 Johnson 等提倡更为科学的口译研究，比如从认知心理学角度去研究。Gile（1995）的认知负荷模型理论（Effort Model）指出了人脑信息处理容量和注意力资源的有限性。在任务处理过程中，图式及图式的自动化有助于降低认知负荷。Spielberge（1970，1983）在其认知心理的研究过程中提出了状态－特质理论，Kahneman（1973）提出了"注意力分配模式理论"（Energy Assignment Pattern Theory），Cassady 和 Johnson（2002）提出了认知测试焦虑模型理论等。这些理论为口译认知心理研究提供了基础理据。

迄今为止，三种不同的心理学研究途径已被应用在口译研究中，它们是心理学方法、心理语言学方法和认知心理学方法。心理学是一门致力于研究人类信息处理机制的学科。心理学方法运用于口译研究是在 20 世纪 70 年代（Gerver，1971，1972，1975；Moser，1976；Massaro，1978；Lambert，1978）。此方法把信息视为口译活动的基本操作对象，把口译过程看作是一个信息处理过程。没有可操作的信息，口译活动就失去了存在的根本。作为心理学的一个分支，心理语言学以揭示人类语言的习得和交际使用过程（尤其是语言的表达和理解）为研究目的（Labelle，2001）。心理语言学方法正式运用于口译研究始于 20 世纪 70 年代中期（Moser，1976；LeNy，1978；Chernov，1979）。该领域的研究旨在阐明口译过程中所涉及的语言处理活动、语言机制和主体的语言能力。认知心理学作为心理学的另一个重要分支以揭示人类信息处理过程中所蕴含的认知机制和它们的相互作用方式为研究目的。认知心理学方法在口译研究中的应用与前两种方法一样早（Seleskovitch，1978），但是直到 20 世纪 80 年代才开始在译学研究中占据越来越重要的位置。此领域的研究以揭示口译员在特定口译环境下认知机制的运作模式为主要目的，这些认知机制主要包括感觉、感知、注意力、记忆、推理、创造性和意识等。

在口译的研究历史上，很多学者从不同的心理学研究途径出发，创建了各自的口译理论模式。Kohn 和 Kalina（1996）对此作了简要总结。基于信息理论，Kirchhoff（1976）从信息编解码的角度提出了以语言处理为中心的口译理论模式。该模式设定说话者为源语编码信息的发出者，这些信息将首先被口译员解码，再被口译员用译出语重新编码，将信息传达给话语对象。两位口译研究的先驱 Gerver 和 Moser 采用传统的、隶属于心理语言学范畴的方法，将口译过程建立在语言处理的时间流程（flowchart）的基础之上。Seleskovitch 从语义学的角度来研究续传翻译，主张只有在特定的上下文或情景中理解的意思才可以作为口译的基础。这种语义学研究方法被 Lederer 扩展应用于同声传译的研究。Lederer 把意义单位和心理语言学中由上及下的语言处理方式考虑在内，把语言单位的语言学意义和上下文及实际交际场景中的意思区分开来，强调认知补充对意思理解的重要性。Gile（1995）同时采用心理语言学和认知心理学的方法，根据自己的翻译和教学实践提出了著名的精力分配模式。Stenzl、Mackintosh、Kurz、Kalina 和 Pöchhacker 基于认知心理学的研究成果，采用动态心理语言学的研究方法把口译过程看作是一个策略性的统一整体，这个整体由一系列由上及下或由底到顶的语言处理活动构成。

以上口译研究的三大心理学研究途径和与之相对应的日趋客观化、科学化的理论模式不仅反映出了口译过程与信息处理、语言处理和认知机制间的紧密联系，也体现了口译认知研究的跨学科性质。这三大研究途径在口译研究中是相互渗透、不可分割的。口译过程实质上是一个以话语信息为处理操作对象，以影像为转换媒介，由口译员的认知和语言处理机制共同参与并控制的一个心理过程。口译任务的成功与否和所达到的效果是由口译员大脑认知机制的运作方式和语言处理效率所决定的。

对于认知心理的研究可以追溯到 17 世纪，当时人们就有对情绪采取理性控制的信念之说，到了 19 世纪焦虑便成了人们无可回避的问题。19 世纪中叶，Kierkegaard 对焦虑进行了直接深刻的研究。20 世纪初，弗洛伊德曾就认知心理学中的焦虑问题指出，所谓的"客观焦虑"属正常焦虑的范畴，是正常焦虑的共同形式之一。它是人类与生俱来的有限性，反映了人类面对自然力量、病痛及终极死亡时的脆弱，这在德国哲学思想中被称作"原始焦虑"。这一焦虑并不隐含自然的敌意，也不会引出防卫机制，除非人类的有限性成为个体内在的其他冲突和问题的焦点。1939 年，著名心理学大师

Mowrer（1939）认为焦虑是人类行为的重要动机之一，人类有机体与其先祖一样，具有对外来威胁进行反应的能力。罗洛·梅（2010）提出了焦虑量（volumes of anxiety）与焦虑形式的问题。他认为，焦虑的能力并非习得而来，然而个体的焦虑量与焦虑形式则由习得所获。关于考试焦虑的研究最早可以追溯到 1914 年，Fenling 等人通过测试医学院的学生，发现他们在期末考试前后尿中糖分的变化。Strom 等（1987）还从课堂性格特征方面对课程程度和考试焦虑的相关性进行了测定。Calvo 和 Carreiras（1993）研究了考试焦虑对学生阅读过程的影响，发现考试焦虑度高的学生比焦虑度低的学生在理解同一篇文章上花费的时间要多，表现出低效的特点。苏联学者 Luria 也注意到考试状态中学生的言语，他的"测验焦虑问卷"的问世，使后来的研究者们开始从不同的角度研究考试焦虑问题。

20 世纪中叶开始，焦虑由潜藏到公开、由隐性到显性，成为共同关注的问题，随之，也就由"隐性焦虑的年代"进入"显性焦虑的年代"（Auden，1947：3）。焦虑是一种反映"情绪状态"的重大现象，被 Freu（1974）誉为"关键问题"，由此焦虑成为西方心理学、哲学、宗教学、教育学、社会学等领域的重大研究课题。Cassady 和 Johnson（2002）通过在认知范围内进行的测量，指出考试焦虑度高的学生情绪不安定，具有神经质的特征，其学习成绩会受到负面影响。这些研究虽然没有明确提出焦虑级度的概念，但是对焦虑等级已开始涉及。

随着西方国家焦虑研究的深入，焦虑逐渐在学习理论与动力心理学中被模因（meme）发展为重要的问题。然而，当时的多数研究显示，焦虑对外语学习的影响是负面的，它与学习成绩、表达能力、自信心之间均存在着负相关。之后，以不同形式和信息增量呈现的模因得到广泛传播，其信息模因深入人心（康志峰，2013b）。21 世纪初，焦虑模因陆续传入中国。纵然认知心理研究起步较早，然而真正意义上的口译与认知心理学的跨学科研究却凤毛麟角，直到近些年才有所推进。

从 20 世纪末起，中国开始对认知心理中的正常焦虑和考试焦虑等问题进行探讨。叶仁敏等人（1989）的研究发现，中国大部分中学生的成就动机很高，考试焦虑度不高，智力水平较高。王银泉和万玉书（2001）、李炯英（2004）、贾飞（2010）等一大批学者从整体焦虑研究的视角切入，指出外语学习焦虑对外语学习所产生的负面影响，这一由国外模因而来的焦虑整体论只谈及焦虑对外语学习的负面效应，而忽视了它的促进作用。郝玫和郝君平（2001）的研究虽然在整体论概念模因基础上产生了信息内容的增量，提及学生英语成绩与成就动机存在正相关，差异均达显著水平，但并没有将其细化，没有分清焦虑的高、中、低三个层次，更没有明确究竟是焦虑的哪个级度与外语成绩产生正相关。邓愉联（2008）将焦虑分成促进性焦虑和退缩性焦虑。其中促进性焦虑使学习者产生动力，迎接新的学习任务；退缩性焦虑使学习者产生反动力，逃避学习任务。这一区分对焦虑研究的学习理论具有明显的进步意义。中国的认知心理研究起步较晚，真正意义上的口译与认知心理跨学科研究就更晚了，近年来产生了一系列相关研究专著，如《同声传译与工作记忆的关系研究》（张威，2007）、《口译中听、译两种焦虑模态的认知心理管窥》（康志峰，2010）、《认知心理视阈下的口译研究》（康志峰，2012）及《口译认知心理学》（康志峰，2013）等，再加上发表的相关论文（康志峰，2011，2012a，2012b，2012c，2013b；张威，2012；王湘玲，2013），从多个方面切入口译的认知心理研究，包括口译焦虑的动因、级度和影响、多模态口译焦虑的级度溯源、口译多模态焦虑、立体论与多模态口译教学、口译研究的跨学科探索，以及认知心理因素对口译策略的影响，等等，从细节上充实了口译认知心理学的研究。

在远程口译中，由远程沟通所产生的距离感和对电信设备的不适感，对口译员的包括焦虑在内的心理有不同程度的影响。因而，从心理学角度对远程口译所进行的探索，能帮助研究者找到远程口译的跨学科研究方法。

二、远程口译研究的方法论

研究方法是指在研究中发现新现象、新事物，或提出新理论、新观点，揭示事物内在规律的工具和手段。对口译研究学科来说，研究方法对于学科发展和学术研究的意义重大，主要体现在两个方面。一方面，研究方法有利于学科的可持续发展。特定学科研究方法的完善在一定程度上代表了该学科的完善程度。另一方面，研究方法有利于学术规范的形成。研究方法是人们解决科学问题时所采取的基本手段、途径和规则，对于学术规范的形成和完善有很重要的意义。

方法论是关于研究方法的理论，是指导科学研究的基本假设、逻辑、原则、程序、方法等问题，是指导科学研究的一般思想方法或哲学观点。简而言之，方法论就是对研究方法的科学性、客观性、有效性的讨论和论证，而研究方法则是研究的具体操作方法、技术、程序。任何科学研究都要求遵循一定的方法论，通常包括探求的模式（演绎推理或归纳推理）、数据的性质（定量或定性）、研究目的、总体方法论策略等。传统的探究模式多以演绎推理居多，即从理论到数据，先在理论框架内确定一个假设，然后确定可测量的变量，通过实验、观察、调查等方法获得定量数据来证实假设的真伪。与演绎相反的是归纳推理，即通过观察、实验和调查来获得定性数据，然后概括出一个理论。研究目的总体上是探究、描述或解释。根据具体目的，研究者会采取一个整体的方法论策略来处理实证数据。方法论通常分为三种：观察法、实验法和调查法。观察法又称为实地考察（field work），是指当研究对象发生时在现场对它进行观察或收集数据，如研究者亲眼实地观察、录音或录像等；实验法是指在实验室中模拟真实场景获取数据；而调查法主要是通过访谈或调查问卷的方式获取数据。

口译研究自身也展现了其方法论的多样性和不断发展的潜力，既有偏"实证科学"的，也有偏"人文科学"的。如下所示，口译研究按研究目的、研究用途、研究性质等不同标准可分为不同的研究方法类型：按研究目的可分为探索性研究、描述性研究、解释性研究、预测性研究；按研究逻辑可分为归纳研究和演绎研究；按研究用途分为理论研究和应用研究；按研究性质可分为定性研究和定量研究。具体方法有观察法、调查法、实验法、文献研究法、理论思辨法、经验总结法等。

远程口译中多实证研究，以下将具体阐述。

（一）观察法

观察法是研究者为了描述口译行为和活动并发现口译现象的本质和规律而采取的研究方法。观察法实施的关键步骤包括：

（1）进行大略的调查和试探性观察。这一步工作的目的不在于搜集材料，而在于掌握基本情况，以便能正确地计划整个观察过程。

（2）确定观察的目的和中心。根据研究任务和研究对象的特点，考虑要弄清楚什么问题，需要什么材料和条件，在此基础上确定观察的目的和中心。如果目的和中心不明确，观察便不能集中和深入。

（3）确定观察对象。一是确定拟观察的总体范围；二是确定拟观察的个案对象；三是确定拟观察的具体项目。

（4）制定观察计划和提纲。观察计划除了明确和规定观察的目的、中心、范围，以及要聊什么问题、搜集什么材料之外，还应当安排好观察过程，包括观察次数、密度、每次观察持续的时间及如何保证观察现象的常态等。在观察计划的基础上，应对每次或每段观察提出具体提纲，以便使观察者对每一次观察的目的、任务和要获得什么材料非常明确。观察提纲应包括每次观察的具体问题。

（5）确定观察手段。观察手段包括两个方面：一种是获得观察资料的手段；一种是保存观察资料的手段。获得观察资料的手段主要是人的感觉器官，但有时需要一些专门设置的仪器来帮助观察，如录像、观察屏、计算机终端装置、动作反应器等。这些仪器主要起两方面作用：保证观察的客观性与提高观察的精确性。在保存资料的手段中，人脑是天然的器官，但这种与观察主体连在一起的保存手段缺乏精确性和持久性，也不能实现资料的客体化。因此，我们可利用文字笔记等书面手段及摄影、录音、录像等技术手段，把观察时瞬间发生的事物状况准确、全面地记录下来，供研究中反复观察和分析所用。

对远程口译活动进行现场观察，能够对口译行为的功能及通过这些行为显示的文化背景进行描述和分类。将翻译的话语和未经翻译的话语进行归类，可划分为协调（Wadensjö，1998）或整体融合（Angelelli，2004）、促进对话者的积极参与（Baraldi，2012；Gavioli，2012）、进行文化预设（Mason，2006），以及不同话语和文化社区之间的调和（Angelelli，2004，2012）。

（二）实验法

实验法是指研究者依据一定的研究假设，主动操纵研究变量，并对非研究变量予以自觉、明确和适度的控制，分析和统计研究数据，从而检验研究假设的一种研究活动。

通俗地说，这是一种先假设后检验的研究方法。假设就是从已有的理论和经验出发，形成某种思想和理论构想，即假说；检验就是将形成的假说在有计划、有控制的实践中加以验证。通过对实验对象的观察，确立自变量与因变量之间的关系，有效地验证和完善假说。

所谓假说，就是根据事实材料和一定的科学理论，对所研究问题的因果性和规律性在进行研究之前预先作出一个推测性论断和假定性解释。假说的形成是一个理论构思过程。一般经过三个阶段：发现问题—初步假设—形成假说。

所谓变量，即在研究过程中，需要进行操纵控制和测量的诸因素，主要有自变量、因变量和干扰变量。

自变量又称实验因子或实验因素，即由研究者认为可以操纵控制的、有计划变化的因素。它由实验者操纵，由于其自身独立的变化而引起其他变量发生变化。它有如下特征：（1）它的变化会导致研究对象发生反应；（2）它的变化能够被研究者所操纵控制。

因变量又称应变量或依变量，它随自变量的变化而变化，是研究者打算观测的变化因素。它有如下特征：（1）随自变量变化而变化，或对自变量作出反应；（2）根据需要，有待观测的因素；（3）以某种反应参数来表征的可测量因素。

干扰变量：又称控制变量、非实验因子或无关因子，指除了研究者操纵的自变量之外，其他会引起研究对象因变量变化的影响因素。干扰变量在实验中必须严格加以控制，为了更好地探索因果关系，以切实保证因变量的变化是由自变量的变化所引起的，就必须排除其他无关因素的影响，控制无关因素，使实验除了自变量以外的其他条件保持一致，这样才能保证实验研究具有一定的效度。

实验法操作过程的主要步骤为：

（1）形成假说。

（2）制定严谨的科学实验方案（选择被试、确定对比组、实验方法过程的设计、实验材料和工具的选择、研究无关变量及其控制措施、实验的阶段划分、原始过程性资料积累的方案与分工、成果形式的确定等）。

（3）按照方案实施实验。

（4）形成实验的阶段性报告和总结性报告。

（5）对实验进行评价论证。

学者们十分关注远程口译双语转换过程中体现的语言现象，包括用实验的方法来比较远程口译中自然口译员（未经培训）和受过正式培训的专业口译员、工作语言和方向。此外，心理语言学分析也有侧重于远程口译时的理解和产出所涉及的认知和信息过程、认知负荷和大脑功能。相关的实验性远程口译研究还分析了口译中涉及的各种同步过程，包括听力和口语以及输入和输出（也称为耳声跨度或时滞）。例如 Isham 和 Lane（1994）、Hyönää 等（1995）、Massaro 和 Shlesinger（1997）以及 Englund Dimitrova 和 Hyltenstam（2000）。学者们还探索了远程同声传译中工作记忆、短期记忆、长期记忆和/或注意力资源之间的关系，并以口译表现的测量为因变量。采取实验方法来研究远程口译通过对口译产品的评估来关注口译的质量或有效性，包括分析源语和目标语的词汇或语义对应、传递特征、源语言影响的表现、接受者/客户的理解或对功效和/或专业性的判断（Pöchhacker，2001；Shlesinger et al.，1997）。

（三）调查法

调查研究是研究者采用问卷、访谈、观察、测量等方式对现状进行了解，对事实进行考察，在收集相关材料和数据的基础上对口译问题和口译现象进行探讨的研究方法。

调查研究包含两层意思。一是调查，指运用观察、询问、测量等方式收集事实和数据；二是研究，指对数据资料进行思维加工。

调查法的基本操作过程为：

（1）确定调查的目的。确定问题，形成假说。

（2）确定抽样总体。要从中进行抽样的总体应与要得到的信息的总体一致。从样本得出的结论适用于被抽样总体，超出这个范围的结论的使用程度取决于被抽样总体与目标总体的差异程度。

（3）确定待收集的数据。一般只收集与调查目的有关的数据，过长的调查表会降低回答的质量。

（4）选择抽样方法。

（5）确定需要的精确度。因抽样调查是要由样本推断总体，会带有某些不确定性。一般是对相对误差或绝对误差作出概论水平上的要求。

（6）抽样调查实验。在小范围内试填调查表，对调查表进行必要的改进。

（7）实施调查。

（8）进行数据分析。

（9）写出调查报告。留存有关调查对象总体的信息，可能对将来的抽样起指导作用。

调查法可用于研究远程口译中的许多主题，例如质量评估、培训、口译员的角色、口译员的社会地位，以及口译策略。调查法多用集中在翻译行业。例如，调查远程口译员作为职业群体的职业、身份和地位。调查法一直是质量评估研究中最有效的方法之一。基于问卷调查的会议口译质量研究可以侧重于用户期望和/或用户响应。Angelelli（2004）的口译研究中详细介绍了口译员的人际角色量表如何开发，并描述了改进和测试测量量表的可靠性和有效性的方法。她利用调查、同行在研讨会上的反馈、文献综述和对口译员的采访进行材料整理和编写，然后根据专家意见和专项小组来确定量表的内容效度。

以上三种研究方法在远程口译研究中的特点、手段和作用各异。

第二节　远程口译研究的理论范式和理论模型

　　侧重于信息通信技术支持的口译研究总体上与机器翻译研究不同，但有关质量的研究却成为共同的标准。在会议环境中比较现场口译质量和远程视频口译（同声传译）的研究发现，除了早期的远程口译疲劳之外，这两种模式下的质量几乎没有差异（Moser-Mercer，2003；Roziner & Shlesinger，2010）。相比之下，在法律环境中比较现场和视频口译（交替传译）的研究揭示出两者存在重要的质量差异，且远程口译中较早出现疲劳（Braun，2013；Braun & Taylor，2012）。在医疗保健领域，现场口译（交替传译）和通过音频链接进行的远程同声传译的比较显示，后者具有更高的准确度（Hornberger et al.，1996）。

　　许多研究已经超越了对翻译质量的研究，引出了与人体工程学因素和工作条件等相关的问题。例如，远程会议口译的综合研究指出了口译员的一些心理和生理问题，诸如压力、远程工作时的不适感，以及口译员的疲劳和对自身表现的不满（Moser-Mercer，2003；Roziner & Shlesinger，2010）。医疗保健和法律口译领域的研究开始关注用户的看法和偏好。一些研究者从医疗保健管理的角度调查了医疗口译员、医生和患者的看法，以确定与现场口译相比，远程口译是否具有同样的效率（Azarmina & Wallace，2005；Locatis et al.，2010；Price et al.，2012）。调查表明，口译员和医生通常更喜欢现场口译，也喜欢远程口译中的视频会议口译。值得注意的是，Price 等人对口译员的调查（2012）表明，所有这三种方式都能传达较为完整的信息，研究同时对信息通信技术支持的方法进行评级，但由于与远程参与者建立融洽关系的困难更大，因此远程口译在人际关系的沟通方面不太令人满意。根据一些调查发现，口译员的自我认知中，现场口译和远程口译的准确程度相似（Azarmina & Wallace，2005），但法律环境的研究表明，口译员中存在对口译表现看法的差异（Braun & Taylor，2012）。

　　在第二章远程口译研究发展历程的讨论和本章第一节远程口译方法论讨论的基础上，本节将使用"范式"（paradigm）这一概念来追溯远程口译研究中特定研究模型的出现和发展，并探究他们目前的地位和相互关系。

一、远程口译研究的理论范式

"范式"的概念由美国物理学家 Thomas Kuhn 在《科学革命的结构》（*The Structure of Scientific Revolutions*，1962）一书中首次提出。他认为科学理论不是能被经验证实或证伪的个别命题的集合，而是由许多相互联系、彼此影响的命题和原理组成的系统整体。他将这一系统称为范式，并指出范式是某一科学团体在长期的探索、教育和训练中形成的共同信念。范式理论最初只针对自然科学，后来被应用于社会科学。

范式的概念有广义和狭义之分，广义的范氏指具有共同理念的研究团体，狭义的范式是指研究方法的范例。口译研究者对范式理论的使用各不相同。Moser-Mercer（1994）用范式来区分不同的口译研究群体：社会科学群体和自然科学群体。Miriam Schlesinger（1995）则把范式作为一个理论和方法论模式应用于更为具体的口译研究。最早对口译范式进行系统研究的是 Franz Pöechhacker（2006），他借助 Chesterman 的模因理论和 Kuhn 的范式概念，将 20 世纪 70 年代以来的口译研究归纳为五种研究范式：翻译释意理论范式（IT paradigm，interpretative theory of translation）、认知处理研究范式（CP paradigm，cognitive processing）、神经语言学研究范式（NL paradigm，neuro-linguistic paradigm）、翻译理论研究范式（TT paradigm，translation-theoretical paradigm）和话语互动研究范式（DI paradigm，dialogic discourse-based interaction）。

第一种范式是 20 世纪 70 年代以 Seleskovitch 为代表的巴黎学派所倡导的翻译释意理论范式。该范式的提出主要依据广义上的范式概念，即具有共同理念的研究群体，他们认可基本相同的假设、价值、方法和标准。IT 范式的核心理念是释意模因，强调口译过程中脱离语言外壳的意义的重要性，即口译是意义交流的活动，而不是简单的语言代码转换。这个方法论主要依靠对真实口译实践的观察而非在实验室中进行实验。释意理论非常强调观察法的重要性，不太注重实验等实证方法，因此其口译研究结果大多是规定性的，缺乏一定的科学依据。释意理论范式是最早的口译范式，对当前的口译研究仍然有很大影响。

第二种范式是 20 世纪 80 年代中后期由一部分对心理学和认知科学感兴趣的口译研究者提出的认知处理研究范式。这些学者同释意派学者一样，也试图解释口译员的大脑活动，但不赞成仅仅使用基于本能的自然主义方法，而是希望借助心理学和认知科学的研究方法来达到目的。代表人物包括

David Gerver、Jennifer Mackinntosh、Catherin Stenzl 和 Sylvie Lambert 等人。他们公开挑战释意派理论，称其缺乏科学性，提倡通过跨学科合作来提高口译研究的科学水平。该范式的核心理念是"认知信息处理"，认为口译是一种信息加工活动。这种范式通常使用实验法来验证研究假设，引导了以实验手段为主的实证研究的"复兴"。

第三种范式是在 20 世纪 90 年代 Turku 大会后出现的神经语言学研究范式，主要由 Triest 大学的神经语言学家 Franco Fabbro 和 Laura Curran 提倡。他们依靠更为专业的神经心理学实验研究方法，如近年来运用的大脑成像技术，使"正在翻译中的大脑"得以视觉化，试图解密口译的认知过程。该范式主要用神经科学的方法来研究口译，但是对于口译研究的影响力却是有限的，因为它主要关注大脑的功能和翻译时大脑半球的运作情况，对于研究设备和研究方法要求很高。

以上几个范式考察的都是口译员的心理加工活动，而对口译的社会文化语境未曾提及，与之有关的社会交际问题也鲜有探讨。20 世纪 80 年代，德国功能派翻译理论家 Hans Vermeer 提出了翻译目的论（Skopos Thoery）。他认为翻译行为都是由翻译目的决定的，即译者的目的、译文的目的和翻译手段要达到的目的。这些目的更多由译语接受者的交际需求和期待、情景和社会文化语境所决定，而非传统的翻译原则（原语译语对等、忠实性等）。随着目的论在翻译研究中的广泛运用，口译研究者开始将目的论引入口译研究，认为口译活动是由交际需要、目的语受众或社会文化环境所决定。受 Vermeer 影响，Stenzl 在 Treiste 研讨会上呼吁拓宽口译研究的视野，采用偏重功能性的途径，把口译活动放在整个交际过程中进行研究，将发言人、口译员和接受者都考虑进来（Stenzl，1989）。Poechhacker 则以功能主义理论为基础构建概念模型，对会议口译同传中的互动、情景及其文本特征进行实证分析。总的来说，以功能主义为基础的口译实证研究相对较少，直到该研究途径与翻译学的另一个研究趋势——以译文为导向的描述翻译学——融合后才逐渐形成了口译研究的又一新范式，即以目标语语篇为导向的翻译理论途径，又称为翻译理论研究范式，其代表人物是 Schlesinger 和 Poechhacker（2004）。这一范式已经开始关注文本、交际和社会文化问题，探讨交际各方如何从社会文化立场出发彼此进行互动。

第五种是 20 世纪 80 年代末到 90 年代初产生的话语互动研究范式。以 Roy 和 Wadensjö 为代表的学者从人类学、社会学和社会语言学的研究成果中获取灵感，开始关注各种对话口译类型，并将口译视为发生在一定社会和机构语境下、以口译员为中介、三方参与的交际谈话过程，通过对"作为交际活动的谈话"（talk as inter activity）的分析来弥补"作为文本谈话"（talk as text）的观察视角的不足，体现的是话语产出和协调的模因。他们的研究为口译研究提供了一个新的概念途径和语篇研究方法，从而催生了话语互动研究范式的诞生。话语互动范式在 20 世纪 90 年代不断发展，出现了很多基于话语的实证研究。

根据 Kuhn 的研究，当旧的范式无法解决新问题时，就会出现新的研究模式，挑战旧范式的地位并最终导致范式转换（paradigm shift），从而推动科学的不断发展。虽然 Pöechhacker 的口译研究参考了 Kuhn 的范式理论，但他并不认同范式转换的观点。他认为范式的变化是一种进化（evolution）而非革命（revolution），虽然范式之间存在着争议和矛盾，但也具有一定的互补性，因此口译领域呈现的是多种范式并存且相互关联的局面（Pöechhacker，2006）。正如 Garzone 和 Viezzi 所总结的，"尽管口译研究基于多种范式，但所有的学者都愿意把自己归于这个独立而且自重的研究群体，而且这个群体也越来越得到全球科学界的认可"（2001：11）。远程口译研究的范式也从初始的话语分析逐步转向认知研究和多模态研究。

二、远程口译研究的理论模型

模型是所研究的系统、过程、事物或概念的一种表达形式，是人们根据研究目的，在一定的假设条件下，再现某种事物或现象的结构、功能、属性、关系、过程等本质特征的物质形式或思维形式。模型包括实物模型和理论模型，其中建构模型是一种特殊的理论研究方式。理论模型也可采取多种表达形式，如语言描述、数学公式、图像或图表，其中后两者能够直接形象地表达一种现象，因此成为较为常见的模型形式。模型可用于研究多种目的。理论模型可以对关于某种现象的直觉上的假定和观点进行表达，以直接的观察和实证数据为基础而建立的模型则旨在描述"现实"的某一方面。

远程口译研究的范围较为广阔，从关注围观过程的认知领域到宏观交际过程的社会文化层面均包括在内，因此可以涵盖以下不同的研究焦点：社会—职业角度将远程口译看作一种社会职业来建构模型。如果进一步缩小研究焦点，把关注点放在特定的社会机构上，如国际组织、法庭、医疗机构等，则可以突出远程口译在机构中的功能。如果将视角放在特定种类的交际活动，如会议或访问，远程口译的互动功能就会凸显出来。如果关注语篇作为交际过程中的物质载体这一特性，分析者可以将远程口译视为一种语篇或话语过程。对语言应用中所蕴含的思维过程的兴趣促成了远程口译认知模式的诞生。人类思维活动的物质基础也可以作为建模的对象，其中最重要的是关于大脑组织和脑部活动的理论模式，即神经层面的研究。远程口译中不同的分析层次如下所示：

（一）社会—职业和机构模型

人类学层次中的远程口译研究模型关注历史进程中的社会间关系和文化身份。曾文中（1992）的口译职业化模式是口译研究中社会—职业模式的代表，它以台湾的会议口译市场为参考，从口译作为一个在社会中被认可的职业的角度对其进行描述。该模式概括了口译职业化的四个阶段，描述口译如何从"市场混乱"的阶段发展到拥有"职业自主性"的阶段。如果将特定社会或社会文化的层次进一步具体化，可以从远程口译的发展、功能和经济的角度，也就是从机构的层面对口译进行建模。Agger-Gupta（2001）的研究描述了加拿大和美国医疗机构中发生的与口译相关的变化，在许多同类模型中具有代表性。这些模式描述口译服务在不同的机构背景下，如何从"设法应付"的阶段发展到文化上得到适当关心的、具有成熟特征的阶段。远程口译在过去几年也逐渐发展成一种职业模式。

（二）话语互动模型

互动模式代表了存在于互动过程中参与各方之间的社会、情景和交际关系。这些模式可以进一步分为三类：第一类勾画了互动各方的格局，第二类关注交际过程，第三类描述语篇或话语在交际互动中扮演的角色。

1. 交际各方格局

Anderson（1976/2002）勾画了以口译员为媒介的基本互动格局。在这种互动中，说 A 语言的单语发言人和说 B 语言的单语发言人通过精通两种语言的口译员进行交流。Anderson 的线性格局图突出了双语口译员在交流中的重要地位。其他学者则使用三角模型来描绘口译员的地位和作用。在三角模型中，口译员被置于顶点的位置。随后，学者们从不同角度对基本的三方交际模型进行了延展，解释了更加复杂的互动格局。

Gile（1995b）提出了会议环境下互动格局的简单模式。在该模式中，单语发言人面对人数众多的听众，且部分听众听不懂源语，因此需要依赖翻译。如果将 Gile 模式进一步具体化，则可以将所有对口译员工作造成影响的各方考虑进来，其中包括会议组织人员、文件服务人员和技术员等。Chiaro

（2002）关于电视口译中不同互动方格局的多个模式彰显了特殊机构内口译模式的复杂性。在电视口译中，面对面的交流方式和大众传媒中典型的"一对多"传播方式结合在一起。无论是"一对一"还是"一对多"的口译互动模式，都可以通过添加更多参与方的方式被延伸和具体化，同时也可以将模式进一步完善，从而更好地反映互动各方的相关特征。

这一互动者模型突出了互动中交际"个人"的"角色"，认为个人在交际中的意图定位和对其他参与方的评价是由个人的社会文化背景或视野所决定的，而这种背景和视野优势由多种认知能力和经验所组成。也就是说，从认知的角度来看，一种情景只是在参与方的视角中存在。受到与"感知"和"性格"相关的生理和心理因素影响，个人的定位和评价（包括动机、情感态度、期望值和意图）决定了某个场合的面貌，以及如何在该场合中采取行动。Wadensjö（1998）指出，口译员有着多重听话人身份，并以"接收样式"（reception format）为主题进行分类，包括以"报告者"身份来听取内容（只需要重复所听到的内容），以"裁定者"身份来听取内容（用权威的方式将说话人所讲的内容概括传递出来）和以"回应者"身份来听取内容（听话后需要在输出时考虑整个语篇）。Wadensjö 特别强调"发言人身份"和"听话人身份"的共时性，认为说和听的过程常常同时进行，听的过程也包含了显性的语言活动。Wadensjö 在话语至话语层面解释了"发言人—听话人角色"格局中的动态变化，从而"通过持续的语篇流中可能不断变化的排练组合"来重构交流互动系统。

2. 交际模式

早在 20 世纪 70 年代，Ingram 根据标准的交际模式提出了口译的符号交际模式（1985）。这个模式原为描述手语翻译而设计，它超越了传统口译研究中的"信息转换"概念，指出"信息是由相互交织的不同编码所承载的"，模式提到了"语境"，口译员被描述为"渠道"中的语码转换站。Kirchhoff（1976）参照 Ingram 的模式提出了更为详细的"交际双重系统"模式。在该系统中，信息由语言和非语言信号组成，信息发送人在特定的情境和社会文化背景中对信息进行编码，并传递给目标语境中的主要接收人。口译员是将该系统的两个部分联系在一起的中介。口译员在此过程中成了口译过程的参与者之一：一方面是源语信息的次要接收人，另一方面是目标语信息的次级发送人。Poyatos 的研究中（1987/2002）利用矩阵的方式将口译中出现的听觉及视觉符号系统进行了横向和纵向的排练，形成了不同的听觉/视觉共存格局。

3. 文本和语篇

Stenzl（1983）是口译研究中首个借用语篇理论和翻译理论对口译互动进行理论模式建构的学者。她以翻译过程的语篇理论模式为基础，围绕发言人、口译员和目标语文本接收者对同声传译中的交际信息流进行了描述。尽管这一模式最初是针对同声传译设计的，但因为适用面广，现在已经成为描述口译过程中交际信息流动的一个普遍模式。Stenzl 指出，这一口译过程的步骤之间存在"互动及共时性"（1983：47）。信息流动模式是一个互动模式，也是一个加工模式，不仅描述了各交际方及其互动，同时也展现了口译员本身的信息加工过程。

（三）信息加工模型

早期的口译加工模型主要关注的是翻译过程的性质。

1. 翻译过程

Seleskovitch 对口译任务进行了偏向认知层面的分析，指出交替传译和同声传译的机制是一个"三角的过程"（1962：16），三角形的每个顶点是意义的构建。根据这一模式，翻译中的核心处理过程并非语言的"代码转换"，而是口译员对"意义"的理解和表达。在这一理论中，"意义"是有意识的，由语音引发的语言含义及认知扩展部分组成；同时也是非语言的，即说和认知记忆中的任何语言形式相分离。翻译过程在根本上是根据不依靠语言的话语意义来进行的，翻译并非单纯的语言转换过程。Garcia-Landa（1998）根据心理语言学的研究，进一步分析了三角模型。他认为该模型中包含了两个话语行为，两者是由"意义对等"原则联系起来的，即发言人原本的话语行为意图等同于口译员对于该意图的理解，并随之成为口译员输出目标语语篇的意图。这一意图又等同于客户对于想表达的意义的理解。为了更好地反映语篇理解和输出过程，该模式涉及注意力门槛、记忆结构（工作记忆、长期记忆激活）、语篇组件及情境变量等因素。远程口译由于空间疏远的原因，翻译认知过程受到多种因素影响，从而影响口译员的行为。

2. 多重任务

Ledere 设计了更为详细的同传过程模式，包括八种思维活动。在同一时间内，两种或两种以上的活动同时进行。他将这些活动分为三大类：持续进行和并行的活动（听辨、语言理解、概念形成、以认知记忆为基础形成的表达）；一直"潜伏"并间歇出现的活动（感知情景、自我监控）；间歇出现的活动（语码转换、寻找特殊的词汇表达）。Ledere 将输入语理解、概念形成和表达等主要加工过程与工作记忆和长期记忆的功能联系起来，模式较为全面。Kirchhoff 认为基本的加工模式包括了"解码"（decoding）、"重新编码"（recording）、"输出"（production）和"监控"（monitoring）四个部分。这一模式旨在解释心理语言学层面的处理难点，而不是描述"理想口译"的过程。此后，Gile（1985）认为口译中有三个基本的认知负荷，分别是"听辨与理解"（listening）、"语言表达"（production）和"记忆"（memory）。Gile 用该认知负荷模式来解释口译中的处理难点和失误，他认为可以解释导致口译中失误的原因，例如专有名词、数字和复杂的技术词汇等。

3. 复杂的操作过程

Gerver 首次提出了同声传译的心理加工模式，设计了模式流程图用来描述源语的输入加工和目标语输出过程中的心理结构和步骤。该模式描述了记忆结构（短期缓冲储存、长期记忆体系、输出缓冲）和口译员可控的步骤，如放弃参看输入语、输入前测、输出监控和为了提高输出质量的"反向跟踪"。Gerver 的模式从心理学的角度对口译过程进行了分析，同时区分了语言的表层元素（语音、单词、句子）和被口译员理解的语言的深层含义。到 20 世纪 70 年代中期，Moser-Merser（1978）设计了同声传译的记忆结构和加工过程模式，以心理语言学的话语理解模式为基础，关注短语层和句子层的源语输入加工阶段，同时也反映了源语输入驱动的加工过程与长期记忆的知识之间的互动。该模式假设了加工过程中一系列的决策点，而这些决策点决定了整个加工过程是继续进行还是回到上一阶段。这些决策点之一就和预测有关。如果预测的效果足够大，能够激活目标语中的相关内容，则可以省略中间的许多加工步骤。Hiroaki Kitano（1993）设计了话语至话语的翻译系统 DMDIALOG，能够处理简单的电话对话。该混合体系包括了象征性的信息处理部分，用来解释语法分析等基于规则的活动和联结主义的网络。远程口译中出现的"疏离"会造成口译员认知压力，并加剧疲劳感，进而影响口译表现（Skinner，Napier & Braun，2018；姚斌，2011）。在此情况下，口译员的主体性进一步增强，更倾向于采取增添和解释的翻译策略。

第四章
远程口译研究热点

　　口译是一项非常复杂的认知任务（Gile，2009；Moser-Mercer，2000），对口译员工作环境的任何改变都可能影响其表现和处理信息的方式。针对远程口译员工作的研究，学界主要关注如下几点：存在感缺乏，超负荷认知，口译策略，远程口译所需的知识和技能，以及口译员的权限和角色等。

　　国际会议口译员协会（AIIC，2000）提出了在会议口译中使用远程和电话会议口译的基本准则。根据相关国际机构的研究，Causo（2012）概述了通过视频链接进行远程会议口译的最低技术标准。Hoogen 和 Rotterdam（2012）总结了在法律诉讼中使用视频会议的最低要求。欧盟 AVIDICUS 项目为法律诉讼中的视频会议口译制定了全面的指导原则（Braun & Taylor，2012，2014）。Napier（2012）提出了一套可以在法律诉讼中使用的视频会议手语翻译指南。Kelly（2008）和 Rosenberg（2007）为电话口译提供了指导建议。此外，一些机构已经为电话会议和视频会议情况下工作的口译员和工作人员发布了实用指南（参见附录）。鉴于远程和电话会议口译在设置、沟通目的、参与者数量和分布情况、口译方式和其他变量方面的变化，为具体实践提出一般性建议的难度很大。显然，远程和电话会议口译的可行性取决于一系列因素，而不仅取决于设备的技术水平和链接质量。

　　远程口译中的源语语篇是一个多模态立体语篇，其意义由发言人的语言信息、副语言信息和非语言信息复合而成。同理，口译员产出的目标语语篇也是一个立体语篇，其意义也是由这三类信息复合而成。远程口译中的听众在接收口译员所发布的信息时整合了两个信息来源：一个是听觉感知，其信息来自口译员的语言表达和副语言表达（如口译员的语音、语调、重音、韵律、噪音等）；另一个是通过视频手段接收到的视觉感知，其信息来自源语发言人和口译员的非语言表达（包括表情、手势、身势及其使用的辅助视觉符号，如图片等）。由此可见，口译语篇特征，尤其是在远程传播模式上，具有特殊性，应从多层面进行多模态分析。因此，口译话语研究的另一个重要方面是口译发布特征的研究，包括：口译话语的副语言特征，如语速、音调、重音、停顿等；非语言特征，如口译员的目光注视、表情、手势、身势等。Pasquandrea（2012：150）指出，要全面了解以口译员为中介的动态交际互动过程，就要把语言和非语言资源作为一个整体考虑。

第一节 远程口译的质量

有鉴于远程口译所面临的诸多挑战，口译员和口译服务的质量受到各种因素影响，因此有必要对质量影响因素和质量评估进行系统深入的研究。

自口译研究兴起以来，口译的质量及与质量相关的问题一直是口译研究领域的重要议题。口译作为一种产品，其质量的优劣一直是研究者、培训者、从业者及用户关注的重点。口译研究者和从业者从不同的研究视角和研究目的出发，在不同领域探索口译的质量问题。口译的质量在研究中被视为"完成了质量标准"（Dejean Le Feal，1990：155）、"一个战略过程的结果"（Kalina，1998；Riccardi，2003：257）、"某一遵循规范的行为"（Kurz，1998：392）、"对顾客期望值的满足"（Schmitt，1998；Zauberga，2001：279）、"实际服务与期望服务的平衡"（Kurz，2003：17）、"互动性的概念建构"（Bot，2003：40）。这表明，很难从单一视角去定义或解释口译质量的概念，学界也缺少统一的定义和标准。这一现状限制了对口译质量和质量评估标准的进一步讨论。20 世纪 50 年代出现了以经验总结和规范介绍为主的口译研究，其中对口译员的口译产出的研究已经对口译质量评估的重要指标完成了初步设计。随着研究的深入，学者们观察和测量了质量的各分项指标（Barik，1969，1971），或是有意识地从整体角度探讨口译质量问题。Moser在分析了 94 名口译员在 84 次不同会议上采访的 201 名用户的结果后指出，被访者对口译服务的首要要求就是忠实，其次是内容、同步性、语言使用技巧和声音质量（Moser，1996：145-148）。Kurz 以公式"质量＝实际的服务质量—期待的服务质量"来描述"感觉的口译质量"和"期待的口译质量"之间的关系（Kurz，2002：312-325）。也有研究者指出，用户对于服务的期待往往不现实，所以不应追求口译服务的理想质量，而要考察现实状况下的口译质量。Buehler（1986）对 47 名 AIIC 成员进行了口译质量标准问卷调查，发现大部分成员认为好的会议口译员应具有母语腔调、声音愉悦、表达流畅、逻辑关联、意思连贯、内容完整、语法正确、术语准确、风格恰当等特点。这些特点都涉及译语的表达。

针对视频会议口译设备的关注颇多。无论使用何种技术，视频会议口译都存在着挑战（Moser-Mercer，2005；Mouzourakis，2006；Braun & Taylor，2014），但任何形式的远程或电话会议口译都应以最好的设备和链接来保障诸如清晰的声音和图像、唇部同步性和链接稳定性等方面的服务质量。在法律和医疗保健环境中，远程口译主要还是适用于交替传译。Causo 还指出了其他可能会对视频会议口译的音质和理解产生负面影响的因素，认为"视频会议经常将不适合此目的或设置不合规的地点链接起来，这意味着声音的混响［……］简单全指向麦克风等"（2012：229）。Rosenberg（2007）和 Kelly（2008）在电话口译方面提出了类似的观点。他们指出了远程口译过程中使用普通电话和免提电话的不当之处：普通电话迫使手机在听众之间来回传递，而扬声器电话的背景噪声过多。为解决问题，Kelly 建议使用双耳机手机。

在视频会议口译中，所需的摄像机和屏幕数量是和设备相关的。对一个会议小组来说，每个站点要有一个摄像头和一个屏幕来捕获和显示所有参与者的图像。然而，更多参与者需要多个摄像机和多个屏幕（或显示不同参与者的分屏）。此外，还可能需要单独的多功能摄像机，以便口译员清楚地看到文本、图表和图像。

在一般的远程会议口译中，通常不需要其他参与者看到口译员（远程手语翻译除外），但在医疗保健、法律和商业环境中，所有参与者需要都能互相看到对方。不仅如此，口译员还应该能够看到自己的小图像。该图像是监视非语言交流的重要手段，也是口译员传递多模态信息的重要来源。

Van den Hoogen 和 Van Rotterdam（2012）在讨论法庭环境时建议，使用视频会议不应强迫交际各方改变位置，但这在远程口译中是不可能的。Kelly（2008）也强调了不受干扰的工作环境的重要性，因为呼叫中心（或口译中心）可能出现口译员互相干扰和在家工作时出现背景噪声问题。

与面对面的口译形式相比，在评估远程口译质量时，需要考虑远程口译中涉及的多方位因素，de Boe（2020）通过对医生与病人间的模拟咨询和访谈进行多模态的比较分析后发现，与面对面的口译相比，远程口译可能因为多种因素（设备技术和远距离环境、信息的对等标准、对交际活动的把握）

而影响口译质量，如图 4-1 所示。

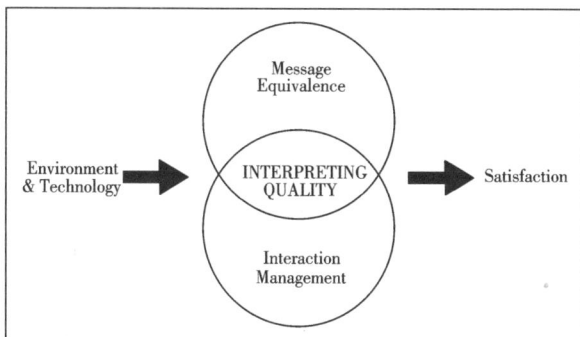

图 4-1 de Boe（2020：88）

Moser-Mercer（1996）针对口译质量评估研究中的方法提出建议，认为口译质量评估的目的取决于评估模式，并将评估目的分为三大类：面向口译实践（包括从用户角度和雇主角度出发）的评估，面向口译教学的评估，以及面向口译研究的评估。与这三类评估目的相应的评估模式分别为评价（即了解自然状态或口译现场的口译服务质量的手段）、评定（即在教学中了解学员对口译技能掌握情况的手段）和测量（即分析语言实验室条件下的口译成品以达到科研目的的手段）。

一、面向实践的质量评估

以用户为出发点的口译质量评估研究经历了一段发展历程。Buehler（1986）就口译质量问题向 AIIC 会员发出问卷，从用户的角度对口译质量进行实证研究。在研究中，Buehler 假设译语用户通过口音是否地道、声音是否悦耳、产出是否流畅等指标来判断口译员的口译质量，要求受访口译员对这些口译质量评估指标进行排序，指标顺序为：源语意思的转译、译语前后的一致性、翻译的完整性、译语语法的正确性、译语与源语风格的一致性、术语的准确性、语音语调的正确性、翻译的流畅性、声音悦耳度。Kurz（1989）进一步从用户对口译质量的期望值的角度进行研究，发现涉及内容的指标，用户与口译员的看法一致，而其他指标，如语音语调、声音是否悦耳等，口译用户与受试口译员有不同的看法。Altman（1990）从口译从业者的角度了解其对决定口译员角色及交流效果因素的看法。受调查的口译员认为，会议口译员必须有效地传达信息，否则极有可能影响交流的顺利进行。Meak（1990）对会议口译专业领域的医生进行的问卷调查表明，即使是同一用户组的不同个体对口译质量指标的侧重也不相同，但在主题知识和术语方面，同一用户组的不同个体基本态度一致。Gile（1990）通过发放问卷，要求用户用不同等级来评价口译整体质量、语言产出质量、术语使用、忠实度、声音质量和流畅性，结果大多数用户认为与内容相关的指标最为重要，流畅性次之。受到 Buehler、Kurz 和 Gile 研究的启发，Kopczyniski（1994）将受试用户分为人文组、科技组和外交组。全部受试小组更倾向于认为评价口译质量的主要指标是内容而非形式，且内容的细节程度和准确程度尤其重要。

AIIC 在 1995 年发布了针对会议口译用户进行的一项调研，提出了一系列问题：（1）从用户角度来看，好的口译要具备哪些因素？（2）用户对口译质量的各项标准如何排序？（3）用户的期望值是否受到不同环境的影响？访谈结果表明，在期望值方面，几乎所有受访者都主动提到了最重要的四项因素：内容准确性、同步性、羞耻技巧和声音质量。其中，初次使用会议口译服务的用户更为重视羞耻技巧，其次才是内容的准确性。

Moser-Mercer 等（1998）从口译质量的定义入手探讨了口译质量问题。她认为，职业口译的最优标准意味着口译员要提供完整、准确的翻译，不扭曲原意，并试图捕捉发言人在某种外部条件限制下传递的全部言外信息。口译的服务对象是不懂源语的人士，因此不能从狭隘和抽象的意义上将质量理解为源语信息固有的内容。1998 年，他们探究了同传时间延长对口译质量和口译员生理、心理压力的影响，认为口译员超时工作可能会带来由生理、心理压力增大而造成的质量下降的风险。Snelling 等（1997）研究了日本媒体的口译质量后指出，对媒体口译员的基本要求包括：听起来便于理解，遵循广播用语规则，在源语播音结束的同时完成口译，即使有时间差也不能相隔太远，对每个源语段落与译语发言同步化，具备接近广播标准的音质、语音语调和发音。Ais（1998）通过设计实验来评估语音语调、译语与源语信息一致性这两个口译质量指标。研究结果表明，实际的口译质量与用户感受到的口译质量差别明显。用户期望值与质量的概念有关联，但与质量或成功的实际感知无关联，并且用户对某些指标权重的判定也具有一定的隐含意义。

AIIC 于 2001 年年底完成了一项针对口译员工作的调查。调查以描述口译员工作中的压力来源及其正面特征、了解口译员工作环境中的物理压力、验证工作特征与口译员生活质量和口译之间的关联性、为口译员工作环境的改善提供可靠依据等为研究目标，通过对物理参数（口译箱内的空气质量、温度、湿度等）的测量、向口译员进行问卷调查或要求其提供自我分析报告、记录口译员的生理参数（包括心率、血压）及其 24 小时内不同时段的表现等研究手段，对口译员生理、心理、物理（工作场所条件）和表现这四组参数之间的关系进行分析。在远程口译中，环境因素对口译质量的影响在口译研究中起到了更为重要的作用。

张威与柯飞（2008）通过对四场国际会议进行问卷调查，了解参会者对口译质量因素的评价情况。问卷设计参考了 Buehler 和 Kurz 研究的重要口译质量因素，选用了信息完整、表达流畅、逻辑条理、专业术语、语法准确、语音语调、声音悦耳和翻译风格等八项因素，然后将反馈数据用 SPSS 软件进行统计分析，结果显示，各类用户将内容性因素（信息完整、表达逻辑、术语等）放在首位，形式性因素（语法、语音、声音质量等）则放在相对次要的位置。用户的不同目的、不同知识背景、外语水平和口译使用经验都对口译质量因素的评价产生了或多或少的影响。Strong 和 Rudser（1985）提出了手语翻译质量评估的模式，研究结果显示，主观评价的可靠性要明显低于客观文本测评的可靠性。因此，虽然主观评价可以对口译评估提供有趣的视角和有用的维度，但不能替代合理的客观测评。

在面向口译职业实践的实证研究中，为尽可能多地获得关于口译服务质量的信息，采用的方法多为现场观察法和调查法。

欧盟 AVIDICUS 2 项目的后续系列实验旨在探索培训过程中使用不同类型设备对口译表现的影响（Braun，2014；Braun et al.，2014）。它涉及与上一轮研究相同的翻译，提供了口译员在参加项目之前通过视频链接进行短期口译培训的资料，还采用了更好的设备。虽然有一些改进，在数据中也可以观察到，不同视频环境对口译员解决问题的策略所产生的结果（Braun，2017）。现场口译和远程口译之间的众多差异在不同视频环境下仍然存在，因此必须保留培训，提高参与者的熟悉度，提供更高质量的设备（Braun et al.，2014）。上述分析尚未研究电话中手语翻译的使用情况，但随着在各类环境中手语翻译使用的快速增长（例如就业、医疗、教育和社会环境），对手语翻译使用策略的认知和理解迫切需要提升。现行的法律，例如联合国公约中关于残疾人权利的条款（UNRCPD），也督促人们加快帮助聋人以平等恰当的语言形式获得公共服务。许多公共机构已经依赖电话网络与公众进行接触和沟通。视频口译服务成为提供平等访问机会的必然选择。

2015 年，为期 12 个月的项目 Insign 在欧盟委员会的委托下进行。这个实验旨在调查提供泛欧水电服务的可行性，增加聋人之间的互动和政治参与度，并改善针对聋人的社会公众服务（Hay & Pabsch，2014）。该项目以一种混合方法来检验口译员的经验和培训需求（Turner & Skinner，2014），用户的使用类型和满意度（Turner et al.，2016），以及平台使用的实际交互情况。该项目录制了一系列视频口译，调用了 6 种手语和 5 种口语，并探究了经验丰富的团队的不同使用策略和方法，为视频口译员提供有意义的借鉴。研究发现，使用平台提供平等访问的真正潜在需求来自公共机构，如欧盟委员会。翻译人员还发现，视频口译的迅速扩展服务在许多专业领域或情境中并不适合远程口译（Napier et al.，2017）。这些要求经常让口译员感到难以适应。虽然这个潜在的需求让视频口译服务工作实现了更广泛的互动，但已有口译员反馈挑战度极大（Wessling & Shaw，2014；NCIEC，2008）。目前尚不清楚什么原因导致口译员的"倦怠"：是呼叫中心的人体工程学因素，公司的政策，译前准备的缺乏，存在感的缺少，还是其他因素（Alley，2014；Bower，2015）。因此，目前尚无法确定能否通过提高呼叫中心设备的人体工程学性能，来改善口译员的工作效率。例如，手语翻译中的口译员需要密切关注视频屏幕，无法分心观察四周情况或放松全身。

二、面向教学的质量评估

Solow（1981）认为口译员将交际各方连接起来，扮演的是类似于联通电话交际双方的角色。他指出，为保证翻译产出的质量，口译员应具备以下素质：（1）灵活性，以便随时适应不同场合、不同性质的活动，以及不同用户的不同需求；（2）客观性，避免个人情绪的介入影响翻译产出；（3）自律性，即能在无监控的情况下维持工作水准。Schjoldager（1995）提出了口译课堂上使用的质量评价模型及四大问题：（1）听众是否能够理解并愿意听口译员口译；（2）口译员使用的语言是否合适；（3）口译员的译语产出是否恰当；（4）口译员是否是忠实的交际者。Sawyer（2004）针对口译员表现测试这一专题，指出了评定（assessment）与评价（evaluation）的区别，认为有必要区分对质量的评价和对表现的评价，即质量是相对于产品而言的，而表现是相对于过程而言的。

在口译研究的初期，针对口译质量的系统性、科学性研究尚未出现，口译质量更多是作为一个子项目出现在口译教科书或培训材料中。在这类教材中，作者多通过经验总结法分析和归纳口译实践，并从中概括出关于口译质量的规定性说明。这种说明，提出了相对最优质量（optimum quality）的概念，为口译质量概念后来的明确与细化奠定了必要的基础。理论思辨法也是面向口译教学的口译质量评估研究中较为常见的方法。研究者从观察入手，对现象进行概括，形成初步理论，推导出相关命题，并通过后期资料分析对理论进行评价。除了上述使用较多的人文主义研究方法外，研究者也常使用实验法进行研究。不同于上述方法中更为全面的探讨和考量，实验法常针对口译质量的某一具体指标或参数进行研究。远程口译涉及的远距离认知问题多采用实验法。

三、面向研究的质量评估

Gerver（1967）的研究表明，在同声传译中，口译员的口译表现受到源语速度的影响：当语速超过每分钟 120 词，听说时间差就会越长，口译员犯错误的概率也越大。Barik（1971，1975）探讨了同声传译中的省略、增添和翻译失误等偏离源语的现象，指出译语产出的总词数与源语产出的总词数的比率可以作为评估口译员表现的重要手段。Goldman-Eisler（1972）通过对比同声传译的源语和译语录音，分析了听说时间差的长度、语言要求、断句、意义单位等因素，认为各种较长的听说时间差和以高频率出现于句末的长时间差与声像记忆（echoic memory）及任务难度成反比，与断句能力和口译质量成正比。

Chernov（1973）找到了衡量口译质量的客观、独立的参数，认为其合理性是建立在说话人口头发言存在犹豫、延迟等成分的基础之上，即停顿时长相对实际发言时长比（pause length/speech length，P/S）。如果口译员的P/S 比超过了发言人的 P/S 比的 0.8，则口译质量达到满意水平或以上；不足 0.8，说明口译质量有待改进。此后，Chernov（1992）又预计到信息技术在今后的同声传译领域中的应用，提出电脑辅助同传时，不仅可以提供与会议流程相关的词汇、会议主题相关术语和会议基本背景材料，而且由于本身可以自动记录停顿和发言时长等参数，因此还能根据对不同 P/S 水平的设定监控口译质量并发出不同信号，给口译员以提示。

胡庚申（1988）提出了口译效果的构想，包括口译效果评估的方法（例如记录检测法、现场观察法、采访征询法、自我鉴定法、回译对比法、模拟实验法、考核评定法等），并在此基础上设计了 CREDIT 模型，明确并定义了影响和决定口译效果的主要因素，且根据其重要程度确定权重，最后以加总求和法计算出口译效果所处的数值空间。Angelelli（2000）从 400 场次的口译活动中选取了会议口译和社区口译场景，从背景、场合、交际各方、目的与结果、信息形式、语气、语篇类型、交际规范等角度逐一进行对比分析，认为对口译员的要求应随着交际场景的变化而有所区别，不能用单一标准衡量口译质量。由于远程口译也涉及社区口译的法律和医学场景，而事实证明，影响口译质量的因素不仅包括现场的各种交际场景因素，还包括远程技术给口译员带来的挑战，因此质量评估需要从多个角度来衡量。

Pöchhacker（2001）从口译质量评估的不同视角、口译产品和服务的多重质量标准、多样性的研究方法出发，指出口译作为不同交际主体、交际语言和文化背景之下进行的一项调节型交际任务，是为了满足某一需要进行的服务性活动。口译员在提供口译服务时，"实际上是提供了一个文本产品，在听众的社会文化空间范围内已有意义、有效果的方式将发言人的源语信息传达出来"（2001：421）。远程口译服务尤其如此。口译员的远程音频和视频语言服务在虚拟空间以有意义、有效果的方式将发言人的源语信息传达出来。

Garzone（2002）认为口译质量问题涉及不同方面、不同主题和不同视角，而且同一小组评估质量的不同指标也不尽相同。在此基础上，Garzone将图里的翻译规范概念应用到口译研究中，认为口译规范可以视为"内在的行为限制，这种限制在不同背景下控制口译员的各种操作，其目的在于达到与社会文化语境紧密联系的、基于规范的质量标准"（2002：110）。根据这一口译规范，Garzone认为口译质量可以被定义为"包含口译规范在内的一种构想，这些口译规范能有效保证某一特定社会、文化、历史环境下理想口译效果应该具备的内在和外在特征"（2002：110）。

Kalina（2002）将口译视为互动性的交际过程，试图提出一个包含口译质量各种影响因素的框架。她认为，口译质量受三方面因素的影响：语义内容（连贯性、逻辑衔接、完整性、准确性等）、语言表现（语法正确、可理解性、文体充分、术语充分等）、表现力（声音质量、演讲技能、同步性、技术熟悉程度等）。Kalina按照时间顺序将口译质量影响因素分为四组，分别为口译前的必要条件、口译过程的条件、口译过程的要求、口译过程的精力。她认为该框架可以继续扩展和修改，作为确定口译活动是否达到质量水平的参考。

蔡小红和方凡泉（2003）从口译的性质、口译质量评估的类别、标准、目的和方式、口译任务、口译员素质、口译效果等方面全面分析了口译质量与效果评估的问题。

Seeber 和 Zelger（2007）从伦理的角度探讨了同声传译中关于准确性的标准，认为所谓准确或真实的同声传译必须包括声音、语义和意图三个方面意思的传达。在远程口译中，意图的传达尤为困难，因为远距离让口译员无法利用情景线索和交际中的非语言线索进行意图猜测。尽管不断改进的电信技术已经让远程口译中的声音表达接近现场口译，但是传输中的电流影响和声像延迟仍然是影响口译质量的重要因素。

第二节 远程口译中的口译员

一、口译员的职业素质和能力

心理学家长期以来一直关注职业口译员的心理素质条件。Sanz（1931）根据对 20 位"国际联盟"和"国际劳工组织"会议口译员的访谈，列举了包括认知能力素质（例如智力、直觉、记忆力）及道德和情感素质（例如机智、判断力、警觉性和镇定）等 12 种素质。1965 年的翻译伦理规范主要关注后者，要求口译员具备"高尚的道德修养、诚实、有良知、值得信赖而且情感成熟"（Cokely，2000：35），类似的条文也常见于针对法庭口译员的法律条文。Van Hoof（1962：59）针对法庭、军事、联络和会议口译员列举了诸多个人必备条件，包括身体素质如毅力和坚强意志，智力素质尤其是语言熟练程度和对广播通用知识的掌握程度，以及心理素质如记忆技能、判断力、精力集中度等。就会议口译而言，Keiser（1978）强调的"知识"（对语言和通用知识的掌握）和"个人素质"包括"凭直觉知道意义的能力"、适应性、精力集中、记忆技能、公共演讲天赋和令人愉悦的嗓音等。

虽然口译界目前尚未就"口译能力"这一概念进行专门的探讨，但从相关研究（蔡小红，2001；仲伟合，2001；刘和平，2005）来看，学者们比较一致地认为，"口译技能"（实指"口译能力"）的构成主要包含三个模块：双语能力、言外知识、口译技巧。这种划分方式与翻译研究中关于翻译能力构成的划分是基本一致的，如 Cao（1996：328）就明确把翻译能力划分为语言能力、知识结构和策略能力三个模块。综合前人的相关研究，我们可以把"口译能力"界定为完成口译行为所需的内在知识和技能体系（王斌华，2007），并把口译能力的构成具体化为以下几个模块："双语能力"、"言外知识"和"口译技巧"。"口译知识"包括百科知识和专业主题知识，"口译技巧"包括听辨理解、逻辑分析和整合、口译记忆、口译笔记、口译转换、口译表达等方面的技巧。

口译是一种复杂的认知活动，口译能力是一项复杂的认知技能。认知心理学的相关研究（Ericsson & Charness，1997）显示，专业技能的学习和进步过程通常会经历三个阶段："认知阶段"、"联系阶段"和"自动化阶段"。口译技能的学习和进步亦是如此：在"认知阶段"，学习者学习口译的相关知识，如源语的听辨理解、分析的程序和方法、记忆的程序和方法、笔记的程序和方法、多任务操作的程序和方法等；在"联系阶段"，学习者主要通过有意识地练习，在不断试验、犯错、发现问题、解决问题的过程中逐步掌握所学的方法，并在方法之间建立关联；在"自动化阶段"，学习者对各种程序和方法的执行达到熟练、快速乃至自动化的程度，且对其认知资源的占用也会逐渐减少。在该阶段，学习者晋级为专家口译员。

根据已有研究，专家口译员和新手口译员的口译专业技能差别存在于多个方面：对知识和知识的组织方式的掌握，口译技巧和策略，信息处理方式，甚至认知神经基础等。Moser-Mercer（1997：257-259）和 Ericsson（2001）等研究者使用"新手/专家比较范式"，发现专家和新手在掌握知识和知识的组织方式方面与口译技巧和策略方面均存在明显差别。就前者而言，专家的"陈述性知识"范围宽广，而且提取速度较快；专家的"事实性知识"有更好的组织、更多的联系（尤其是与具体口译主题的联系）；专家的"语义知识"与语境联系紧密，而新手的语义知识往往与具体语境没有联系。就后者而言，专家不仅在双语理解、表达技巧及记忆技巧上能力出色，而且在以下策略的运用方面也表现突出：在"理解策略"上，专家善于用已知推断未知，且在未知信息冗余或可忽略的情况下会选择跳过未知信息，而新手往往把注意力放在未知信息上并因此而"卡壳"；在"工作负荷处理策略"上，专家善于在口译时进行多任务操作（如一边听辨理解一边作口译笔记），并在任务之间有主有次地分配好认知资源，而新手往往顾此失彼；在"监控策略"上，专家善于在口译过程中监控自己的口译表达，对出现失误或错误的地方进行可能的修正和更正。另外，专家的表现还有一个突出特点，即其技巧和策略运用更为自动化。其他研究虽然并非专门关注口译专业技能，但也从不同角度显示了专家和新手存在的差别（刘敏华，2002）：

（一）讯息处理量的差别

讯息处理速度：专家在同传中的听说时间差比较短；讯息处理量：专家的 65%～80% 相对于新手的 45%～58%；译文长短：专家的译文比较短；错误数量：专家的错误较少。

（二）讯息处理质的差别

分辨讯息重要性的能力：专家更善于分辨主要讯息和次要讯息；讯息处理单位：专家讯息处理单位比较大；口译表达风格：专家比较不贴近原文；

语言流利度：专家的流利度高。

（三）认知神经基础的差别

专家口译员存在由左脑转向右脑的"脑侧化"现象。"口译专业技能"是口译能力的核心和标志（Sunnari & Hild，2010）。口译学习者在完成其正规学习过程（如从口译专业毕业）以后，可能会表现出不同水平的口译能力，但并非所有的口译学习者都具备口译专业技能（Moser-Mercer，2008）。

口译员能力是口译员在口译学习和职业化过程中不断发展的一种能力，由六个模块构成。"双语能力"、"言外知识"和"口译员的心理/身体素质"是口译员能力的基础；"口译技巧"是口译员能力的核心；"口译员职业素质"是与口译员职业相关的素质。口译员心理/身体素质包括：集中的注意力、良好的记忆力、快速的反应力等适合从事口译职业的心理素质和能够从事较长时间高强度脑力活动的身体素质等。口译员职业素质包括：口译员在各种口译现场了解、适用或必要时创造新的口译规范的能力；口译员的角色定位能力；口译员的职业道德素质；口译员与口译活动各方（尤其是口译客户）进行协调、谈判、合作的交际能力；口译员操作口译技术设备的能力；口译员熟练使用 IT 技术工具进行会议准备的能力等。口译员是否具备口译工作所需的"职业素质"、"心理素质"和"身体素质"，是判断其是否成为一名合格口译员的重要方面。

在远程呼叫中心工作的口译员全天都要接听来自各类客户的呼叫要求，他们必须在不同的语言之间切换，呼叫主题和呼叫者的社会语言背景也各不相同（Brunson，2011；Gracia-García，2002；Napier et al.，2017），因此口译员必须采用不同方法来应对（Marks，2015）。为了使口译员能够管理各种呼叫要求并与各类客户打交道，远程口译员需要具备以下基本能力（NCIEC，2008；Taylor，2009）：

- 精湛的口译技巧
- 丰富的口译经验
- 良好的百科知识水平
- 广泛的词汇
- 对不同文化及其差异的了解

呼叫中心的优秀口译员并不仅仅是依据以上能力来评定的，而是更多地取决于能否提供优质服务。研究采访了消费者和口译员，让其列举优秀的远程视频口译所应具有的特点。在美国，远程呼叫中心执行严格的程序，口译员缺少准备时间来保证与来电者的交流，确保通话的有效性（Brunson，2011）。平台提供了一些基本准则，让客户了解具体流程，但许多公司在这些指导方针外还要求口译员在通话前查询通话的性质，厘清呼叫者间的关系，或讨论呼叫的结果（Brunson，2011）。因此，美国对专业的远程手语口译员的经验要求很高。口译员需要面对来自全国各地的呼叫者而无法预知呼叫的主题和性质，需要建立特定的术语，或花时间调整不同方言的差异。相比而言，欧洲的呼叫中心就没有强加这种规定，口译员只需要参与并成功完成远程口译流程（Napier et al.，2017）。

Braun 和 Taylor（2012b）对来自世界各地的 166 名法律口译员进行了大规模调查，发现在法律情境的远程视频口译中，拥有不同工作经验的口译员大多更喜欢现场口译。然而，那些年龄较大、口译经验较多的人倾向于使用远程口译。年龄可能是影响口译员的重要因素。丰富的生活和口译经验可以在某种程度上给口译员提供应对各种沟通所需的弹性情况和主题，应对各种背景的对话者。

研究表明，呼叫中心的工作环境会影响手语口译员的专业自主权（Alley，2014；Brunson，2011），应对客户的期望和工作情绪的压力会影响口译员的口译质量（Wessling & Shaw，2014）。由于呼叫中心在政策法规上与口译员需求存在冲突，且需要口译员在公司模式下运作，因此，尽管呼叫中心的口译员可以在一天内应对大量来电（Brunson，2011），但远程工作环境仍给口译活动带来了巨大挑战。

呼叫中心服务的一个重要特征是按需提供服务或要求口译员临时上岗。每个来电者对服务的期望都不相同，且自有其特殊的风格，口译员需要对这些对话进行一定程度的管理。一些来电者能够意识到口译员的需求并能主动评估其能力。一些呼叫客户希望口译员像机器一样重复所表达的内容，而有些来电者则高度依赖口译员对谈话的翻译和阐述（Braun，2013；Brunson，2011；NCIEC，2008；Tylor，2009；Wessling & Shaw，2014）。呼叫中心的口译员发现，呼叫客户、主题和需求的变化使他们难以严格遵守口译标准。

二、口译员的心理

在使用音视频技术进行远程口译时，"存在感"是影响口译员的最重要因素。口译员"存在感"的强弱，是与其他参与者相较而言的（Short et al.，1976）。与主要参与者同一地点参与会话的口译员，可以利用上下文信息如物理特征、姿势、凝视和面部表情，帮助自己在认知过程中理解说话人的意图和语气（Setton，1999）。当口译员与需要沟通的人员位于同一地点时，他们通常可以利用情境化线索推断出交际互动的特点和对话者之间的人际关系（Dickinson，2014）。相比之下，远距离可能会破坏口译员的"存在感"，并使之处于不利地位（Moser-Mercer，2005）。

在远程口译中，当口译员与部分或全部交际参与者分开时，通常可以使用的一些线索变得不容易掌握和运用。例如，对远程视频呼叫中心工作的手语口译员而言，聋人对话者只有一条线路可以进行视频连接，而另一位对话者则通过电话连接，这对于口译员来说非常不适（Napier et al.，2018）。即使口译员能看到所有远程参与者，但交际参与者的环境也只有部分可见（Braun，2004，2007；Napier，2012a，2012b，2013）。研究表明，这种情况会导致口译员平等参与交流活动的能力降低。与此同时，其他参与者在现场所能看到和听到的内容也非常有限（Braun，2004，2007，2013，2014，2017；Braun et al.，2018）。

在场感的缺乏是否影响口译员的能力仍然是研究者们讨论的热点问题，结果不一而足，可以从主观评分之间的对比来看学习表现，或者实际口译中出现的问题（反映为错误率）与实践和经验的比例。通过与现场口译的对比观察发现，相关上下文信息的缺乏迫使口译员在工作时借助猜测技巧，并在认知处理和自我监控中投入更多精力（Chernov，2004）。这一发现也被证明适用于远程口译（Braun，2004，2007）。也有研究提出，远程口译中的高认知负荷会导致过早疲劳（Braun，2013；Moser-Mercer，2003，2005），增加出错的风险，尤其是在法律环境中。鉴于法律交流活动的结果对于个人的影响巨大，口译错误率的上升无疑是危险的（Braun & Taylor，2012a）。Moser-Mercer（2003，2005）进一步断言，在远程口译中口译员会承受更多的心理压力。与上述研究相反，一些研究者发现，口译员不在现场也有一定的好处。例如，根据某些医学口译员的说法，与医院环境的分离有效消除了干扰和通常的压力，口译员可以更好地专注于口译任务（Gracia-García，2002）。

焦虑是一种由紧张不安的情绪所导致的恐惧心理，这一现象普遍存在于口译员中。其主要原因在于，外语知识非常广泛，而口译员所能掌握的知识很有限。研究者在分析口译员心理素质的过程中特别指出，选择口译职业，就是选择了与压力相伴。有时候由于服务的客户过于强势，口译员会产生压迫感，加重焦虑情绪，因此有必要对口译员的焦虑现象进行研究。口译焦虑自 2006 年起从外语学习焦虑中剥离出来，被界定为一种与口语、听力、阅读和写作等具体外语技能并列的特定情境与技能的焦虑（Chiang，2006）。现有的口译焦虑研究多采用定性研究方法（如理论概括、经验总结、访谈等）探讨口译焦虑的成因，或考察口译课堂、教师行为、口译学习策略、口译困难等因素对口译焦虑的影响，或关注口译焦虑的影响及应对策略，如采用经验性描述方法研究焦虑对口译员的影响，焦虑对口译任务完成情况的影响等（Alexieva，1997；Kurz，2003；Chiang，2006；Bontempo & Napier，2011；龚龙生，2006；康志峰，2010；董燕萍，2013）。现有研究虽已取得较大成绩，但大多还只停留在定性分析上，定量研究尚不多见，定性和定量相结合的研究更是阙如。此外，多数研究所关注的只是口译焦虑这一单一角度，而从口译学习策略、工作记忆、学习动机等多个视角综合调查和研究口译焦虑的形成机制及认知影响的成果尚不多见。远程口译中尤其如此。由距离产生的技术畏惧感和对会话参与者的不确定感，增加了口译员的心理压力，也加重了心理焦虑。

三、口译员的角色空间

在漫长的口译历史中，口译员多由双语者担任。他们扮演如向导、谈判人、信息传达者等中间人的角色。直到 20 世纪，随着口译活动的职业化，口译员的角色开始有了明确的规定。会议口译员的工作环境多为同传箱，很少与讲话人和听众有面对面的交际沟通，且口译活动的主要目的是信息的传递，因此口译员被理解为应该保持中立和"隐形"的角色（Goffman，1981），只是充当语言传输的"管道"（Reddy，1979）。口译员不应当对谈话的内容、观点、进程等发表任何看法、提出任何建议，要严守中立，在口译活动中充当被动的"传声筒"。口译员被看作单纯的"语言转换器"，完全没有主观能动性，只能像机器一样机械地翻译，甚至完全字对字的翻译。众多研究表明，远程口译过程因受到技术设备、环境、语境等因素的影响变得十分复杂，进而产生了一些限制因素，如角色矛盾、现场压力、权力平衡等，最终影响到口译员对自身角色和社会对口译员角色的期待。比如在法律情境下的远程口译中，口译员的表现很大程度上取决于法官、法庭工作人员、警官等各方的期待。

随着全球化发展及随之而来的频繁的双语交流的增多，口译员开始更多地主动参与到讲话双方的交流中。他们在适当的时候主动地掌控交际过程，充当了"文化经纪人"（cultural broker）或"调解人"（conciliator）的角色。通过研究对话者在口译活动中的行为方式，Goffman（1990）和 Malone（1997）提出，口译员的参与方式与以往不尽相同，他们真正参与到口译的互动活动中（Wadensjö，1998；Metzger，1999；Roy，2000），通过相应的活动对口译的结果产生影响。Wadensjö（1997）认为，如果将口译看成一种互动活动，那么口译员参与的对话就有其特定的交流原则，而口译员的角色也应包括两种主要功能：一种是翻译，另一种是协调对话。Angelelli（2004）指出，口译员不仅要参与对话中的语言构建，更要消除文化和语言障碍，减缓对话中的压力，通过支持乙方或建立联盟关系来保持对话关系的平衡。

Llewellyn-Jones 和 Lee（2014）研究发现，口译员需要了解并熟练运用交际互动惯例，同时还必须对工作的语言和文化有一定的了解，以保证双语交流的顺利进行。口译角色空间模型提出了三个相互关联的维度，即互动管理（interaction management）、参与者联盟（participant alignment）、自我展现（presentation of self）（参见图 4-2）。口译员可以沿着这三个维度在口译活动中作出相应的决策，并掌控整个口译过程。该模型的核心原则是，口译互动是可以协商的，口译员在互动中占据着与其他主要参与者不同的位置。口译员不仅参与了意义的共同建构，还参与了内涵的共同建构（Bélanger，2004）。由于加入了技术的因素，远程口译中的距离因素会对口译员可能采用的策略产生较大影响。

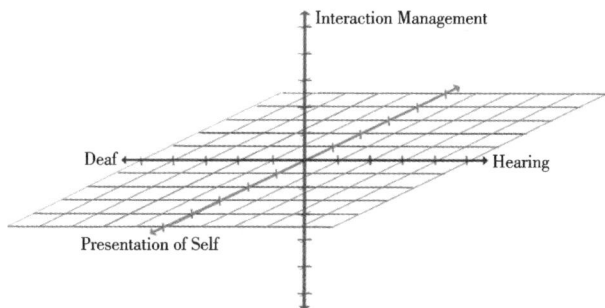

图 4-2　（Robert Lee，2020：115）

角色空间模型中的纵轴（Y 轴）是互动管理，指的是口译员在管理参与者之间交际活动中所做工作的程度。例如交替传译（告诉发言者暂停）、澄清要求、转述或重复。低度互动管理例子包括不问问题、不澄清或重复源语信息的某些部分。模型中的水平轴（X 轴）是参与者联盟，指的是口译员在与主要交际双方建立信任方面所使用的策略。由于交际双方不使用共同的语言，他们必须跟口译员建立信任，以确认信息得到忠实传达，同时也能准确地收到交际另一方传达的反馈信息。与参与者高度紧密联系的例子包括与交际方在距离上接近，眼睛与交际方凝视并微笑、皱眉头或适当地回应。在传译之前或传译过程中，口译员会向交际方提供相关背景信息。此外，口译员还可以采取比较隐蔽的策略，例如手势语等。

与参与者联盟较弱的例子包括：主动避免与他人的眼神接触，身体姿势非常封闭（如双臂折叠、双腿交叉）。在某些情况下，口译员可能被交际一方视为紧密联系，而被另一方视为联系较弱，这会对翻译的公正性和对口译员的信任产生重要影响。

Z轴是指口译员的自我展现。与此相反的是对口译员仅有"管道作用"的先入为主的成见（Roy，1993）。尽管与主要参与者的互动方式不同，口译员作为口译活动的一部分，积极地参与到整个交际过程中。高度自我展现的例子包括口译员主动将自己介绍给交际各方，直接接受（或拒绝接受）食物，适当地回答（或推迟）交际方的问题。低度的自我展现包括无视交际方的直接问题等行为，将自己称为口译员，而不是用第一人称（例如："口译员想休息一下"或"口译员没有听到最后一句话"）。

使用角色空间模型来分析远程口译，不仅可以与面对面的口译进行比较，还可以分析远程口译中需要特殊考虑的领域。受到远程距离和技术的影响，远程口译中限制了口译员某些策略的使用。为了使远程口译互动尽可能取得好的成效，口译员尝试主动参与互动，与交际方保持紧密联系，并适当地展现自己。这些策略的使用都是为了提供准确有效的信息、技术服务和优质的口译服务，以满足交际各方的需求。

第三节　远程口译中的话轮转换

现代语言学鼻祖索绪尔首次区分了"语言"（language）和"言语"（parole）这对语言研究中的基本概念。索绪尔当时是从结构主义的角度出发来研究语言的，其哲学基础是社会心理主义。他认为语言存在于一定的社会当中，是纯心理的、抽象的，而言语是个人的，是心理的、物理的。语言要成立的前提条件应该是言语。随着语言研究的不断深入发展，现在语言学界一致认为，语言是指人类各民族自成体系的交流符号，由语音、字词、语法和带有民族文化特征的习惯用法等一系列规则所构成。言语则指的是语言在不同个体的交际习惯中的体现及表达语言的方式，它与主题、语境和相关知识相互关联，明显地带有使用者的个性特点。

由于口译所接触的往往是与某一主题相关、存在于具体语境中的信息，因此口译研究更加重视言语的研究。作为术语的"话语"实际指的是言语在具体语境的运用。从根本上说，口译活动是一种人类的言语交际活动。语言与语义之间约定俗成的联系建立在言语交换的基础上，言语传递的对象都是以交际为目的的语段。在口译过程中，由于各种语言具有各自不同的表达方式，因此某种意义，语言的相异性又给交际活动制造了障碍。作为口译活动中唯一的跨语言跨文化协调者，口译员必须对两种语言的社会文化背景有深刻了解。

口译活动是通过口头翻译手段来实现不同文化间交流的一种方式。对口译的认识不应该仅仅停留于语言符号的简单转换，而应把口译行为视作一种动态的交际行为。由于语言会随着交际内容和语言使用者的改变而改变，且交际环境也处于动态之中，因此口译员的理解和表达也应该处于动态之中。口译员在口译过程中必须重视源语的文化背景，消除由社会环境与文化背景的不同所带来的交际隔阂，要时刻牢记口译活动中所翻译的语言是实际的社会文化交流话语，而不仅仅是两种语言之间简单的符号转换。

由于口译是不同语言和文化系统的人通过口译员进行的口头话语交际过程，因此谈话的参与者交替发言是谈话话语中最显著的特征。对谈话中的参与者来说，都有可能出现进入或退出谈话、保持或放弃发言权的现象。许多社会学家和社会语言学家认为，会话是一个参与者发话、停止，另一个发话者开始的过程。但是日常会话并不是以问题与回答一一对应的序列形式展开，实际情况要远为复杂，因为日常会话中还广泛存在着"重叠"和"沉默"现象。除了通过翔实的语料分析一般日常会话中存在的话轮系统，还可以通过口译语料来分析话轮转换系统在口译过程中的交际运用。

在谈到日常会话的进行方式时，Sacks（1974）和他的同事们通过一些口头交际数据发现了两个明显的现象：在绝大多数情况下，一个时间点内只有一人发言，且会话参与者通常交替发言。为了进一步解释说话者是如何不断进行话轮转换的，分析者们将会话视为完成两项主要任务的生成机制。第一项任务是，说话者必须能够找到适当的时间转换其说话人角色，也就是要把说话的权利出让给下一个说话者。Sacks 等提出，说话者应该能识别出哪些可能出现话轮转换的位置。会话的第二项任务是要制定确定下一个说话者的规则。他们同时还发现，在话轮构成单位的末尾进行的话轮分配通常有两种情况：一是现时说话者通过点名、凝视、手势或其他方式（例如对特定的会话参与者提问）将下一话轮分配给所选择的说话者；二是会话参与者自选为下一话轮的说话者。

一、话轮转换规则和信号

社会语言学家通过研究会话结构，试图找出话轮转换中出现的种种问题的解决方法。Sacks 等人同时提出了制约话轮的结构、分配新的话轮给另一个会话参与者并且协调话轮转移以减少间隔和重叠的一系列规则。这些规则可以运用于任何可能出现话轮转换的转折点上。它们总共可分为两类；一是现时说话者选择下一个说话者；二是会话参与者自选。

规则 1——应用于第一个转换关联位置：

a. 如果现时说话者选择下一轮说话者，那么现时说话者必须停止说话，被选的说话者必须接着说话。话轮转换出现在下一轮说话者被选择后的第一个转换关联位置。

b. 如果现时说话者没有选择下一轮说话者，那么任何其他谈话参与者都可以自我选择，第一个自选者成为下一轮说话者。

c. 如果现时说话者没有选择下一轮说话者，其他谈话参与者也没有进行自我选择，那么现时说话者可以（但并非必须）继续说话，即要求获得下一轮说话的权利。

规则 2——本规则适用于第一个转换关联位置以后的所有转换关联位置：

如果规则 1c 生效，在以后的各个关联位置规则 1a—c 可以循环使用，直到实现话轮转换为止。

这些规则的核心是话轮转换关联位置（transition relevance place），即某人话轮可能终止并出现话轮转换的位置。转换关联位置体现了话轮组成单位的多样性，可以是词、短语、分句或句子。一般来说，正是由于话轮的不断替换，才能不断产生新的话轮。

在话轮转换系统中，会话参与者尽量减少了会话可能出现的停顿、沉默或是重量，使会话得以顺利进行。要做到这一点，说话者和听话者必须配合默契，尽可能准确地判断话轮的过渡关联位置，即某个话轮可能终止的位置。实际上，一方面，说话者不断有意无意地发出各种各样的言语和非言语信号，暗示他即将终止话轮，帮助听话者找到该话轮的过渡关联位置；另一方面，听话者也在不断捕捉、追踪和分析说话者所发出的各类信号，从而作出正确的判断，以确定说话者可能终止其话轮的位置。

在话轮替换系统中，说话者发出的信号可分为：放弃话轮信号（turn-yielding signal），表示说话者意欲放弃话轮；保持话轮信号（turn-holding signal），表示说话者无意放弃该话轮。

Duncan（1973）提出判断放弃话轮信号的六大线索，这些线索可以单独发挥作用，但在多数情况下往往是一起出现并发挥作用。这些线索是：

- 语调，在音位从句（phonemic clause）的末尾使用非平声调（non-level tone）；
- 辅助语言——延长，在最后一个音节上的延长或在音位从句重读音节上的延长；
- 身体移动，任何手势的停止或者放松手的某种紧张的姿态，如松开握紧的拳头等体态动作。
- 社会中心序列（sociocentric sequences），某些套语的出现，如 but what、or something、you know 等。
- 辅助语言——音高/响度和某些套语同时出现的音高/响度的降低；
- 句法，包含终止一个完全的语法小句，即会有主语与谓语的句子。此外，使用反义疑问句也是一种常见的信号。

另外，说话者的目光凝视也是判断说话者是否会放弃话轮的一个重要因素。说话者在说出一段较长话语时往往目光离开听话人，而在快要结束说话时才转而以目光凝视听话人。这往往可以作为听话人判断说话人是否要说完话的重要信号之一。

英语日常会话中常见的保持话轮的方式可以使用话语来完成成分，如 and、but、however 及未完成标志（incomplete marker），如 if、since 的句子或句子组合。由于说话者使用了 before 一词，就意味着他的话尚未结束。听话者就不会在他说完"I'll crown that bastard."后立刻通过自选来争夺下一个话轮。

来自听话者的信号也分为两种：索求话轮信号（turn claiming signal），表示说话者意欲占有下一话轮；反馈信号（feedback signal），表示听话者无意占有下一话轮。索求话轮可以是打断现时发言人的说话，也可以改变目光凝视方向，提出一种想要发言的势态，发出某种不耐烦的反馈，如 yes、yes I know，以及使用类似于 well、but、so 之类的词语。谈话话语中听话人的反馈并不构成一个话轮，也不构成对发言权的要求，而只是听话人向现时说话人提供有用信息的一种方式。

二、远程口译中的话轮转换

口译是不同语言和文化背景的人通过口译员进行的口头话语交际过程。作为一切会话中普遍存在的基本言语转换机制，话轮转换规则也同样适用于会话口译。在远程口译活动中，口译员与原始会话者之间的话轮转换原则是对日常会话话轮转换规则的延伸和补充。两者的区别在于，尽管话轮的大小长短并不固定，且话轮转换主要以上述规则为主，但口译员由于是整个口译活动中唯一的跨语言跨文化者，因此话轮转换能否顺利进行，不同语言和文化背景下的原始说话者能否实现成功和有效的交际，达到各自对话的目的和期望，在很大程度上都取决于口译活动的中介人，取决于口译员能否有效而合理地使用话语策略，以协调不同原始说话者之间可能出现的停顿、沉默或是重叠话轮现象，消除原始说话双方可能出现的误解和会话过程中的冷场尴尬情境。

以下将通过口译实例分析口译员如何在口译活动中具体运用话轮转换规则。

（一）制造话轮

在口译过程中，当口译活动的参与者意识到话轮转换的关联位置或某一话语结构存在话轮转换可能时，就会把话轮转换给下一个说话者或继续下一话轮。

Sacks（1968）认为，言语不仅仅是由一连串合乎语法结构的句子组成。听话人必须经过一番理解才能掌握说话人所要传达的意义。研究日常会话就要分析说话者的话语和听话人对这些话语的解释和反映。此项研究主要涉及如下问题：怎样区别有意义的接应得很好的谈话与接应得不好的谈话。

实际上日常会话不仅仅是一连串发言权的简单轮换。尽管人们有时相见只会说些应酬寒暄的话，但在多数情况下人们的互相交谈都有实质内容，因而需要建立交谈话题（topic）。Sacks认为，在日常会话中，所有会话的参与者"通过引入话题，展开话题又集中话题"的方式来组成对话。会话参与者相互交谈的发展是由会话的话题所指导的。关于话题，首先要注意哪些是可以会话的话题。一般而言，说话人不必告诉听话人已经知道的事情。话题是否恰当取决于会话的对象是谁。更重要的是话题的选择很大程度上为社会文化规范所制约。因为口译不仅仅是两种语言简单的编码转码，更是两种文化之间的交流。因此，有些话题可以是两种文化都能接受的，而另一些话题只在一种文化中经常提到，而在另一种文化中根本不涉及，或即使涉及，其谈论的方式也大不相同。

由于不同的文化对特定情境中的话语和行为有不同的理解，不同文化背景中的人之间的交际必然容易产生困难和误解。在口译交际过程中，由于原始说话者一方（或双方）对另一方的社会文化传统缺乏了解，因而可能会出现交际中断。

就此一方面而言，口译活动的参与者（包括口译员在外）根据有关话语规则，通过了解特定情境下会话发展的方向和各位说话者进行对话的目的，来参与话轮转换。整个口译所涉及的话题并非事先确定，而是在会话过程中协调而成。会话话语便是一个双向动态的协调过程。每个会话参与者一方面为正谈论的话题提供新的信息，另一方面也从自身话题的角度提供新的信息。各方的发言都可以看作是对所谈话题的协调。协调会话的目的是要使会话顺利进行，最终实现交际。但由于口译中的原始说话者语言不同，文化背景存在差异，因此口译中难免会出现疑惑或误解。跨语言跨文化的口译员虽然不能总是预测到原始会话者的话题内容，但是可以使用一定的话语策略发现话轮转换的契机，在适当的时候制造话轮，进行话轮的转换。

一般来说，在口译员协调的会话中，由于原始对话者之间语言不通，在日常会话中产生迷惑或误解，可能在口译过程中出现暂时的沉默或停顿现象。在这种情况下，口译员就应该使用恰当的会话策略来协调话语交际过程中出现的误解和故障。口译员制造话轮必须先参与前一轮的话轮转换，然后通过自己的协调作用将下一话轮分配给另一方的原始会话者。口译员通过这种协调话语的行为来积极地参与口译的交际活动。

（二）打断或忽视话轮

口译中常常会发生同一时间内两个（或几个）原始说话者同时说话的现象，这种情况出现的原因有二：其一是根据话轮转换规则，现时说话者没有选择下一轮说话者，那么任何会话参与者都可以自我选择成为下一轮说话者。这就必然鼓励会话参与者尽早开始说话以取得新一轮的发言权，由此便产生了重叠发言现象。其二是会话参与者对当下话轮会何时结束或转换关联位置的预测所引起的。由于在口译话语过程中，两个（多个）原始说话者使用不同的语言，口译员的协调作用显得至关重要。口译员应该在出现重叠说话的尴尬局面时打断或忽视其中一个原始说话者的话轮，并把下一话轮指定给另一个原始说话者，以推动原始说话者之间有效而成功的交际。

口译员处理重叠说话现象的第一个策略是打断话轮。口译员既可以打断一个原始说话者的话轮，让另一个原始说话者说话，也可以同时打断两个原始说话者的话轮，然后把下一个话轮指定给其中一个原始说话者。口译员打断话轮不是任意的，是受会话话题、情景语境、原始说话者双方的地位和关系等一系列因素影响的。这个策略还取决于口译员对会话整体的认识，对话语的功能性和语境中话语目的的解释，以及从相互作用的角度来确定会话中所涉及的"礼貌原则"和"言语行为"。由于远程口译具有虚拟场景的特性，口译员往往需要不断地打断讲者，以确保信息准确无误地传递。

口译员处理口译中重叠说话现象的另一个策略是忽视话轮。在一些口译场合中，口译员可以暂时忽视一个原始说话者的重叠说话，把这部分说话储存在脑子里，同时让另一个原始说话者继续说话，并翻译他的话语。在传达了后一个原始说话者的信息之后，口译员再将刚才储存的话语表达出来。这种处理策略基于几方面的考虑：口译员通过观察确定某段话语在当时并不重要，不必马上翻译出来，或者这段话语简短而容易记住，或者口译员预测到其中一个原始说话者会很快完成他的说话。

（三）接受话轮

不同语言和文化背景下的人们在交际时会受到某些系统性差异的影响，如情境及在此情境中对恰当行为和意向的不同文化假设，或是会话中组织信息或记点的不同方式，以及不同的说话方式，都可能造成日常交际中的失误。口译中的原始说话者由于不同的文化背景和个人会话的倾向性，同样会给口译中的交际制造障碍。作为口译活动的中介调解人，口译员不应只承担信息传递的任务，还要协助原始对话者之间实现更好的理解和交际。口译员要适时且恰当地处理原始对话者寻求帮助的言语行为，就必须掌握一定的话语常识，通过会话的具体情境和对话语内容的准确分析来确定相应的处理策略。

根据话轮转换理论，日常会话中（包括口译过程）存在一些重要特征：话轮的顺序和大小是不固定的、可采的。在绝大多数情况下，一个时间点里只有一个人发言。既无间隔又无重叠地从一个话轮向下一个话轮的转换是经常的现象。这一类转换同带有间隔和重叠的转换一起构成话轮转化系统。话轮的分配事先没有规定，由所有会话的参与者在会话发展的过程中使用各种话语策略来相互协调。

为了灵活机动地处理口译中可能出现的两个原始说话者同时说话所造成的短暂沉默，或是口译信息传递过程中所遇到的文化障碍，口译员要发挥自身的能动性，通过观察原始说话者的话语来预测其交际目的，充分考虑交际中原始说话双方的身份地位，同时也要把握整个会话交际的话题，并在此基础上寻找口译的恰当时机，通过制造话轮、打断话轮或接受话轮的方式来协助交际的顺利进行。这就要求一名合格的口译员不仅有深厚的双语功底，同时也懂得观察口译具体进行时的语境和原始说话者的话语特点。口译员在口译中所面临的问题主要是确定传递哪些信息，因为他不仅仅是个"传声筒"，更是被原始会话者视为整个口译会话中的一员。他通过各种方式参与话轮转换系统，实现口译各方面的交际目的。

第四节　远程口译中的策略

作为一种有目标的活动，口译在根本上是一种"策略性"的过程；对口译研究者而言，口译是一种复杂的认知信息处理任务或语篇加工技能（Arcais，1978：398f）。作为该领域内深具影响力的学者，Dijk 和 Kintsch（1983）提出了话语产出的策略模型。研究者在"策略"的范畴下，对大量的心理语言学加工步骤展开讨论，"策略"因此被定义为"意图控制下的目的性过程"（Kalina，1998：99）。

20 世纪 90 年代以来，口译策略的研究日益丰富。有的关注口译策略分类；有的关注预测、压缩、重组等一些具体的口译策略在特定场合的使用；有的通过实证方法，调查在特定口译任务中所有或部分策略是如何共同作用推进口译任务的完成。此外，不同口译形式中口译策略的使用也是研究的重点之一。如同传策略研究关注的是记忆、断句、预测、缩短听说时差等策略，交传策略研究则更侧重转换语序、增加、句法转换等策略（Donato，2003；Chernov，2004；Lim，2011；Seeber/Kerzel，2012；Liontou，2012）。口译策略的研究方法也呈现出多样性。有的运用追溯性工具，采用追溯、监控、内省式表达等心理研究实证方法，了解研究对象在口译认知加工过程中所遇到的困难及采取的策略；有的运用语料研究方法分析口译产品，探讨口译策略的使用特点；有的采用对比研究方法，探讨职业口译员与非职业口译员等不同群组在口译活动中策略使用的差异，并将相关成果运用于口译教学及培训（Donato，2003；Liontou，2012；Bartlomiejczyk，2006；Ricardi，2005）。就口译策略的研究方法而言，最具代表性的应该是 Gile（2009）的研究。该研究依托精力分配模式理论，通过分析口译认知过程中口译员精力分配的特点和口译困难的处理技巧，探讨了口译策略的使用情况。

一、规范、任务相关策略

　　口译活动中处理策略的问题始终与口译员输入中产生的困难紧密相连。特别是表达的高速度和结构的复杂性（尤其是在同声传译速度和认知制约的情况下），都被认为是造成高度加工负荷从而要求采用应对策略的因素。在有关以加工为导向的口译活动研究文献中，"压缩"和"预测"等策略是最常被讨论的问题。然而，正如 Schlesinger（1999，2000）的研究所表明的，不能仅以输入负荷的形式来解释策略。口译员认识到客户对其口译产品和表现的期望，并试图满足这样的期望，也就是 Chesterman（1993）所提出的翻译"期待规范"，在形成口译员策略性反应方面和认知制约因素同等重要。例如，内化为口译员培训课程和专业精力一部分的口译表现标准，如流利和顺畅的口译输出等，可以成为允许某些类型的省略和增补策略的理由（Schjoldager，1995/2002；Schlesinger，1999）。这表明，在以应对高负荷输入为目标的口译过程策略和以目标语听众有效交际为目标的口译产品策略之间存在差异。然而，两者之间的界线殊难划定。例如，在强调处理策略和以规范为指导的行为之间的相互作用时，Gile（1995）指出，口译员对处理技巧的选择可能会受到各种规则的指引，如"使话语交际影响最大化"或"自我保护"（1995：201）。

　　许多口译活动中成为技术或技巧的特有策略，都可以用不同的方式加以分类。就整个任务而言，可以分为在线策略（口译员在口译活动当下所考虑的）和离线策略（在翻译的认知加工之前或之后的策略，如准备词汇表或在文件做上标记）。在线策略反过来也许是一种特定方式的口译活动所特有的典型策略。交替传译中的笔记和同声传译中的滞后调整，就属于特定方式口译活动特有的在线策略。在面对面的交际活动中，口译应用多种多样的策略来进行互动话语，尤其是保护各自的面子（Mason & Stewart，2001），以及言语的、非言语的话轮线索和交际反馈（Dimitroa，1997）。尽管这些应用已经非常广泛，但目前绝大多数有关策略的研究都集中在会议同传上，尤其是对源语和目标语之间结构差异这一经典问题的关注。远程口译中，由于缺少现场的情景线索，口译员更多采用增添和解释的翻译策略。

二、句法结构的应对策略

　　自从 Glemet（1958）把同声传译中的产出过程描述为"把语法的未来抵

押出去"，学界就已经对不同语法结构造成的语言挑战进行了研究。Kade（1967）和 Kirchhoff（1976/2002），以及一些其他学者研究了德语作为源语的情形，论及了等待策略，认为等待的目的如果不是像一般情况下所认为的"等待动词"，至少也应该是让输入信息清晰化。Herbert（1952：65）认为口译员不能因为等待而停顿，那么等待进一步输入就可以采取口语中支支吾吾的形式，即放慢速度或者使用"不改变意义的冗赘表述"或"补白"（Glemet，1958：121；Kirchhoff，1976/2002：116）。然而这种滞后策略导致更大的储存负荷，反而限制了等待策略的使用，并要求口译员进一步采取先发制人的行动，比如切分。切分技巧也被称为"意大利香肠技巧"（Jones，1998：101）。Kirchhoff（1976/2002）等学者认为，切分是在复杂的输入结构结束之前，在短语或分句层面上对输入信息进行提取和翻译。这种被广泛传授的策略，被 Seleskovitch 和 Lederer（1995：125）称之为"处理意义的子单元"。之后，Goldman-Eisler 的实验研究也发现作为切分策略的"裂变"得到了普遍采用。研究者还根据实验数据和实地调研数据，对切分和重组策略，特别是译出语为亚洲语言的同声传译进行了研究（Setton，1999；Ishikawa，1999）。

　　研究者们讨论最多的同传策略是预测。除了在更广泛意义上，在期待加工基础的意义理解中发挥根本性作用之外，预测被具体定义为在相应成分出现在源语输入之前，同传口译员就产出了句子成分（Setton，1999：52）。Wilss（1978）和 Lederer（1978/2002）等研究人员已经就各种句法预测进行描写和分析，并区分了"语言预测"和基于"意义期待"的"言外预测"。"语言预测"主要指基于熟悉的词汇—语法模式的"词语预测"，而"言外预测"则是基于语境所进行的"隐含或未知意义预测"。大部分德语圈学者认为"任何同声传译都具有语对特定性"（Wilss，1978：35），但释意派理论研究传统的学者则不重视语法不对称的作用。除了理论思考，学者们通过各种实证研究来讨论这些策略。Gile（1992）对日语中可预测句子结果的长度和功能进行了数据库分析，Joerg（1997）研究了德语和英语语对在同声传译中的动词预测，探讨了专业知识和方向性的问题。Van Basien（1999）使用 Lederer 的语料重新分析预测时也提到专业知识和方向性的问题。Setto 将 Joerg 的研究成果运用到德语和英语语对与汉语和英语语对的语料分析中，质疑了"为了结构而使用策略"的提法，指出"单就有标记的句法结构本身而言不会阻碍同声传译"（1999：82），突出的反而是语言和语境线索的认知和语用加工。远程会议同传中对预测能力也提出了更高的要求。

三、内容改编策略

与各种形式的内容改编加工有关的策略，关系到口译表现标准和"质量"等基本课题。但是有关内容加工的策略，尤其是"简约"类策略，主要是作为应对认知处理制约的方式进行分析的，比如在同传工作中，尤其是远程视频会议环境中，为应对输入的高速度和信息的高密度而运用的压缩或"摘要提炼"策略。早在20世纪后期，Chernov（1978，1994）就讨论过为应对高输入速度而采用的词汇和句法的压缩及省略策略，东欧的几位口译研究者（例如 Alexia，1983）也研究了同一问题。Kirchhoff（1976/2002：116）则以类似的思路探索了"通过选择（省略无关的信息）对信息进行简约"的策略。

压缩不仅可视为"挽救技术"，而且也可以视为支撑翻译过程的策略导向。这在交替传译中可以得到最好的证明。Herbert（1952：67）认为，由于完整的交替传译应当只占用发言人所花时间的75%，因此口译员必须加快说话速度，避免重复、迟疑和冗余，才能实现压缩。根据10位学生口译员和2位专业口译员进行交替传译的实验语料，Dam（1993）认为，通过各种类型的替代和省略所实现的篇章压缩在策略上不仅是必需的，通常也有着上佳的效果。Viaggio（1991：51）也指出，口译员要"传达所有的意义"，并不意味着要"说出全部"，即不必把源语信息意义连同风格和语义上的细微差别完全翻译出来。因此，"传达所有的意义"，主要是对口译过程中以意义为基础还是以言语转换为基础的观点，同时也是有关基于形式和基于意义的口译方法之间的基本区分。对于这种区分，Gran（1989）和 Isham（1994）等学者都持有相同观点。

因此，采取"合成"的方式而不是"说出全部"的方式进行口译是建立在"压缩"或"隐含化"这一基本策略之上的。"隐含化"强调了各种压缩的方法和所涉及的语对之间的联系：什么需要直接说、什么可以不直接说是由具体的语言和文化所决定的。与此相反，尽管被认为是翻译的普遍性特征，明晰化可能是一种规避语言和社会文化差异的策略。由此，Kohn 和 Kalina（1996：126）提出，根据目标语的话语规约采取改编策略的必要性包括"恰当的文化改编和顺应"。

第五章
远程口译教学

　　向新入职的口译员传授必备的知识和技能，是远程口译职业化过程中的重要一环，其主要传授途径为教学和培训。教学和培训意味着要完全了解职业的整体内容和全部程序，因此许多口译研究都以教学和培训为背景，直接或间接地为之服务。多数远程口译研究者或是口译教学人员，或是正在接受口译教育的学生。大学层次的远程口译教学目前还在发展阶段，欧洲各高校在这方面始终居于领先地位。进入互联网时代以后，随着远程口译的职业化和制度化，新一轮远程口译教学和培训浪潮正在兴起。目前，口译研究中针对远程口译教学方面的系统研究并不多，大部分是关于研究者的经验描述和总结，主要涉及的方面包括：学生筛选、课程设置、教学内容和方法，以及表现测评等。以下章节摘自 Braun 教授调研和总结的有关远程口译教育领域的现状。

第一节　远程口译教育

　　以往的研究表明，口译教育较少尝试远距离模式。目前比较有名的远程口译教育机构主要有三家：温哥华社区学院（Carr & Steyn，2000），南非大学（Moeketsi & Wallmach，2005），阿德莱德培训和继续教育学院（Rowan，1998）。日内瓦大学(2005)也曾制订包含若干远程学习模块的口译员培训计划。Language Line Services、AT & T（2004）和 Berlitz Interpretation Services（2001）等美国语言服务机构在提供口译服务的同时也会适时召开培训研讨会。

一、远程口译教育机构教学

(一) 温哥华社区学院

温哥华社区学院在世界范围内首先开展口译教学实验。1997 年，学院开始通过电信手段提供正式的法庭口译服务；2000 年，又采用远距离模式开设课程。学院的 1 年或 200 小时课程包含 4 个科目，其中包括 6 小时电话口译练习和发送给学生的录音带、录像带练习（Carr & Steyn，2000）。该课程分配给口译实践的时间远远低于校园计划的 123 小时。这个差距表明学院无法提供培训计划中与现场教学相同的练习时间，并让教育工作者意识到口译实践的重要性。正如 Carr 和 Steyn（2000：85）所说："以远程教育形式保存该模型的构想，很快由于天文数字般的成本而被认为是不可能的。"但是，没有研究指出提供如此昂贵的远距离模式练习和练习时间的减少可能对培训质量产生影响。口译实践之外的教学主题，主要通过印刷材料、视频音频材料及电子邮件进行教学。视频会议研究中心用于视频电影展示和相关讨论。在电话口译实践中，网络链接 3 名参与角色扮演的学生和 1 名进行评论和指导讨论的监督老师。

2002 年，学院提出了一个完整的社区法律口译在线培训计划，包括使用互联网、视频音频和打印材料来说明课程的关键点，并在一系列音频片段中开展口译练习，培养学生在理解、记忆、笔录和释义方面的技能。计划包含 49 分钟的口译职业素养录像带和 2 个视频会议，给受训人"会见"教师的机会，并练习交替传译；同时还提供 12 小时由语言专业小组和双语口译教师组织的交替传译、电话会议练习，并通过 PureVoice 文件进一步练习口译。学生们在听完练习对话并在每次演讲后启用这些文件记录他/她的口译问题和答案。然后，将文件附加到电子邮件中，由指导员在每次口译后进行更正，给出建议，再将文件返还给学生。目前，以课堂为主的课程有 279 小时，其中包括 150 小时的口译练习。

由于该项目是第一次尝试远程口译服务模式，因此大量的时间都被用来教授与口译相关的材料，音频、录像带的内容主题，以及网络相关的设备组件。尽管报告认为项目取得了成功，但该教学计划尚未处理远距离模式下如何教授核心口译科目这一关键问题。在初始阶段，教学中使用的主要口译媒介是电话，只有 6 小时的现场口译实践，对培训专业口译员来说实践时数过少。口译练习的时间随后增加到 12 小时，仍远低于课堂计划中的 123 小时或 150 小时。因此，学生必须依赖录音带、录像带或 PureVoice 自行练习，提高口译技巧。在教学计划初始阶段的视频会议中，一般只有 3 名学生在线，也缺少规定的口译练习。之后的视频会议采用交替传译，但也只有 2 个视频会议为教师和其他学生服务，并提供口译实践。这无法构成口译教学的主要渠道，对较大学生群体教学所要采用的技术及其教学适用性也有待进一步调查。非正式的报告结论是，"基于网络的远程教育口译培训目前不能在课堂上提供相当于课堂水准的口译培训"，并指出电话会议有几个缺点，包括缺乏视觉互动，接触时间短暂，以及"经济方面的考虑"、"调度的困难"等问题。

目前尚不知晓应如何解决视觉交互的问题，也不清楚这种模式下学生是否可以达到与普通校园课程中的学生同等的能力水平。尽管如此，温哥华社区学院的经验表明，以电话口译作为教学媒介是可行的，至少对少数学生来说是可行的。但通过远程模式教授口译，无论是通过视频会议还是电话会议都很昂贵。

（二）南非大学

南非大学是世界上最大的远程教育大学之一。1999 年，它推出了提供专业化法庭口译教育的文学学士学位，并于 2000 年正式纳入学制。该计划通过传统远程教育（学生使用纸质版学习指南进行自学和写作后授课）、现代远程教育（使用电子邮件、互联网、音频和录像带及视频会议），以及线下方式进行教学（在各个中心举办讲座，学生前往比勒陀利亚主校区并参加冬季和夏季学校的讨论课）。学习中心还有辅导员，由他们在工作时段和周末开展讲座，并与学生讨论问题（Moeketsi & Wallmach，2005：81）。Moeketsi 和 Wallmach 承认，主要的挑战是以远距离模式教授口译本。为了让学生有机会练习口译技巧，必须提供录音带的口头文本，并要求他们完成学习指南中给出的快速练习口译任务。口译任务是在录像带上提交的，讲师会提供详细的书面反馈。对于学生来说，讨论课是练习口译技巧的机会。讨论课采取扩展研讨会或夏季/冬季学校的形式，并定期举行（每个教学模块至少 10 个小时）。

因此，该计划中口译相关科目要通过各种形式的互动，实现远程教育最大化，同时兼采传统方法和现代技术。但是，教授口译的程序很大程度上依赖于不同形式的面对面教学。例如：老师和前往学习中心的学生进行面对面研讨会，辅以学生的自我实践。该计划尚未充分解决通过远距离模式教授口译的根本问题，这可能和南非的技术环境有关。由于大多数学生无法使用电脑或视频播放器、CD，使得视频不能构成核心课程学习的一部分，只能用作附加材料。在线提供课程也不太实际，因为南非很少有家庭用户可以访问网络线路，可用带宽非常有限（有些用户甚至无法使用普通电话）（Moeketsi & Wallmach，2005：84）。显然，在这种技术环境中，面对面教学更具灵活性，足以满足学生的需求，是理想的解决方案。

另外，南非大学教学计划中针对学生录音口译任务提供详细书面反馈的做法非常耗时。假设一个班级中有 15 名学生，他们每人提交 1 小时的磁带，教师就需要花 15 小时听磁带和更多时间写评论，而这还只是口译任务中的一项，因此这种增加的工作量必须在主要预算项目中仔细考虑。

根据 Wallmach 的说法，2004 年，南非大学在南方提供了为期一年的非洲手语翻译课程，也使用类似的教学方式和远距离模式。但由于该教学计划有更多的资金，同时按比例提供了更多的现场时间，讲师们得以在计划开始之前前往南非一些省份采访和测试学生。培训计划包括 160 小时的现场教学，平均每周 20 小时。为方便现场教学，不同地区的学生被安置在一个中心位置。除了正式联席会议期间，讲师们还在周末观察了学生们的口译实践。因此，该教学计划具有强大的面对面特色，再加上讲师的现场教学，投入达160 个小时，这甚至高于澳大利亚一些为期一年的口译课程所提供的接触时数。例如，西悉尼大学、昆士兰大学和麦考瑞大学的口译教学时间为 72 小时到 94 小时不等。由于手语翻译的教学可能需要更多的时间，因此课程的教学内容通过远距离模式进行，并非满足教育的要求。此外，运行此教学计划所涉及的成本也必须考虑在内，在没有足够资金的前提下这样的计划是不可行的。

（三）阿德莱德培训与继续教育学院

阿德莱德学院的旅游与国际语言中心培训和继续教育学院（TAFE）提供口译文凭课程。虽然这门课程并未定位成远程学习计划，但它的确具有远程教育的一些特点。学习资料由四部分组成：学习指南、语境研究之文化与社会、语境研究之工作手册、未来意义之口译技术。前三部分是印刷文本，最后一部分是 3 个录像带或 2 张 CD。未来意义之口译技术部分包含六种不同语言的六种口译方案，反映六个主题的口译。每个场景之后是一些用于讨论目的的不同材料，某些课程材料具有远程教育的特色。例如，学习指南和语境研究之工作手册提供了明确的说明，用于指导学生的学习过程，并给出了一些参考用于自定进度指导学习的问题和作业（Rowan，1998）。核心口译教学在根本上是课堂教学，学生必须参与进来，不能单独依靠学习资料。学生学习要以课堂教学为中心，同时必须参加校内课程，练习口译。因此，归根结底，虽然学习材料可以帮助学生回顾所学，但课堂的中心地位不可取代。可见，该教学计划仅适用于校园学习。

（四）日内瓦大学

2005 年，日内瓦大学开始为口译员提供继续教育课程并发放证书，课程中包含了远程学习模块。这个课程设计通过远距离模式教授口译，为口译员提供在线技术知识、班级信息规划、研究项目等的培训。例如，"远距离基础课程"学习模块将帮助学生熟悉证书中使用的学习环境。同时特别关注用于支持学习活动和流程的在线工具论坛、聊天或期刊。"交替传译教学"概述模块包括：（1）确认交替传译口译员所需的技能并开发相关练习；（2）设计交替传译课程的介绍；（3）识别关键笔记的原则；（4）计划练习和不同材料的进展阶段。

虽然通过远距离模式教授口译，但这些尝试都没有充分应对口译科目教学核心的关键挑战，或提供可与课堂教学相比的口头和视觉互动。在口译实践方面，教学仅限于极少数参与者和极短的时间，远低于正常标准的校园培训计划。此外，这些尝试还普遍存在自学的特点。在这种情况下，电话是主要的口译实践媒介。在日内瓦大学的模式中，口译主要是在基于课堂的现场会议中讲授，口译相关的主题则通过远程学习来教授。虽然通过远距离模式教授口译在某种程度上是可行的，但口译中的视觉互动问题几乎没有得到解决。

二、语言服务机构教学

AT & T 公司在美国的语言热线中提供电话口译服务，并对电话口译员进行认证。这包括通过短暂的电话培训课程来为有意加入的口译员提供技能服务（2001），帮助其为电话口译考试做准备。培训课程持续数小时，时间视具体情况和口译员的口译经验而定，内容涵盖交替传译、道德守则、一般和行业特定的口译协议、术语等。认证测试也通过电话进行。该教学计划更像是一项针对口译员的在职培训计划。但是，受训的口译员不同于没有口译经验的学生，因此用于训练的远程教学课程等教学因素也有所不同。系统的教学对于口译学生来说很重要，因为口译员可能没有联络口译方面的丰富经验或未参加过正式的培训计划。语言热线服务计划由于是出于特定目的，专为执业口译员而设，因此很难被认为是适当的远程口译教育计划。在技术方面，Language Line Services 也像温哥华社区学院一样使用电话进行口译实践，但是这两个机构都没有解决口译教学中的视觉交互问题。

Berlitz GlobalNet 是国际翻译和语言服务提供商。像 Language Line Services 一样，它也有自己的独立认证体系，要求所有候选人完成资格认证（Berlitz，2001）。他们为住在偏远地区或无法前往特定现场的专业口译员提供"远程学习课程"，帮助其进一步完善口译技巧。这些课程通过电话进行，一般持续两小时到一两天，是关于特定口译的研讨会或讲习班，诸如"连续成功战略"等问题的考试和"同声传译和交替传译工作坊"。

例如，"医学口译：远程学习音频"研讨会系列，包括在 2001 年 7 月和 8 月中举行了关于医学口译员的道德准则、角色定位、美国医疗保健系统、医疗程序和条件等问题的研讨。据 Berlitz GlobalNet 在墨尔本的代表 Andrew Lee 所说，无论是在特定场所还是通过远距离模式，Berlitz 都不提供标准口译培训计划。2002 年，Berlitz GlobalNet 的翻译、本地化、技术写作和口译服务被提供商 Bowne Global Solutions（2004）收购。2005 年 9 月 1 日，Bowne Global Solutions 又被 Lionbridge（2005）收购。自 2002 年以来，Berlitz GlobalNet 已不再为口译员开设培训研讨会，而是专门提供语言教学、跨文化课程培训、翻译和口译（Berlitz，2004）。Network Omni Multilingual Communications（2004）是美国另一家提供电话口译服务的公司，其电话口译认证计划开始于 2003 年。这个计划和 Language Line Services 和 Berlitz 的计划一样，使用电话进行培训，其目的并不是为了远程口译培训。

以上介绍的教育培训都试图找出哪些技术能满足实时远距离模式口译教学的口头和视觉互动要求。理想情况下，传播手段应该随时可用、方便、有效且价格合理。上文梳理了最有可能用于远程口译教学的三种媒体：电话（电话会议、本地区域网络）、视频会议和互联网视频会议。远程课程的运行成本及其对学生的影响取决于许多变量，包括设施和设备的可用性、技术的结合、设施和设备的初始投资、远程程序交付的技术环境、服务提供商的收费、计划的持续时间和注册的学生数量，等等。

第二节 远程口译教学课程设置

欧盟 AVIDICUS 远程视频口译项目设计了三种培训核心模块：法律从业人员专用模块（包括警察），法律服务部门的口译员专用模块，翻译学生专用模块。

本章将介绍三个培训模块，并根据培训需要和培训技术，分别介绍学生口译员，法律口译员，及该模块所针对的法律从业人员。视频会议口译使用者位于两个不同的地方，例如通过远程视频链接的法院和监狱，口译员与非母语人士一起在法院或监狱中使用扬声器。在这种情况下，诉讼程序在其中一端（例如法庭）进行，同时通过远程视频链接另一端的口译员（例如另一个法院）。目前几乎没有法律方面的职前和在职口译培训，更不用说以视频为媒介的口译培训。欧洲的高等教育机构最近才开始提供本科和研究生级别的培训和专业口译员的法律口译短期课程。关于认证或认可的相关规定也很少，主要是由英国语言学家特许学院提供的公共服务口译文凭（DPSI）。自 1994 年以来，英国的情况更加不稳定。为解决法律口译员和法律人员的缺乏问题，欧洲委员会开始资助英国司法部的刑事司法项目，针对法律从业者和警官进行相关培训。

欧盟 AVIDICUS 项目在口译员和法律从业人员的培训上迈出了一步，但是随之出现了两个问题：首先，由于缺乏最基本的法律培训，可能导致此类口译培训提前。但更关键的是，各种形式的视频口译的使用可能会由于以下情况变得越来越频繁：新的欧盟立法，尤其是欧洲议会和理事会关于解释权和刑事诉讼的翻译；欧洲努力加强合作与互助绿皮书中反映的跨境刑事诉讼；欧盟《2009—2013 年欧洲电子司法年度行动计划》的推行。所有这些举措都鼓励在法律诉讼中使用视频会议。2008 年进行的法律数据调查表明，视频会议已在刑事诉讼中得到广泛使用，能够有效加快跨境合作，降低成本，提高安全性。AVIDICUS 项目在 2009—2010 年度进行的调查中确认，刑事诉讼中以视频为媒介的口译也在不断增加。

其次，关于视频口译的研究很少。在 AVIDICUS 项目中进行的研究明确指出，视频媒介的口译尤其具有挑战性。AVIDICUS 项目的研究结果表明，视频会议技术可以为当前的一些问题提供有效的解决方案和相应的口译服务，利用相关研究提高对视频媒介的理解并减少实践中的困难，同时还强调了特定情况下以视频为媒介的口译的局限性。研究成果将有助于完善解决方案，更好地规划口译员的工作。在这样的背景下，AVIDICUS 项目旨在开发一系列以视频为媒介、具有不同解决方案的口译培训模块，针对不同的目标群体，包括法律口译员、口译学生和法律从业人员（含警察）。在 AVIDICUS 中采用的培训方法，其优势在于具体实践与项目研究成果的结合。培训中以研究为导向的指导有助于反思实践，并为适当的解决方案提供良好的基础。此外，模块的互动是灵活的。可以在一天或更短的时间内互动，也可以扩展为适合不同需求的课程。学生口译模块旨在成为更广泛的模块或法律口译课程的一部分，但是该模块试点项目的反馈表明，视频口译需要投入更多的时间。以下章节将对该项目的具体远程口译教学进行介绍，以期为国内的远程口译教学提供思路。

一、教学的技术基础

基于实践的培训模块在任何情况下都要考虑三个重要的技术要素。首先是至少两个远程口译"站点"的可用性。为了模拟和培训，需要将两个（或多个）站点放置在同一座建筑内，以便课程参与者（和导师）在培训课程中进行更改和定位。培训课程也可以作为两个机构之间（例如两所大学之间或大学和公共服务提供者之间）的协作活动来组织兼容的视频会议设备。其他两个关键要素是远程口译链接和设备的质量。最低的技术规格源自视频会议手册。该手册由欧洲法律数据处理工作组提供，具体内容可从欧洲电子司法门户网站（http://e-justice.europa.eu/）获得。以下是这些规范的概括：

- 视频会议系统：应使用专门的"空间系统"，或者使用基于电脑的系统，前提是该电脑具有合格的处理速度，当没有其他"繁重"的视频会议会话正在进行时，应用程序将在此电脑上运行。
- 基于口译 ISDN 的链接：如果使用 ISDN 链接，则最少 6 条通道（3 条 ISDN 线路）可以实现。
- 带宽 384 kbit/秒，传输速率为每秒 30 帧。如果使用大屏幕，则可能不够。H.320 或 H.310 视频标准应该使用 ISDN 链接（H.310 能提供更快的链接）。
- 基于网络的链接应通过互联网使用 H.323 视频标准。至少应有 1Mbit/秒的带宽。

- 图片：系统应将 H. 263 和 H. 264 标准用于保障图片质量，每秒 30 帧的帧速率可确保接近广播质量的图像质量。

- 最常见的音频传输标准是 G. 711 和 G. 722，提供 128 或 64 kbit / 秒的 7 kHz 音频编码。但是国际会议口译员协会（AIIC）认为，范围为 7 kHz 的音频不足以进行远程会议口译。

- 屏幕：应使用尺寸合适的 LCD 屏幕。屏幕应该大到可以识别面部表情并用于展示。

- 麦克风：具有全双工音频的回声消除麦克风并且应该使用音频静音。

- 相机和照明：可控相机应该要远程使用。视频会议房间中的灯光应创造自然的氛围，尤其是面部表情清晰可见，无阴影。

- 就座安排应尽可能仿造现实生活，并为口译员提供符合人体工程学的座椅。

在培训中，上述规定可以适当调整或去除。例如，就座位安排而言，无须在训练环境中重建法庭或监护室，但条件应当足以提供培训体验。尽管设备和链接质量极其重要，但是参加培训模块的人可以从视频会议系统中使用质量不高的链接方法，例如 ISDN（2 至 6 个通道，即 128 至 384 kbps），Skype 或类似的基于网络的视频电话服务。在法律环境下使用质量不高的链接和外围设备（屏幕、麦克风和扬声器）进行交流和口译，毫无疑问会出现质量问题。但是随着高质量设备和链接更容易获取，"不良"的技术体验在训练中可以大幅减少。例如，英格兰的许多治安法庭都配备了用于"法院监狱视频链接"的视频会议系统，其中多数用于延期听证会，而该设备中的参与者在远程站点（监狱）中基本看不到。

所需设备取决于口译模式（交替传译、同声传译或耳语翻译），据此选择培训课程，并在所在国家/地区进行相关培训。调查表明，至少在欧洲，新兴的视频会议主要采用交替传译模式，即口译员先听然后翻译简短的语音。在这种口译模式中，可以考虑为口译员准备耳机，以降低噪声水平。调查显示，一些国家也使用同声传译，即口译员在聆听时进行翻译，扬声器不必暂停。同声传译通常需要特定的附加设备，特别是在视频会议情况下需要为口译员提供隔音间，且隔音间要与视频会议系统相连。相比之下，若同声传译以"耳语"的形式传递口译，或者口译员在旁边口译，通常不需要额外的设备。在视频会议情况下，这种口译模式仅适用于与口译员在同一地点的参与者。培训必须涵盖不同的口译模式，因此参加培训的人可以根据每种模式的具体细节来评估不同模式的适用性，从而寻找适合特定视频会议情况的口译模式。

用于视频会议的技术可以依托局域网或互联网。使用这些技术的视频会议也可以被广泛用于"桌面方式"和"基于工作室"的会议（Wang，2004b）。桌面会议是指使用个人计算机的参与者在自家或工作场所参加会议。基于工作室的会议是指参与者前往为会议专设的工作室或学习中心。在教学方面，视频会议由于可以容纳口头和视觉互动，是一种理想的教学方式。教师在配有视频会议设施的演讲室中，可以在远程学习站点与学生互动。

局域网通常由某些群体特别设计和开发，也称为内联网。它拒绝从网络外部访问的用户，以保证沟通的质量和安全性。在数字通信时代，宽带技术通常用于局域网以确保即时通信的带宽。Wang（2004a，2004b）通过局域网内的视频会议进行语言教学实验，发现图像质量和即时通信与声音一样，几乎没有问题；"视频和音频都是与清晰度、一致性和实时标准同步"（Wang，2004b：94）。但由于是内部网络，只能通过特殊链接访问，灵活性不够，无法让参与者在旅行时使用。局域网视频会议是基于工作室的会议，因此有高昂的设置和运营成本。局域网支持的基于工作室的视频会议"经常涉及更复杂的设置和技术，例如编解码器、多点控制单元、工作室和可视化工具……显然，最初的投资和长期维护的成本巨大"（Wang，2004b：93）。

互联网具有电话会议无法提供的优势，是远程口译的理想载体。互联网由卫星或电缆支持，有时也由两者结合。卫星互联网通常用于铺设电缆成本较高的地方（Phan，2002）。例如，在荷兰，休斯网络系统（2004）为 800 所学校安装了卫星互联网。在国外的城市中心或没有电缆连接的城镇，卫星互联网得到广泛应用。卫星技术也适用于互动通信，它允许参与者成为信息的发送者和接收者。

互联网通信可分为三种形式：文本、语音、视觉。最流行的形式是文本通信，例如电子邮件。在目前的技术条件下，文本通信可以实现实时和同步。例如，在使用 ADSL5 技术的聊天室中，参与者可以立即收到短信。但是，语音和视觉的通信使用较少，部分原因是语音和视觉交流的同步并不有效，也难以掌握延迟状况。在 20 世纪 90 年代末的远程口译研究中，Fors（Niska，1999：117）发现视频会议有"令人恼火的延迟"，因此需要更高级的技术解决方案．

进入新世纪，情况并没有得到显著改善。例如，O'Hagan 和 Ashworth（2002）使用电脑和互联网上的配音设施进行了为期 10 周的试点，远程教授学生翻译。他们指出，"远程口译平台是基于语音的课程，但这些课程不够可靠"（2002：xii）。他们在电脑上通过互联网对许多 VOiP 应用程序进行的实验表明，"一般来说，他们〔VOiP 申请〕无法提供口译所需的质量水平"（2002：62）。O'Hagan 和 Ashworth 认为"互联网偏爱文本通信模式，而语音通信尚未发展到相同的程度"（2002：94）。他们解释说："在我们的课程中，我们出现了声音的突然消失等众多的问题。中断通常意味着讲师需要为特定参与者所丢失的部分重新开始讲课。互动环境中的这种不一致性，也给教师和学习者带来了额外压力"（O'Hagan & Ashworth，2002：119）。

值得一提的是，O'Hagan 和 Ashworth 的实验完全为语音沟通，主要关注如何向学习者远程教授翻译。理想情况下，口译教学会涉及参与者之间的口头和视觉互动，这需要更先进的技术环境和更宽的带宽以消除长时间的延误。

Wang（2004b）采用互联网的远距离模式进行中文教学实验。虽然是为语言教学所设计，但她的实验还是为口译教学提供了有用的信息。实验进行时，Wang 和其他老师在格里菲斯大学讲学，学生则分散在澳大利亚其他地方。Wang 使用 Netmeeting7，测试了以下三种环境：

- 拨号调制解调器（教师）—互联网—拨号调制解调器（学生）；
- 宽带（教师）—互联网—拨号调制解调器（学生）；
- 宽带（教师）—互联网—宽带（学生）。

实验是一对一进行的，即一名教师对一名学生。因此和课堂教学相比，它与个人辅导更相似。

在拨号调制解调器—互联网—拨号调制解调器环境中，音质差且不稳定，有时声音会冻结一两秒钟；视频质量也差，而且"视频的一个主要问题是由于互联网流量不足或参与者计算机的容量有限而导致的图像冻结。冻结的时间可能从 1 秒到 10 秒"（2004b：101）。

在宽带—互联网—拨号调制解调器环境中，老师能体验到更清晰、连续性更强的声音和更好的视频质量，延迟也较少，但学生的成绩仅略高于以前的环境。结果表明，由于教师使用了更多流量、更宽的带宽而取得了更好的体验，学生由于继续使用相同的拨号调制解调器，情况保持不变。

根据 Wang 的研究，使用 Netmeeting7 非常实惠。该软件可以从互联网上免费下载，但用户需要购买网络摄像头，并支付互联网链接费用。Wang 的研究为远程教育中的言语和视觉互动提供了宝贵的意见。研究也指出，不安全的带宽会导致时间延迟，这会影响视频会议的有效性和可靠性。为解决延迟问题，Wang 建议在互联网流量足够大的时间内安排会话。

其次，在三种技术中，宽带链接似乎是口译教学唯一有效的选择。鉴于宽带的可用性，有线连接到因特网是一个重要的限制因素。2002 年，在澳大利亚进行的一项研究中（Ko，2004），只有约 12.5％的参与者有线连接到互联网。此外，大多数发展中国家的学生只能访问拨号调制解调器。这大大影响其速度、可访问性和费用。在视频会议中，如果要将宽带电缆链接用于互联网，这些因素必须考虑在内。

第三，基于一对一辅导的视频会议是一个主要缺点。教学口译涉及的互动人数在两人以上，这反过来又需要更大的带宽。互联网视频会议的有效性和可行性尚未得到明确的评估。

从上面的实验和互联网视频会议的报告中可以看出，通过互联网进行语音和视觉传播，包括之前所提到的图像电话，其主要问题都与带宽有关。带宽与信息传播的数量和速度之间的关系，可以用高速公路上的交通来比喻：文本通信，如同一条每个方向只需要两个车道的高速公路；语音通信，如同一条每个方向要有八个车道才能保证车流顺畅的高速公路；视觉通信，则是一条每个方向要有一百个车道才能完成车流处理的高速公路。

传统拨号调制解调器连接到电话线的速度是每秒 56 千比特。对于典型的电缆调制解调器，最大速度为 1.5 兆比特。但 1.5 兆比特是理论上的最大速度，实际速度不可能随时达到，因为不能确定互联网是否为专用网络，也不能保证足够的带宽。当互联网一次传播的数据量过多时，其情形类似于高速公路上的交通堵塞。由于互联网的局限性，带宽已被确定为影响视频会议质量的主要因素（Buckett et al.，1999；Chou，2001；Kötter et al.，1999；McAndrew et al.，1996；Wong & Fauverge，1999）。因此，Wang（2004b）建议互联网视频会议应在上午 8 点之前或周末举行，且所有学生都要同时听到并看到老师。在对话口译练习中，所有参与者都必须能听到和看到对方，带宽的要求会更大。

随着电信技术的发展，宽带也可以使用传统的铜质电话线链接作为 ADSL。根据产品的不同，ADSL 的速度可达到每秒 1.5 兆。另外，和有线调制解调器一样，产品的速度越快，价格越贵。但 ADSL 技术也有几个限制：并非所有电话服务都可用；它的带宽无法保证；它不如专用宽带可靠；它的高速度体现在下载方向上，其上传速度要慢得多（Internode，2004）。因此，使用 ADSL 进行网络视频会议会比使用电缆调制解调器有更多延迟。

另一种可用于互联网视频会议的技术是专用网络。这便是在高速公路上建立特殊车道，以拒绝其他车道车流的汇入。专用网络类似于局域网，可以保证带宽。目前一些商业提供商和有此类需求的组织已经在使用这项技术进行视频会议服务。但是，这项技术的费用极高。例如，澳大利亚迪肯大学提供用于教学目的的视频会议服务，其报价是每小时 210 澳元。

从技术上讲，更宽的带宽可达数百兆位甚至千兆位，但普通用户或者无法使用，或者不能负担如此昂贵的费用。因此，虽然技术存在，但基础设施仍未准备好。换句话说，我们尚不能将高速公路连接到我们自家的车道。

在电脑上使用连接摄像机的互联网视频会议时，老师和学生之间几乎看不到彼此；顶多只是看到其他人的面孔。即使学生可以看到老师，老师也无法清楚地看到所有学生，因为"每个工作室一旦超过 6～7 人便很难保证链接质量"（Mouzourakis，1996：27），"当越来越多的人出现在同一屏幕上，他们的形象就越不清晰"（Tiffin & Rajasingham，1995：112）。这也会降低两种教学视觉互动的有效性和学习效果。

我们可以依靠多种技术通过互联网进行视频会议。专用的网络是最有效的，其次是宽带电缆，而通过传统电话线连接的拨号调制解调器是最慢的。成本是使用快速专用网络的主要限制，而其他选择则可能会有延迟问题。以上技术问题和成本花费都给远程口译教学带来诸多限制。

二、教学课程内容和方法

（一）针对口译学生的模块

这部分内容主要介绍针对口译学生尤其是硕士水平的学生的模块。学生一般要求具有一定的语言水平和面对面口译的经验。同时还应对有关的法律制度和普遍存在的实践问题有充分的了解。因此不建议将此模块应用在硕士课程的第一学期。

1. 教学目的和学习成果

该模块的具体目标是：

提高对以视频为媒介的新型口译的认识；详细介绍各种视频会议形式和法律程序中的远程口译，概述目前的做法和未来的趋势；使学生能够探索视频媒体与面对面口译中的特定挑战（例如通过技术渠道感知对话者，处理因缺乏视觉线索、技术设备和通信控制而产生的问题）；向学生解释造成这种情况的原因，充分理解视频交流和口译作为司法部门应用手段的理由；为不同形式的实践提供视频口译机会；鼓励讨论和反思实际经验；提供以视频为媒介的口译研究领域的新问题。

在学习成果方面，将让学生充分了解远程口译，懂得在远程视频口译中使用相关技术。学生还将学习相关的初步知识，从而评估进行视频会议和远程口译的具体工作模式和工作时间。

2. 课程大纲

该模块的课程大纲分为 6 个主要单元。主要由教师主导、学生探索和发现、学生在课堂上的实践练习几部分内容组成。此外也鼓励学生随时参加讨论，提出问题，从而创造一个积极的学习环境。

单元 1：简介

该单元旨在概述最新的远程视频会议在刑事诉讼中的使用情况，介绍欧洲法律框架内的相关新法律及其含义，并解释视频会议的技术基础。首先，该单元强调了司法部门采用这些口译服务形式的动机，如加快诉讼节奏的需要、节省成本的要求和合格法律口译员不足等。它还可以吸引学生注意利益相关者在使用或不使用视频会议时的紧张关系，包括视频会议口译员的表达可能会降低口译质量，其工作条件可能对口译产生不利影响等。其次，该单元为学生提供与欧盟法规相关的信息，其中包括在刑事诉讼中对视频会议的提倡，尤其是"程序路线图"，以加强对嫌疑人或被告人的指令。这将帮助学生了解刑事诉讼中使用视频会议的立法和政治背景。第三，介绍视频会议相关的术语，并参考各种用于视频会议的技术，指出这些技术的适用性。该单元的预期学习成果是提高学生的意识，了解采用视频会议口译形式的动机。

单元 2：视频会议和口译

该单元旨在提醒学生注意参与者和口译员所处的不同位置。视频媒介口译形式在这里称为视频会议口译，口译员需要参与到视频会议中，例如听需要翻译的远程见证人说话。在视频会议中，口译员通常与某些参与者在同一地点，此设置与远程口译相反。远程口译的主要目的是解决本地口译员的短缺问题或节省其旅行费用。作为本单元的成果，学生将能区分不同的环境并了解其不同的动机。这可以帮助他们认识到不同的设置通常不能互换，每个人都有需要面对的问题。

单元 3：目前的做法

该单元旨在介绍在目前的诉讼中使用视频会议口译和远程口译的示例。首次动手实践课程：视频会议口译和远程口译的目的是双重的。首先，概述视频会议口译和远程口译在当前法律诉讼中的用法。其次，整合本模块中两个练习课程中的第一个。在第一部分中，该单元确定了视频会议口译在当前实际使用的示例和远程口译在欧洲的法律诉讼中的使用情况（基于AVIDICUS项目对欧盟法律从业人员和口译员所做的调查）。该单元把重点放在刑事诉讼上，但也包含其他情境，例如移民诉讼。该单元在不同的时间和地点下使用不同形式的视频口译，例如视频会议口译第一次听证会和还押延期听证会，还有警察采访远程口译。提供的例子来自不同的欧洲国家，并强调实践中的异同。通过以下内容，该单元尤其可以适应本地环境，从国家或地区环境中获取其他材料。单元的第二部分包括实操练习。这需要一个至少包括 3 名学生的小组、法律程序脚本和使用视频会议的技术。建议学生练习视频会议口译和远程口译时积极应用上几个单元学到的知识，但动手部分应当适应当地情况、考虑相关性和可用时间。以下是两个如何练习的例子：

（1）视频会议口译实践

由一名学生担任检察官或法官并在视频会议室 1 中。另一名学生在视频会议室 2 担任见证人，说另一种语言。说远程见证人语言的学生担任口译员，口译时间大约 10～15 分钟，其他学生现场观摩，也可以互换角色重复练习。

（2）远程口译实践

由一名学生担任警务人员，另一名学生扮演犯罪嫌疑人或受害人，他们在同一间屋子里。第三位学生使用犯罪嫌疑人或受害人的语言，担任口译员，使用另一种语言。学生可以练习口译大约 10 到 15 分钟，然后将角色交换给另一名学生。没有角色的学生在不同的站点观摩。

这些例子建议使用至少两种工作语言。如果条件不具备，也可以用一种语言进行练习。随后进行小组讨论，分析实践经验和观察结果。应鼓励学生将两种设置相互比较并通过面对面的口译来讨论他们所遇到的问题，观察并确定解决这些问题所需的条件。最后学生可以发现视频会议口译和远程口译能够满足不同需求。学生也可以了解当前尚未获得普遍接受或认同的视频会议口译和远程口译实践标准。实操练习应让学生体验面对面口译和视频媒介口译之间的差异，并反思自己的做法。

单元 4：从实践到研究

视频会议口译和远程口译其他领域的研究结果可能会提出单元 3 中出现的一系列问题。鉴于缺乏视频会议口译和远程口译的通用标准，方法论意识就显得格外重要。另外，口译课程的毕业生将来可能会将新口译形式引入他们的工作机构。在这种情况下，评估技能至关重要。因此，第 4 单元让学生熟悉调查结果，综述关于视频口译不同用途的研究，其重点是研究和评估方法。作为该单元的成果，学生有望对研究和评估视频会议口译和远程口译的不同方法作出区分，并进而提高对特定事物之间联系的研究和评估方法及研究成果的认识，使其找出以往评估方法的缺点。学生在该模块中获得了视频会议口译和远程口译的初始实践经验，未来还可以结合具体需要对视频会议口译和远程口译实践开展进一步研究。

单元 5：对未来研究的启示

该单元的目的是确定与视频会议口译和远程口译有关的研究问题。这样可以让学生注意潜在问题，并比以前的单元更注意系统化整理自己的意见。该单元首先确定视频会议口译和远程口译的主要研究领域，包括技术对口译员表现的影响，法律诉讼中视频会议口译和远程口译的社会文化特征，视频媒介对交流的影响，对参与者进行管理并保持他们之间的融洽关系。完成本单元后，学生可以增加对视频会议口译和远程口译中潜在问题的认识，并思考有助于解决此类问题的策略。该单元还将为第二次实操练习打下基础并鼓励学生发现问题，并更好地解决问题。

单元 6：总结

最终单元的目标是双重的。一方面，它包含了两次实践；另一方面，它得出了有关视频会议口译和远程口译在刑事诉讼中的新用法。建议重复第 3 单元中的练习，使用不同的法律情境设置和脚本，鼓励学生积极思考，通过实践让学生熟悉视频会议口译和远程口译中仍然存在的困难，口译或沟通交流的策略，视频会议口译和远程口译的进一步培训应包含的要素，对口译员和法律人员的指导方针和对从业者的建议。最后一个单元突出了模块的要点，并提出了解决这些问题的建议。视频会议口译和远程口译的实用指南是口译员的练习模块（参见附录），可以包含在总结单元里。

3. 教材

该模块的教材经过多次开发，初步版本已在试点使用。教材的最终版附录中提供的内容，在结合了学生的反馈意见后形成。但也应看到，一方面，考虑到视频会议口译和远程口译的当前实践、趋势和使用频率，需要及时更新教材以反映其变化。另一方面，实践、不断变化的法律框架和新的研究成果也在促进教材的更新开发。该材料包括：

涵盖教学大纲各部分演示文稿。每个单元的一组练习：练习包括每个单元末尾的演示文稿。讲义提供了以视频为媒介的口译，以支持第1单元中讨论。视频会议口译和远程口译的参考书目，也可从 AVIDICUS 网站获得（www. video conference-interpreting. net）角色扮演会话的脚本：角色扮演应基于真实可能且适当的材料。

演示文稿提供了教师主导的摘要、教材和模块。教学风格应该相应地侧重互动/反思和讨论。每个单元中包含的练习旨在推进此过程。

单元 1：简介

本单元的幻灯片概述了使用视频会议口译和远程口译的主要动机，列出了有关的主要立法框架。幻灯片还包括相关法律文本的链接，以供参考。有关视频会议的欧盟法规试点课程表明，让学生一开始参与是不错的方法。在诉讼程序中引入视频媒介进行口译可以要求学生学习这些课文并评估他们的态度。视频口译中学生可能会发现媒体经常热衷于报道新颖但过分简化的口译形式，并对视频口译的可行性、优势和潜在成本进行分析。这种见解可以与第1单元中提出的观点进行对比，特别是专业口译员对视频会议口译和远程口译缺点的认识。这样的讨论提醒学生注意对视频会议口译和远程口译的反应，并为后续单元提供重点。入门单元的另一项练习将鼓励学生研究关于视频会议的立法文本。

单元 2：视频会议口译

本单元的幻灯片以图形表现不同的设置并提供使用示例。视频会议口译示例练习，要求学生找出其使用的地点，然后鼓励其思考法庭环境下视频会议口译不同变体（如同声传译）的优缺点，并从远程口译员、其他参与者和法官的角度来综合评估。这项练习要求学生充分运用现有知识对视频会议口译的新情况进行分析。

单元 3：目前的做法

本单元对比了不同国家和地区视频会议口译的不同做法。例如，对比在英格兰/威尔士的首次听证会中视频会议口译的不同做法，介绍了法律从业者在欧洲使用视频会议口译和远程口译的频率和原因。本单元包括一系列具有挑战性的练习，以提高学生的评估能力。如要求学生讨论当前做法中有争议的部分，口译员对视频会议口译和远程口译的反应，法院和警察局的视频会议口译，以及远程口译中的座位安排问题。如上所述，实操练习应基于脚本。为了更加贴近现实，脚本应反映具体情境。学生可以是角色扮演者，且需事先接受一些指导。或者由另一位导师、合法从业者或警务人员志愿者参加角色扮演，利用其优势帮助学生扮演并体验不同的角色。

单元 4：从实践到研究

本单元概述了视频会议口译和远程口译迄今为止的研究成果，比较了欧盟/联合国关于远程会议口译和医疗保健业务中的研究方法，提供了有关研究的信息，及视频会议口译和远程口译实践的评估方法。相关练习要求学生评估这些研究和方法，并提出自己的方法论。

单元 5：对未来研究的启示

本单元的幻灯片确定了相关研究领域，并划定了每个领域的研究范围。练习包括让学生思考如何研究选定的问题，鼓励学生讨论影响视频会议口译和远程口译过程的各个方面。

单元 6：总结

本单元旨在对从第二次实操实践课程开始到第 3 单元第一次会议的教学过程进行总结。幻灯片着重于总结、备注并提出对视频会议口译和远程口译的要求及其存在问题。幻灯片还可以进一步扩展，将视频会议口译和远程口译的实用指南包含在内，加入口译员的练习模块中。

4. 萨里大学的实验

学生口译模块在英国萨里大学翻译研究中心的试点项目课程中于 2010 年和 2011 年举行了两次。该课程目前已纳入第二学期的模块，标题为"公共服务口译——趋势和问题"。2010 年，该模块有 9 名学生参加，2011 年有 22 名学生参加。同时，该模块和教材的版本也于 2010 年试用。

第一场

第 1 单元（简介）以演讲形式进行，随后进行了宣传，通过收集新闻稿来提高水平。第 2 单元（视频会议和口译）以研讨会形式呈现，讨论视频会议口译和远程口译的不同配置。相关练习成了讨论的一部分，学生要考虑不同的视频会议口译变体的优缺点。

第二场

首先讲解作业，然后以研讨会的形式提出问题并进行讨论，再次将练习第 3 单元的内容纳入研讨范围。学生亲身实践视频会议口译，两种实践都有这种口译的形式，而不仅限于远程口译。

在进行口译练习之前，先简要介绍设备。用于会议的视频会议会话套件配备了访问网格节点（http：//www.accessgrid.org），支持网络视频会议。学生可以看到另一个房间（总览图和 2 个不同角度的特写镜头）和自己房间的照片，该图像被投影到电视墙上。在角色扮演中，采用模拟试听脚本，证人使用远程口译。涉及的所有角色：口译员，法律专业人员和非母语演讲者均由学生扮演。若是法律从业者能参与角色扮演，学生将获得更多经验。萨里大学的学生还有和法律从业者面谈的机会，硕士课程其他部分也可以接触到法律口译员。

所有学生都收到了模拟审判的简介，部分学生在其中扮演角色。在此之前，学生接触过英语法律体系和法庭口译的介绍，也曾以角色扮演的形式在以前的课程中使用过类似的脚本。在视频会议口译中，一名学生担任裁判官（说英语），而一名波兰学生自愿去另一个地点扮演见证人的角色，其他波兰学生与见证人一起在远程站点轮流翻译。使用的其他语言包括汉语、希腊语和意大利语。会议结束后，探讨学生观察到的现象。

第三场

学生进一步获取远程口译的实践经验，并再次扮演所有角色。本次会议采用了警察采访脚本，以与会议 2 相区别。最后的讨论汇集了学生们的看法：在课程中拥有自己的视频会议口译和远程口译经验；对视频会议口译和远程口译存在的问题和未来发展方向的研究；关于一般性问题的结论性发言和潜在的解决方案。学生进行了许多有趣的观察，发现实际会议后的讨论有效地丰富了模块的"理论"部分。例如，一些口译员扮演者注意到话论转换上的困难（"我不知道何时该说话"、"应该何时开始口译"）。与远程站点对话者的沟通及座位安排问题也得到了关注。例如，一名学生评论说，"口译员应该与证人视线接触"。另一名学生表示，对话者在视频会议情况下具有不确定性的特征："我不知道从哪里开始。"还有学生提出了技术上的问题，并询问视频会议链接或技术设备出现故障时的解决方案。在远程口译环境中，一名学生承认自己因独处一室而感到孤独，进而产生远离人群的感觉。总的来说，学生对视频媒介的新形式持积极态度。一名学生总结道："因为我们是口译新手，我们能更轻松地掌握视频会议口译和远程口译。有人做到二十年或更长时间，可能就不那么容易了。"学生的态度与某些专业口译员的态度形成了鲜明的对比。

5. 试点项目的评估反馈

最终评估结束时，在两个试点课程中都分发了评估问卷，总计 26 份，由参加课程模块的学生完成。萨里大学的学生来自不同的语言背景（包括汉语、波兰语、俄语和土耳其语）、不同的国家，他们都志愿成为公共服务口译员。法庭口译的某些方面可能与他们的原籍国或多或少相关，但是法律诉讼中的视频口译会议使学生的学习范围超出了各个国家的语境。会议的参加者众多，反馈也很积极。

在开始该模块之前，学生对视频会议口译和远程口译的知识水平各不相同。据报道，学生对两种口译的认识来自"常识"、新闻、本科学业和网络研究课程。大多数受访者认为，视频会议口译和远程口译需要某种形式的专业培训，并且这种口译形式在公共服务口译内表现良好。是否应将视频会议口译和远程口译会议做成独立会议模块，反馈回来的意见并不清晰。大多数参与者还认为，视频会议口译和远程口译的时间虽短但足够（16 人），其中 7 人感觉时间不足，另外 2 人认为太多。学生通常对自己的学习充满信心且较为积极。但在真实口译环境下，他们的信心相对较差，因而希望得到更多的练习。课程参与者最重要的反馈是：实践是课程中最有用的部分，而且时间也很充足。在萨里大学，该模块作为通用模块提供给同一组学生中的不同语言对，但在分配的时间内，无法保证班上的每个学生都能积极参与。一些学生很高兴有机会观察他人，并进行视频会议口译和远程口译，因为他们学到了如何在视频链接中进行自我展示并解决问题。正如一位与会者所说的，"所有语言都需要有实践的机会并体验挑战"。总体而言，学生的反馈意见表明，视频会议口译和远程口译的主题可以扩展，从而为实践部分提供讨论话题。

（二）法律口译员模块

本节概述了面向法律口译员的模块。它针对刑事司法环境中具有一定口译经验的口译员而设。在模块的设计中，参与者已熟悉法律口译中的职业道德规范和实践问题。

1. 目的和学习成果

该模块的目的是提高口译员对采用远程口译的动机和理由的认识；概述在各种环境下，不同国家和地区电视会议远程口译在当前和未来可能的用途；讨论电视会议所面临的问题和挑战，及法律环境中进行远程口译的可能性；介绍技术和视频口译实践；为如何处理使用过程中出现的各种问题提供指导性的媒体采访视频；为进一步的讨论和研究提供基础。完成模块后，参与者可以理解不同形式的视频口译。此外，也能够为远程视频口译的使用提供建议。

2. 教学大纲

与学生口译模块相反，练习模块口译的设计时间为半天或者最多一天。这是为了使口译员在不严重影响其工作的情况下安排时间表。它既可以作为课程，也可以根据当地情况调整现有的长期专业发展计划。口译员模块由五个独立的部分组成。该教学形式为混合方法，将演讲的部分与研究和讨论相结合。

单元 1：简介

该模块首先提供不同口译形式的背景信息，视频口译的原因及用途。模块首先概述了采用这些口译形式的理由，例如需要减少诉讼程序的延迟，合格的法律口译员的短缺，以及在当前经济形势下不断攀升的成本压力。在学生口译模块中，鼓励参与者思考这些变化引起的问题和紧张关系。例如，如何在确保司法公正的同时节省费用。该部分将关键概念定义为视频会议口译和远程口译，然后介绍法律程序中与之有关的欧洲法规，这包括仍在使用的旧法规和欧洲在刑事司法中使用电子工具的倡议。本部分的目的是让口译员了解使用视频口译的经济、政治和法律动机。该单元应根据本地的情况量身定制，例如通过增加相关的国家立法，以便让参与者了解自己国家的立法。

单元 2：视频会议和口译

该单元专门研究新兴的法律环境，并给出了更深层的定义。首先，该单元指出了视频会议口译和远程口译之间的区别。它提供了更详细的定义，并提请参与者注意使用视频会议口译和远程口译的不同动机。该模块明确表明视频会议口译是为了让口译员能进行远程口译而提供的解决方案。视频会议口译意味着口译员与某个视频会议的部分参与者（例如在法庭或监狱）分散在不同地点，而远程口译则要求口译员是唯一与其他人地点不同的参与者。在本部分的最后，参与者将深入认识不同类型的视频媒介之间的区别，了解使用不同设置的原因。

单元 3：目前的做法

视频会议口译当前的示例是诉讼中的远程口译。本节概述了当前的做法，并介绍了实际使用时，视频会议口译和远程口译在法律程序中的行为，给出了视频会议口译的各种示例和远程口译在欧洲不同国家和地区的使用情况。

这些示例来源于法律专业人士和法律口译员的回应，涵盖了刑事司法程序的各个阶段。目前在欧洲各地使用视频会议口译和远程口译示例的目的有二。首先，通过概述欧洲范围内视频口译的发展情况，帮助口译员评估视频口译在各个国家的潜在用途。其次，它提供了进一步观察第 2 单元中情境原型的方式，从而在实践中实现这个做法。同时鼓励口译员反思自身的优缺点，发现能替代面对面口译的方法，找出与视频会议口译不同的实际解决方案。同时邀请他们探讨当前解决方案的适当性问题，例如关于口译员相对于其他参与者的位置、口译方式、融洽关系等方面。完成本单元后，课程参与者将认识到面对面口译和远程视频口译所适合的不同情况。该单元尤其可以让执业口译员为司法人员提供建议，确定视频媒介口译的相关解决方案是否适当。

单元 4：实践演示

课程参与者可以参加任何一个视频会议或远程口译，或两者兼有，具体来说，它可能取决于听众和视频媒介练习形式的特定要求，也可能取决于当地设备、房间和人员的可用性。为了使角色扮演尽可能的现实逼真，课程应该尽可能引入真正的法律从业者。在视频会议口译的角色扮演中，法律专业人士（例如检察官或法官）应位于一间视频会议室中。其中一名课程参与者扮演其他语言使用者，例如刑事案件中的证人，并位于第二个房间。扮演法律专业人士的人员（例如警察）应与其中一名"嫌疑人"待在一起。与"嫌疑人"使用相同语言的其他参与者，应在第二个视频会议室进行口译。对那些使用不同工作语言的学员和其他语言的发言人，角色扮演应在同一种语言中进行，例如检察官和证人都使用同一种语言。参加课程的口译员应使用各自的工作语言，这为他们增加视频口译实践经验提供了机会。

在每种口译场景中，不参与课程的人员在角色扮演中应观察并反思整套程序，尤其应思考视频口译与面对面口译的差异，口译员遇到的困难，以及可能的解决策略。

以下单元提供了讨论上述策略及课程参与者所提问题的机会。

单元 5：讨论和指南

最后一个单元的目的是让口译员反思角色，系统地播放视频会议口译和远程口译及其自身的经历，并为口译员提供应对视频媒介的口译所面临的各方面问题的初步指南。该单元的第一部分通过确定视频口译中经常遇到的困难展开讨论。讨论的要点包括，沟通和协调对话，声音、可见度、凝视和目光接触，以及融洽度和情境化（Braun，2006）。尽管讨论的目的是系统地概述此类问题，但在单元开始时留出若干时间进行头脑风暴，让参与者报告他们在实际会议中的看法会很有效。之后，系统将上述潜在的困难概述为讨论摘要。该单元的最后部分提出了对口译员的建议，并提供实用指南和针对不同阶段问题的解决策略作为本单元的结果，参与者能够了解视频会议口译和远程口译中现有的问题，而有效的培训和不断提升的熟悉度将有助于改善这一点。这在一定程度上可以帮助他们在特定挑战中制定应对策略。

3. 教材

在试点的不同阶段，根据课程导师的观察和参与者的反馈，采用相应的教材。教材不是静态的，而应及时进行调整以适应新的发展和所在国家和地区的情况。该模块中供口译员使用的其他幻灯片曾提及在波兰使用视频口译的情况。如有需要，可以将其替换为国家和地方信息。详细的材料旨在平衡概述信息的演讲风格，提供讨论、反思和自我学习的机会。材料包括：涵盖教学大纲各个部分的演示文稿；待进一步研究的问题；现场演示脚本；角色扮演者的说明。

每个模块单元的教材概述如下：

单元 1：简介

幻灯片描述了当前的视频会议技术可能具有的司法服务口译潜力。除此以外，还介绍了一些基本定义和关键概念；用于视频会议不同类型的链接和硬件；提供详细法律的网站，使课程参与者可以进一步探索。有关波兰立法的信息包含在此单元中，作为材料本地化的示例。本单元最后一张幻灯片提出了需要进一步研究的问题，特别是口译与欧盟法律的关系，要求参与者进行视频会议，然后探索本国的立法进程。

单元 2：视频会议和口译

幻灯片所包含的图像表现了视频会议口译和远程口译之间的差异，不同的使用动机，以及各自的特色。在最后两张幻灯片中，再次鼓励课程参与者开展进一步研究：确定自己所在的国家，探讨设置的动机和潜在用途，从法律服务的角度和口译员的立场分别思考其优势和劣势。此外，请口译员观察视频会议口译的不同参与者，并比较法律口译员在法庭中和与远程证人在一起时各自的优缺点。

单元 3：目前的做法

幻灯片提供了当前用于欧洲各地不同法律环境下视频会议口译和远程口译的示例。这些例子超越了刑事司法环境，因而有更丰富的讨论内涵。幻灯片还包含照片和图像，可以说明在本地或国家范围内使用视频会议口译和远程口译的情况，并使用示例作更深入的考察。

单元 4：现场演示

该单元中使用的角色扮演脚本要充分考虑实际情况。脚本应反映国家背景，并尽可能让真正的法律从业者参与。另外，角色可以由其他课程参与者扮演。相关的幻灯片包括参与者在观察或参加实际会议时要牢记的问题。同时邀请与会口译员就以下方面作出回答：

- 远程视频口译最困难的方面是翻译吗？
- 比您预期的困难多还是少？
- 您观察到什么好的解决方案？
- 您可能有什么不同的处理方式？
- 您在哪里看到潜在的问题？

这些问题可以在单独的讲义中提出，供参与者在实际演示和观察过程中做笔记。

单元 5：讨论与指南

幻灯片旨在集思广益，并在实际演示之后进行讨论。第一张幻灯片总结视频口译的潜在问题。最后的幻灯片为口译员的每个阶段提供初步指导。在会议期间讨论从当前情况和观察中得出的要点。

口译练习模块已在英国和波兰试行。以下三节介绍每个试点项目。

（1）与警察认证的口译员一起参加的培训课程

在英国举行的会议由伦敦大都会警察局的语言和文化服务部门负责，面向警察局认证的口译员，并使用具有相关功能的视频会议设备。目前设备已在警察局安装，用以准备远程口译试点项目。警察局目前正在使用远程口译，使分散在多个工作中心枢纽的口译员为伦敦地区各个警察拘留场所提供口译服务。大都会警察局认为，名单上的所有口译员都应该有机会熟悉这项技术，了解视频口译的概念，并通过视频链接进行实际操作。

熟悉情境可分为两个阶段。阶段 1 提供了对设备的概要，阶段 2 涵盖了视频口译的细节。因此大都会警察局迫切需要为口译员提供培训模块。试行培训课程包括警察学院举行的五个半天课程。41 名获得大都会警察局认证的口译员参加了会议。口译培训课程时长半天，如果当地情况允许或有此需要，该模块可以扩展为一天或更长时间。培训模块的第 1、2、3 单元主要以讲授方式进行，但鼓励课程参与者讨论视频会议口译和远程口译的各种用途。参与者会彼此分享经验。如在 Braun 和 Taylor 关于两次 AVIDICUS 调查的报告中所描述的，口译员对视频媒介口译的态度差异很大。在英国，大多数口译员对这类形式的口译毫不奇怪，仅有部分口译员在讨论中表达了对引入远程口译的关注和不满。在练习的第 4 单元，邀请参与者模拟警察采访犯罪嫌疑人的过程，并进行口译。这就是远程口译场景。角色扮演牵涉一名真正的警察，"嫌疑人"是由面试官的同事扮演。警察和"嫌疑人"坐在伦敦市中心的查令十字警察局内。练习口译的参与者在警察学院的口译中心里轮流口译。开始之前先进行介绍，让志愿者有时间在工作空间里安顿下来，并由采访人通过视频链接作简要汇报。所有工作语言的参与者与口译员角色的扮演者会有一些练习，但是所有会议均使用多种不同的工作语言。为了向小组中的其他口译员提供机会，警察将英语设定为工作语言。该模块的第 5 单元是会议讨论，重点是口译员在视频会议口译和远程口译中的先前经验和在第 4 单元的实践会议上所获得的经验。讨论将分析视频口译的细节，并提出法律口译的基本问题。

（2）培训课程的评估反馈

给所有参与者分发会议评估问卷，鼓励他们立即填写。问卷旨在收集口译员的背景信息、口译经验（尤其是视频口译实践方面），以及他们对口译的感受。培训讲习班收到了 41 份问卷调查表。在反馈表中，参加课程的口译员均大于 30 岁。因为成为会员需要一定的经验，而经验总是与年龄有关，换句话说，会员在刑事司法服务中已经积累了经验。鉴于培训模块是为大都会警察准备的，因此所有参与者都曾经在警察工作的范围内进行口译。此外，他们还接受了一些法庭口译实践。39 位受访者完成过检察院和 32 家监狱的口译工作。与会者还指出，他们在上诉法庭（1 名）中提供试用服务（2 名），也为律师（3 名）提供过服务。其他类型的口译经验包括"其他法律"领域（29 名），医疗（16 名），会议（15 名），商业（14 名），移民（5 名），民法（1 名），家庭法（1 名），社会安全（1 名），社会服务（1 名），精神健康法庭（1 名），等等。几乎三分之二的受访者认为视频会议口译和远程口译需要接受专门培训。

在确定了口译员的背景、知识和经验后，大都会警察局继续使用反馈调查表获取每个培训模块的信息和意见。首先，向参与者调查对模块长度的看法。差不多所有口译员都认为培训的时间长度合适，仅有 1 位口译员认为时间不够，2 位认为时间太长。多数人对模块所有部分的质量都感到满意。与会者还提出了一系列其他的建议，例如，"口译员的工作机会在减少"，还有"更多采用口译员的实用方法"。然而，如何改变模块内容中的时间比例问题，仍然存在分歧。18 位参与者"完全"或"基本"同意，表示应将更多时间用于介绍背景信息。

在视频会议口译和远程口译上，21 人认为实用课程应该占有更多的时间份额；19 人认为讨论和指南应该在课程表中更加突出。总体看来，该模块满足了不同的需求和兴趣。尽管 60％的口译员希望有更多的时间参加实际会议，但大多数人在会议过程中只观察同事而不是练习口译，这也与口译学生的行为形成鲜明对比。在视频口译中学生将会议视为获得更多口译经验的机会，而执业口译员不太可能需要额外的练习。此外，为学生提供的模块营造了一个封闭的培训环境，鼓励学生在同学面前口译。专业口译员处于竞争激烈的环境中，当他们在同事面前口译时，可能会感到不适。问卷还调查了口译员对该模块材料的意见。大多数人认为，这些材料是适当和充分的。大多数参与翻译的人似乎都觉得该课程有助于在实际情况下运用视频会议口译和远程口译。借助评估表，我们可以从口译员那里得到关于该模块的评估，特别是关于模块最成功和最不成功方面的评估，以及他们认为应该包含在未来指南中的内容。另外，以下问题：会议的哪个方面效果最好？为什么？回答包括"全部"（3 名），"实操实践"（11 名），"讨论"（3 名），"相关技术"（1 名）和"欧盟法规"（1 名）几个方面。关于可以改进的问题，回答包括"成功且无须改进"，应该解决"个人口译问题"，"讲义可以改善"，"应该花更多的时间来熟悉并调整音量和视频设置的操作方法"。但是，这些评论仅由少数参与者发表。在论及可用时间的练习时，要求"更多地练习或实操经验"，并且应该给口译员"更多的时间来学习实际工作，以便知道如何正确使用"。尽管许多口译员倾向于观察他人的口译，但是另一些口译员仍提出了更具体的建议。在实践方面，要求"有机会练习语言"。

当被问及会议中哪些方面应在远程口译指南中涉及，一位口译员要求更多地提及"肢体语言和面部表情的潜在问题"；另一位口译员认为为了更好地完成工作，应在视频链接中加入"案情概要"。关于这个问题，大多数其他评论都涉及以下方面：通过视频链接进行口译时，必须对超出了会议范围的工作进行重新评估，口译员在完成这部分工作后"应该加薪"。虽然不是直接与培训课程的目标有关，这些评论表明口译群体中与视频媒介有关的焦虑，反映在法律口译员的态度上。评估显示，就课程内容和结构而言，大多数参与者对试行的培训课程感到满意。一名口译员也评论说远程口译要"容易得多，具有良好的图像和语音质量"。但答复还表明，仍存在一些根深蒂固的问题。口译员在实际进行视频会议口译和远程口译时仍有畏惧心理。增加培训和教育，可以缓解其中一些问题。

（3）与波兰的口译员一起进行的培训课程

除由大都会警察局举办的培训课程，在波兰还试行了由 TEPIS（波兰经济、法律和法院译者协会）撰写的口译服务模块。TEPIS 是欧洲最大的法律口笔译协会之一。该模块是训练专业人士内容的一部分。7 名口译员参加了该课程，其中包括 4 名获得认证的法院口译员。他们在波兰被称为"宣誓口译员"（sworn interpreter），这意味着他们已通过国家口译考试，持有与波兰硕士学位相等的学位，并因此获得了在警察、检察和法院机构中从事口译工作的资格。这 4 位参与者拥有 2 年到 4 年不等的法庭口译员经历。其余 3 名参与者在课程开始时尚未经过口译员认证，但他们都计划成为正式的口译员。所有课程参加者都缺少视频口译方面的经验。口译员分布在两个课程地点：其中一个地点有 5 名（3 名英语和 2 名荷兰语）口译员，另一个地点有 2 名（意大利语和俄语）口译员。该模块分为两拨参加为期两天的测试。因为视频会议设备仅在课程的第一天可用，因此在信息和理论部分之前必须首先进行实际练习。但是，理想的课程至少应该在课程提纲中的实际练习之前介绍部分理论性内容。在实践会议开始时，要让参加者熟悉视频会议设备。来自两个检察官办公室的口译技术人员在视频链接现场展示设备，并解答参与者的疑问。检察官在会议开始时也在场，以提供有关当前视频会议实践的信息，概括其优缺点，并介绍使用视频会议技术获取证据的方法。然后，参与者有机会在两种情况下练习视频会议口译：第一种情况，口译员和检察官一起，而证人在其他地方；第二种情况，口译员和证人在一起，检察官在其他地方。

该练习缺少真正的法律专业人员参加，检察官和证人的角色由 TEPIS 的成员扮演，负责英语、俄语和意大利语的翻译，并由口译员自己为荷兰语口译。脚本由检察官起草，内容包括贩毒和车祸案件中证人的预审。在练习开始之前，口译员得到了关于案件基本情况的简短介绍。该课程组织者报告说，视频会议链接的质量远不如计划中的完善，在某些时刻，链接会完全中断。另外，在图像和声音之间有时也会有明显的迟滞。该模块的理论性内容分为两个主要部分，并具有演讲风格。两部分内容中的第一小节，专门介绍波兰的法院口译员参与法律诉讼时所使用的现行法律概念、术语和措辞。

该模块在结束时会讨论实践会议中出现的问题，以及刑事诉讼中与视频口译有关的问题。为了能够吸引更多的听众，还需要进行管理和笔记记录。与大都会警察局会议一样，鼓励参与者思考自己提出的问题，并在结束时填写课程问卷。在大多数情况下，参与者认为培训模块非常有趣，因为它更强调动手经验，特别是针对特定语言的培训。此外，还介绍了培训模块中作为修订课程的理论部分。约 80 名笔译和口译员参加了课程，讨论了视频会议口译在犯罪诉讼中的运用，欧洲和波兰采用视频口译的法律背景，以及目前欧洲和世界其他地区的使用惯例。问卷还追问了一系列问题，如视频会议口译是否需要培训，是否应组织此类培训，是否应将视频会议口译培训与任何其他实践相结合，等等。共有 37 位参与者填写了问卷，其中 25 位是宣誓口笔译员。在这群人中，只有 3 人拥有视频会议口译经验。在回答视频会议口译的通信质量可能与哪些因素有关时，3 名完成过视频会议口译任务的人提到了设备、视频会议链接，以及人为因素（例如言语举止、口音、发音和语速）；另一位有过两次视频会议口译经验的参与者，强调了在重要的电视会议中使用高质量设备的重要性；第三位参与者则认为，口译质量可能会受到口译员的位置及耳机使用的影响。全部受访者都认为进行某种形式的视频会议口译培训非常必要，并且所有培训都应包括和技术有关的培训。

（三）法律从业人员模块

本节介绍法律从业人员（执业者）如警务人员、调查法官和律师等的模块。许多法律从业人员确实在刑事诉讼中与口译员有过合作，但到目前为止还很少有人了解甚至熟悉视频会议，更不用说在刑事诉讼中进行视频会议口译或远程口译了。他们的经验可能受限于工作所在地区的法律制度或是相关技术的可用性，因此可以根据其已有经验进行调整。

1. 目的和学习成果

该模块的目的是：

提高法律从业人员对视频口译的基本原理和使用动机的认识。提高对以视频为媒介的口译新形式的认识。详细介绍各种视频会议形式和法律程序中的远程口译，概述当前的做法和未来的趋势。概述视频会议在各种环境和不同国家及地区进行远程口译的潜在用途。提供视频口译的动手实践技术和机会，以适应当地具体情况。处理视频媒体采访在使用过程中出现的各种问题并提供指导。为各种形式的视频口译实践提供机会。为进一步讨论和反思实践奠定经验基础。

在学习成果方面，可以使学员深入了解各种基于视频的口译中的技术、工具和使用的动机，以及由翻译带来的特定挑战。此外，还将采用恰当的工作模式让他们能够评估视频会议和远程口译的专业知识。

2. 教学大纲

培训模块的课程表分为 3 个部分，每个部分都包含 2 个主要单元，因此教材总共有 6 个部分。为了使模块适应执业者的时间安排，该模块设计为最好在三个半天内进行一次会议或一整天会议，然后是半天会议。该模块既可以单独作为专业课程，也可以视本地情况而定，还可以适应现有的专业发展计划。从广义上讲，培训模块是由第一部分的理论、第二部分的实践和第三部分的讨论观察组成，并最终得出结论，提出建议。

单元 1：简介

该单元旨在概述视频会议口译和远程口译在刑事诉讼中的应用情况及其最新发展，介绍欧洲框架下的新兴法律及其含义，并解释视频会议中所使用的关键术语的定义。该单元首先会为执业者提供一些与视频会议相关的背景信息和关键术语，介绍视频会议所使用的各种技术，并指出它们在适用性方面的差异。该单元还提出了不同形式口译（交替传译、同声传译等）的行为准则和进行良好的口译练习所要遵守的准则。

该单元指出了视频会议口译和远程口译的基本区别。在视频媒介形式的口译中，口译员需要参与到视频会议中，例如看见有翻译需求的远程见证人。在视频会议口译中，口译员通常与某些参与者在同一地点。此设置与远程口译形成对比，后者主要是为了解决当地口译员短缺问题或节省口译员差旅费用，且口译员是唯一一个身处不同地点的参与者。该单元探讨了每种视频媒介形式的潜在用途，并进行比较。最后，该单元还给出了不同的欧洲国家和地区的视频会议口译和远程口译在当前用途中的各种示例。到本单元结束时，从业人员将对不同类型的视频媒介口译之间的区别和使用原因有深刻的了解。

单元 2：视频会议和口译

该单元重点介绍欧盟各国采用这些形式的口译的法律原因，如需要加快国内和国际法律程序沟通，降低费用和提升效率，某些语言的合格法律口译员缺乏，以及安全原因等。此部分还请执业者注意利益相关者之间关于使用或不使用视频会议口译和远程口译而产生的问题，例如警察对何时使用此类口译服务的关注或口译员对维护口译服务质量的恐惧。该单元指的是当前和新兴的欧盟法律中提及并推进在刑事诉讼中使用视频会议的部分，特别是《刑事法中笔译和口译指令》中的诉讼程序，及与受害人权利有关的立法，如知情权等。该单元应始终与国家法律相适应。从业人员和口译员采用了不同形式的视频口译，例如在首次听证会和还押延期听证会中采用视频会议口译，在警察采访中采用远程口译。口译重点是刑事诉讼，但也提及其他情况，特别是移民。这部分内容尤其可以从中提取其他材料，以适应当地情况。欧洲委员会应对儿童司法问题的部长要求所有专业人员进行跨学科交流培训，与未成年人一起工作，同时，也必须考虑未来的视频会议口译和远程口译培训。

单元 3 和单元 4：实际演示

这些单元由实操练习组成，需要较多参与者组成的团队，法律诉讼的现实场景，以及使用视频会议的技术。建议执业者在视频会议口译和远程口译中探索和应用学到的知识，但实操部分可根据内容的相关性和可用时间的多寡适当作出调整。需要添加若干视频，对这些单元进行图示、演示和比较，并与角色扮演交替进行。之后课程中的角色扮演项目，可以作为执业者培训的模型。该项目由 16 个角色组成，每个角色需 25 至 30 分钟，如讲荷兰语的官员（在这种情况下是警察）与讲匈牙利语的犯罪嫌疑人或证人。4 个角色为面对面的形式；4 个属于视频会议 A 型（视频会议口译 A，即当嫌疑人或被告在另一地点时，口译员与警察同处一室）；4 个属于视频会议 B 型（视频会议口译 B，即口译员与嫌疑人或被告在同一地点，警察在不同位置）；4 个是远程口译设置（口译员与其他参与者，即警察、嫌疑人或证人，处于不同位置）。角色扮演的主题取材于现实生活中的警察所提供的材料。总共要处理 4 种情况：警方对信用卡欺诈嫌疑人的讯问；审讯人口贩卖嫌疑人；面讯一场酒店宴会的目击者；讯问嫌疑人的犯罪阴谋。角色扮演没有剧本，但参与者在简要介绍主题后，会在审讯中进行质询或面试。角色扮演是在荷兰语和匈牙利语之间进行的。由于后者是警察完全不了解的语言，这迫使他们完全依靠口译并杜绝以猜测危害任何人的情况。角色扮演者首先是 4 名荷兰—匈牙利口译员，他们拥有 5～15 年的口译经验，包括法律口译经验。扮演犯罪嫌疑人和证人的都是匈牙利人，几乎完全没有荷兰人。2 名警官（1 名首席督察和 1 名督察，男女各一名）在采访和与法律口译员合作方面有丰富的经验。所有角色扮演活动都录制了视频，以供以后分析和作为培训模块中的插图。

在这两个单元中，执业者必须探索和反思视频会议口译和远程口译相对于面对面口译的优势和劣势。技术本身，如声音和图像的质量、照明和摄像机角度等，是值得讨论和反思的重要方面。而沟通的流程本身也存在着话语重叠、犹豫、误解、目光接触等问题。特别是该单元将使律师事务所和司法服务机构了解视频口译的适用性（尤其是实现正义的目标、口译模式和地点）。参与者会认识到视频会议口译和远程口译能满足的不同需求。目前也还没有一种能被普遍接受的视频会议口译和远程口译实践的方法和标准。练习应该让参与者同时体验到面对面口译和远程视频口译的局限性，并反思自己的做法。

单元 5 和单元 6：

目的是引起执业者对潜在问题的关注，系统分析视频会议口译和远程口译，并以更高的系统化程度概述自己的意见。这些讨论侧重于立法、在不同国家和地区根据欧盟指令和建议进行的实践、技术的影响、口译员的表现、社会文化的影响、参与者之间的沟通和关系调解等。要允许执业者反思视频会议口译和远程口译的经验，并系统地提出能最好应对视频媒介的指南和建议。

3. 教材

上述材料不是固定不变的，而应当根据新的发展情况和当地的立法环境做出调整，并投入实践。材料应该包含：

关于视频会议口译和远程口译的演示文稿，包括以说明性链接呈现的视频会议口译和远程口译的示例，相关国家和地区的概述，有关视频会议口译和远程口译的欧洲和国际法规。许多由讲义提供的视频会议口译和远程口译有关的文本。视频会议口译和远程口译的参考书目。角色扮演的主题、脚本和说明。角色扮演课程的说明。反馈表格和问卷。

单元 1 和单元 2：

本次会议的幻灯片概述视频会议口译和远程口译的关键概念和基本定义、硬件情况、当前两种口译形式的使用情况、采用视频会议口译和远程口译的主要动机，以及欧盟对两种口译形式进行立法的情况。幻灯片包括供参考的法律文本，以使课程参与者进行进一步探索。同时，它也收录了不同国家和地区在当前实践中的例子。例如，英格兰或威尔士地区，口译员通常在法庭上，在比利时，口译员通常与法官同位；在荷兰，口译员可以选择地点，但通常与非母语人士位于同一地点，并使用低声口译；在波兰，未指定口译员的位置，这些是使用视频会议口译的不同做法。插图可以让那些不太了解设置的人知晓房间的配置和参与者的位置。

这一部分内容展示了在本地或国家范围内使用视频会议口译和远程口译的实例，特别适于进行更深入的说明和调查。从针对法律从业者陈述内容的调查，还可以了解全欧洲使用视频会议口译和远程口译的频率和原因。

单元 3 和单元 4：

这些单元中的实践应使用角色扮演脚本，或根据实际情况设计的场景，包括具有现实感的实践活动和能反映国家背景的文本。活跃的法律从业人员和法律口译员可以扮演任何其他角色，如嫌疑人、被告、证人等。这些角色也可以由其他参与者扮演。积极参与角色扮演或以观察员身份参加的执业者应反思以下问题，以获取进一步指导：

- 什么是执业者在视频口译中最感困难的方面？
- 比您预期的困难是多还是少？
- 您观察到什么好的解决方案？
- 可能/应该以不同的方式处理什么？
- 您在哪里看到潜在的问题？
- 面对面口译是否更有利于特定设置？
- 不同口译形式在程序上（法律）的要求为何？
- 视频会议口译和远程口译技术在多大程度上是劣势的？哪些技术可以调整或改进？
- 技术是否影响正常程序或工作安排？
- 需要哪些口译和一般交流方面进行掌握和管理？

这些问题可以在主要课程的单独讲义中提出。观察者在观察角色扮演时也要做笔记。

单元 5 和单元 6：讨论，指南和建议

在此，首先是一般性的建议，其次是作为集思广益和讨论的总结，最后是扮演实际角色的示范。这些幻灯片总结了视频口译中执业者在交流和口译时存在的潜在问题和关注的领域。在完成执业者的角色扮演后，项目团队组织了三次汇报会议，其中一次征询了警方的书面反馈，另一次是执业者的培训课程，最后由执业者、口译员与项目合作伙伴一起召开汇报会议。

三、教学评估和测试

测试和评估（简称测评）是根据特定的目标，用可以比较或者量化的尺度进行的合理评判。测评的目的主要包括三个方面：筛选合格的适合接受教育的学生、检验教学结果、决定可否授予职业证书。由于远程口译涉及一定的责任和潜在的风险，因此在学生上岗之前客观地测评其口译技巧至关重要。测评的主要内容包括：相关服务领域及其组织结构（政府机构、法律领域、医疗服务领域等），工作程序和人员的知识，双语听说的流利程度（包括语域和术语），使用交替传译、耳语同传、视译等准确地进行双语双向转换的能力，对职业伦理规范及相应策略的理解，职业和个人继续发展的计划（Corsellis，2008：60-61）。

测评通常可以分为总结性测评和形成性测评。总结性测评又称"事后评价"，主要是概括或总结学生的最终学习效果，一般在教学活动告一段落或课程结束后进行评价。总结性评价重视的是结果，借以对被评价者作出全面鉴定，区分等级，或决定可否授予证书等。对于学生来说接受总结性测评是被动的，而且是在课程结束后，因此这种测评对学习尤其是某一阶段的学习作用不大。但是总结性测评也有概括水平较高、测评范围较广等优点。翻译研究中提倡使用 Baker（1989）的语言测试模型来对口译进行总结性测试，该模型主要使用行为相关和系统相关测试、直接和间接测试两组对比参数。行为相关和系统相关测试旨在衡量技巧和知识的掌握，前者更倾向于具体测试，如专业领域内的知识（法律情境下的远程口译可以用于测试法律领域的专业知识）；而后者更倾向于评价综合语言技巧和能力的掌握。直接测试与测评目标有直接关系，而间接测试则主要涉及分析的过程。口译员的测试从性质上更加接近行为相关测试。形成性测评是相对于总结性测评而言的，是对学生整个学习过程进行的评价，对学生日常学习过程中的表现、所取得的成绩及所反映出的情感、态度、策略等方面的发展作出评价。其目的是激励学生学习，帮助学生有效调控的学习过程，获得成就感，增强自信心。形成性测评不单纯从评价者的需要出发，也注重从被评价者的需要出发，重视学习的过程，重视学生在学习中的体验；强调人与人之间的相互作用，评价中多种因素的教育作用，以及师生交流。如 Niska（1998）指出，"任何测试都不能替代必要的培训，也不能弥补口译员的缺失，更不能培养出口译员，只有必要的教育才能做到"。因此，远程口译教学测评更多地使用形成性测评（例如上一章节提到的不同教学环节中学生对自己学习的思考、比较和评价），把测评融入整个教学过程，成为教育的有机组成部分。

形成性测评包括标准的设定、学生间测评、自我测评和反馈。即使是经验丰富的学生口译员也经常意识不到自己在口译过程中省略、添加或者误解等错误，要求他们进行自评和互评时，也不知道什么实用、要使用什么分析工具或以什么标准进行。因此，教师有必要先将自己设计的评价标准明确告诉学生，以便其做练习和测评时心中有数，指导如何根据标准去做及如何进行评价和反馈。随着熟练程度的增加，符合标准就会内化为学生的本能反应。如 Bruner（1966）所说，教师指导学生的目的是让他们最终学会指导自己，否则所谓的掌握不过是在导师帮助下的结果。Sadler（1989）也认为学生能够不断进步的必要前提是他们的质量概念要几乎和老师所知道的一样，并能够在产出的过程中持续不断地进行质量监控，随时调用已有的技巧和策略。学生互评和自我测评是紧密相关的，学生需要大量地练习评价同伴在口译中的表现，评价得越多自己学到的就越多。不断听取别人的评价才会知道如何评价自己，因此合格的互评才能产生高质量的自评。学生间测评和自我测评能提高学生的判断能力，是未来良好职业习惯的基础和必备技巧。大多数口译员都是独立工作的，如果缺乏自我监督和测评的能力，就很难发现自身缺点，改进口译质量。反馈也是形成性测评的关键组成部分。首先要告诉学生如何进行书面或口头反馈和接受反馈。有时学生会倾向关注他人口译表现中的缺点而不是优点，这会让被评价者产生逆反心理，因此要告知学生尽量使用委婉的语气和较为正面的词语批评他人，同时也要把批评或者错误当成提高的机会而不是一种失败。评价和反馈的重点可以放在意义、清晰度、风格和表达等重要方面（Sawyer，2004）。其次，教师的反馈也至关重要，包括三点要素：认同学生的目标，指出目前所处的阶段，指出目前阶段与目标的差距（Black & William，1998：6）。

荷兰乌特勒支专业教育大学开设的口译课程穿插着测评，包括三项内容：语言水平、口译水平和职业水平。初期有老师测评，后期有导师测评，还有学生之间的互评，其间穿插老师和学生之间大量的交流反馈。学生还需要评价自己，制定学习目标并监控自己的进度。测评的主要工具是测评表，包括语言和口译技巧测评和互动技巧测评。每个分项都有各自分数和所占权重。

Corsallis（2008）认为，测评应贯穿整个口译教育和职业的全过程，分为四个阶段，即入学筛选测评、本科阶段测评、研究生阶段测评和继续教育阶段测评。本科阶段的测评主要是看学生是否掌握了语言转换的最基本技巧，包括双向对话交替传译、独白耳语同传、快速视译等。每项测评都使用测评卡，评分标准包括准确性、流利性、选词、文化理解、风格、发声、表现、职业化水平和交流合作。对于开始阶段的任务，评分标准可以仅限于准确性、发声和基础的口译技巧。随着学生水平的提高及任务难度的加大，评分标准的范围也随之扩大。例如更注重职业化的表现，关注学生解决实际问题的能力、与各交际方沟通的能力、是否遵守职业规范等。口译技巧方面要求也更具体，加入更多的标准，如语音、韵律、停顿、眼神、姿态等（Riccardi，2002）。测评选取的材料也更加接近真实场景下的语料。由于开设远程口译教学的学校较少，研究生阶段的测评重点可以放在口笔译的高级技巧及理论和专业方向的论文。

Chen 和 Ko（2010；2011）研究了在线学习结束时与翻译学员一起试用在线测试的问题。他们的研究基于对话口译、视听翻译、交替传译在线测试时的相同数据样本，记录了口译考试所有部分的在线传递。

研究总结了测试样本的关键属性。首先，被测者使用自家计算机按网络教室的组织进入指定"坐席"。审查员向其提供对话口译等测试部分，然后以电子方式打开；由被测者访问并管理对话，且能够选择开始录制的时间。被测者相对独立，他们能够以自己的速度工作，在需要时重复分段，并在完成后通过短信向审查员发出信号。审查员可以随机访问被测者的座席，观察其表现，记录所有被测者的音频和视频形式的口译输出。源文本在白板上提供，被测者无法以任何方式（以电子方式）进行标记，必须在另一张纸上做笔记。

总体而言，Chen 和 Ko（2010）在测试中使用的技术能够满足口译口语测试记录被测者表现的要求。此外，还应注意测试中出现的其他问题，例如难以在整个测试过程中监控每个被测者的行为，确保其不使用在线词典或从其他来源获得帮助等。另据被测者的报告，对技术设备的熟悉非常重要，在测试过程中，不仅要能确保所需的录音程序，还要减少技术问题出现时可能的紧张情绪。Chen 和 Ko（2010，2011）的研究表明，通过计算机进行视频链接测试是一种现实的发展，应该将其视为允许使用计算机进行翻译测试的一部分。

第六章
远程口译实践与研究趋势

20世纪中后期，远程会议口译研究在许多方面都取得了重大进展，其成果在全球范围内得到越来越多的认可。进入21世纪，科技革新一日千里，远程口译研究也出现了增长和融合的趋势。这不仅体现在各国远程口译政策和相关规定的完善、专业服务机构的发展和国际学术交流的增多等方面，也体现在远程口译研究理论和途径的不断深入发展上。远程口译研究未来的发展趋势有两个特点：学科交叉和技术转向。一些有较大影响力的变量，如翻译学科的技术转向、全球化、科技进步等，都直接或间接地影响着远程口译职业的发展，从而改变其研究方向。

远程口译领域的多元化趋势在20世纪末开始出现，如法庭口译和手语翻译开始以远程方式进行，大量的学术论文和相关文献相继出现。全球范围内对远程口译职业和学术研究的重视使其研究的发展势头强劲并成为口译研究中不可或缺的部分，也是目前最具活力的领域之一。得益于对翻译学及其他相关学科如神经学、心理学等的大量借鉴，并且专注于话语、互动、环境因素等热门话题，远程口译研究成果丰硕，并具有极大的挑战性和发展潜力。远程口译研究的巨大影响力和作用不再局限于学术圈，许多研究成果对远程口译职业的发展，远程口译职业培训和行业准则等的制定，起到了积极的推动作用。与此同时，现代科技的日新月异也不断改变着口译员的工作方式和环境，衍生出更多的研究课题。在理论和方法论层次上，也呈现出多元化趋势。社会互动语境中的话语分析视角、神经语言学视角为远程口译研究注入了新的活力，并拓宽了其研究基础。

第一节 学科交叉融合

远程口译改变了口译员习惯的工作方式，带来了额外的心理和生理压力，因此其发展过程必然伴随着诸多挑战，其中之一便是对口译员认知资源的挑战。对同声传译活动过程的认知心理学研究表明，同声传译是典型的"多任务处理模式"（multi-tasking），是一种认知处理过程（Moser-Mercer，2005：728），因此必然要遵循人类普遍的认知处理规律，即需要处理的认知对象信息流量不能超过自身认知资源的总和（Gile，1995，2009）。

在此情况下，远程同声传译就面临着多重挑战。

首先，与现场条件相比，远程口译员面对的不是实际的参会代表和其他各种辅助设施（如背板、海报、装饰等），而是要借助多媒体视频会议系统观察现场、摄入视觉信号。这种行为本身就会给口译员带来认知方面的挑战，比现场工作耗费更多的认知资源。而现有技术条件还无法完全消除显示屏幕眩光等干扰因素给口译员造成的如头痛、恶心或眼睛不舒服等生理不适，进而影响口译员认知功能的发挥。

其次，远程信号传输技术给口译员带来的认知压力不仅来自生理不适，更源于感官分裂所导致的问题。在通常的沟通环境下，人类的感官系统是通过相互协调来感知外来信息的。如果是面对面的交流，不同感官对同一信号的感知在时间和空间上是一致的。在心理学上，这种时空一致性所造成的是中枢神经系统内的"感官间协同相互作用"。因此，会议口译员往往会坚持要看到发言人和会场的正面图像（Sumby & Pollacek，1954；Moser-Mercer，2005：728-729）。在现有的技术条件下，音频信号与视频信号还不能完全同步，口译员的"感官间协同相互作用"会受到妨碍，从而需要口译员分配更多的认知资源。

远程口译员面临的另外一大挑战是我们常说的"不在场"（not being there）。这一挑战更侧重于口译员的自身感受，即由于口译员与现场的物理距离而导致的"距离感"和"失控感"。前文提到，这两种感觉是在远程实验中发现的口译员感受方面的最大挑战。对口译员来说，"在场感"或"临境感"（presence）是确保口译活动顺利进行的重要前提。在心理学上，对"临境感"并没有一致的定义，但一般认为"临境感"是"一种心理状态，即个体通过自动的或有控制的心理加工所获得的身处某地或某环（情）境中的主观体验，而这一环境并非一定是个体所处的实际物理环境"（zhou & zhang，2004：201）。而根据个体身处环境的不同，临境又可以分为现实临境（real-world presence）、虚拟临境（virtual presence）和远程临境（telepresence）（zhou & zhang，2004：201）。远程口译员身处远程的虚拟会场环境中，面对二维视觉信号，"临境感"的获得取决于其注意力在多大程度上从身处的环境转移到虚拟的环境中。心理学研究证明，"介入"（involvement）和"沉浸"（immersion）是产生"临境感"所必需的两种心理状态（zhou & zhang，2004：202）。如果口译员能够实现完全的"沉浸"，那也就意味着他在认知上会认为自己是在与虚拟环境直接互动，而非间接或远程互动（Moser-Mercer，2005：731）。与"临境感"相对的恰好是远程口译员感受到的"距离感"和"失控感"。"距离感"的产生是由于口译员自身与会场的物理距离，而"失控感"出现的原因则有着更为复杂的认知背景。

同传口译员在工作的过程中，除了传达发言人的语言信息，完成同声传译工作外，也在不断地观察发言人的非言语行为和现场正在发生的种种情景。借助此类观察，口译员可以弥补言语信息传达的不足，并同时预测将要出现的情况。对于同声传译来说，"预测"是口译员应对现场各种情况的重要策略之一，更是他们调配和节约认知资源的重要手段（Moser-Mercer，2005：732）。然而在远程口译中，口译员的"预测"能力往往受到多重制约，既有外在技术设备的制约，也有个人心理因素的制约，从而成为产生"失控感"的重要原因之一。由此可见，远程口译的研究具有非常明显的跨学科特点。

第二节　研究的技术转向

Braun（2006）指出，需要对远程会议口译可能带来的社会文化影响予以足够的重视，因为远程口译的方式不仅是技术问题或口译员自身的感受问题，更是一个涉及诸多社会文化因素的系统性问题。因此，远程口译一直受到口译从业者不同程度的抵制。例如，欧洲议会的全职口译员和自由口译员曾就议会推动引入远程口译一事表示明显的拒绝（Resolution，2002）。国际口译协会下属的以保障口译员工作条件与身心健康为己任的技术与健康委员会也曾得出结论："远程会议不会替代配备现场同声传译的真实会议，就像电脑打字不能代替手写一样。"（Bros-Brann，2004：1）虽然远程口译对技术设备和同传口译员都提出了很高要求，且现阶段仍然存在各种各样的不足，然而，从欧盟、联合国等国际组织和学术界对远程口译的浓厚兴趣可以看出，新兴的远程口译有着广阔而光明的发展前景。

首先，对欧盟来说，远程口译目前看来是解决现场同传工作室不足的最佳选择。在欧洲议会主席 Pat Cox 致国际口译协会主席 Jean-Pierre Allain 的一封公开信中，Cox 请求国际口译协会会员以远程方式协助欧洲议会完成一次涉及多国的重要辩论。在信中，Cox 强调远程口译的技术方案虽然还未完全成熟，但却是目前所知的各种选择中风险最小的一种。不过他也强调，采用远程口译必须事先征得协会和会员的同意，而且还要就各种相关的技术与医学层面问题开展系统性的实验（Cox，2002）。另外，从长远来看，远程口译对节约资源和保护环境具有重要意义。

其次，采用先进技术手段的远程口译较之现场口译，也有其独特优点。例如，通过会议视频系统，口译员可以用同样清晰的方式看到所有的发言人、发言人在现场演播的幻灯片或其他视频资料，这是现场口译员所不具备的优势。现场口译员一般只能从会场的角落看见一些发言人的侧脸甚至背影，且如果现场的投影屏幕位置较远，口译员可能还需要借助望远镜才能看清幻灯片显示的内容。

最后，对于远程口译这一新的形式，口译员自身也需要具备"适应性专家能力"（adaptive expertise）。所谓"适应性专家能力"是相对于"常规性专家能力"（routine expertise）而言的。口译员的"专家能力"一直是口译界的重要研究话题，然而大多数研究集中于"常规性专家能力"，也即口译员应对常规挑战的能力。从未来口译的需求与发展来看，口译员可能更需要"适应性专家能力"，也就是能"从多种角度看待同一任务，……随时准备尝试探索完成任务的其他新途径"（Moser-Mercer，2005：728）。不言而喻，新途径之一就是远程口译。新兴技术的时代，研究领域也开始转向。

结　语

　　在信息化时代，口译形式、口译员的技能、口译设备等都在发生巨大的变化，口译服务内容和服务语言呈现多样化趋势，口译活动中不断引进先进的口译技术和设备，口译服务模式呈现新的变化。这些变化促进了远程口译的职业化，也吸引学界进一步研究新形势下的口译现象。远程口译领域的研究范围从最初关注围观过程的认知领域到宏观交际过程的社会文化层面均包括在内。远程口译研究的兴起带动口译研究从传统的关注语言的性质和转化，发展到关注跨文化语言转换、言语和非言语交际，以及技术与语言互动的跨学科研究。某种意义上，远程口译研究拓宽了口译研究的视野，推动着它的技术转向，不断丰富其内涵。

　　为了指导新进、规范行业，许多机构和学者都曾提出指导性的文件或意见。例如，国际会议口译员协会 AIIC 曾在 2000 年编写过会议口译中远程和电话口译的初步使用指南，不同研究者也为远程口译提出过指导意见，部分机构已经为电话或电视会议工作中的口译员和工作人员发布了使用指南。但由于远程和电话会议口译在设置、交流目的、参加人数、口译模式和其他变量方面的差异，这些实践中的建议往往不具备普遍的意义。

　　远程口译在实践中的可行性取决于一系列因素，而不仅限于设备或链接的技术质量。例如，远程和电话会议口译设施使用频率的高低和使用目的的多样性或单一性，都会影响远程口译的实践；参与者的人数和分布，尤其是口译员的可能位置、主要的沟通需求和口译方式，会决定口译需求和投资规模。

　　本书以互联网新技术为切入点，回顾了远程口译的发展历程和研究现状，探讨了远程口译在未来发展的趋势。总体而言，远程口译是技术进步和社会发展背景下不可阻挡的潮流，因此对广大口译从业者而言，不仅要重视以往实践中积累的"常规性专家能力"，更要着重培养"适应性专家能力"，积极适应未来可能出现的新型工作环境。另外，考虑到远程口译所面临的众多挑战，对使用口译服务的用户也应当有适当的培训，以便在远程或电话会议口译的情况下与口译员一起高效工作。

参考文献

一、普通图书

[1]曹嬿.法庭口译员角色研究[M].上海:上海人民出版社,2018.

[2]弗朗兹·波赫哈克.口译研究概论[M].仲伟合,等,译.北京:北京教学与研究出版社,2010.

[3]江晓丽.口译课堂教学研究[M].杭州:浙江大学出版社,2017.

[4]焦丹.口译教育研究:理论与实证[M].北京:科学出版社,2017.

[5]康志峰.认知心理视阈下的口译研究[M].北京:国防工业出版社,2012.

[6]康志峰.口译认知心理学[M].北京:北京燕山出版社,2013.

[7][美]罗洛·梅.焦虑的意义[M].朱侃如,译.桂林:广西师范大学出版社,2010.

[8]刘建军.全球视域下的社区口译研究[M].北京:中国社会科学出版社,2014.

[9]任文.联络口译过程中译员的主体性意识研究[M].北京:北京教学与研究出版社,2010.

[10]王斌华.口译理论研究[M].北京:北京教学与研究出版社,2019.

[11]王建华.口译心理学[M].北京:外文出版社,2013.

[12]颜林海.翻译认知心理学[M].北京:科学出版社,2008.

[13]仲伟合,等.口译研究方法论[M].北京:北京教学与研究出版社,2012.

[14]AGGER-GUPTA N. From "making do" to established service, the development of health care interpreter services in Canada and the United States of America: a grounded theory study of health organization change and the growth of a new profession [M]. Santa Barbara: Fielding Graduate Institute, 2001.

[15] ALTMAN J. Error analysis in the teaching of simultaneous

interpretation: A pilot study[M]// Bridging the Gap. Amsterdam: John Benjamins, 1994: 25.

[16] ANGELELLI C V. Invisibility [M]// Routledge encyclopedia of interpreting studies. London/NewYork: Routledge, 2015.

[17] OKBAIGORRI-JALÓN J. From Paris to Nuremberg: The birth of conference interpreting[M]. Amsterdam: John Benjamins, 2014.

[18] BAKER D. Language testing: A critical survey and practical guide[M]. London: Edward Arnold, 1989.

[19] BARALDI C, LAURA G. Coordinating participation in dialogue interpreting[M]. Amsterdam/Philadelphia: John Benjamins, 2012.

[20] BEAUGRANDE R D, DRESSLER W U. Introduction to text linguistics [M]. London: Longman. 1981.

[21] BIRDWHISTELL R L. Kinesics and context: Essays on body motion communication[M]. Philadelphia: University of Pennsylvania Press, 1970.

[22] BOT H. The myth of the uninvolved interpreter interpreting in mental health and the development of a three-person psychology[M]// The critical link 3. Amsterdam: John Benjamins, 2003: 27-35.

[23] BRAUN S. Kommunikation unter widrigenumständen? Fallstudien zu einsprachigen und gedolmetschten videokonferenzen [M]. Tübingen: Narr, 2004.

[24] BRUNSON J L. Video relay service interpreters[M]. Washington DC: Gallaudet University Press, 2011.

[25] BRAUN S. Multimedia communication technologies and their impact on interpreting [M]// Copenhagen: Proceedings of the marie curie euroconferences mutra: Audiovisual translation scenarios, 2006.

[26] BRAUN S. Recommendations for the use of video-mediated interpreting in criminal proceedings[M]// Intersentia: Videoconference andremote interpreting in criminal proceedings, 2012: 301-328.

[27] BRAUN S. Comparing traditional and remote interpreting in police settings:Quality and impact factors[M]. ESaint-Étienne: UT Edizioni Università di Trieste, 2014.

[28] BROWN G, BROWN G D, YULE G et al. Discourse analysis[M].

Cambridge：Cambridge university press，1983.

[29]BRUNER J S. Toward a theory of instruction[M]. Cambridge：Harvard University Press，1966.

[30]CHIANG Y. Connecting two anxiety constructs：An interdisciplinary study of foreign language anxiety and interpretation anxiety [M]. Austin：The University of Texas at Austin，2006.

[31]CHIARO D. Linguistic mediation on Italian television：When the interpreter is not an interpreter：A case study[M]// Interpreting in the 21st Century. Amsterdam：John Benjamins，2002：215-225.

[32] CHERNOV G V. Inference and anticipation in simultaneous interpreting：A probability-prediction model [M]. Amsterdam，Netherlands：John Benjamins Publishing，2004.

[33]COKELY D. Exploring ethics：A case for revising the code of ethics [M]. Sheffield：Direct Learn，2000.

[34]COLLADOS A Á et al. Laevalución de la calidad en interpretación simultánea：Parámetros de incidencia[M]. Granada，Spain：Comares，2007.

[35]CORSELLIS A. Public service interpreting：The first steps[M]. Berlin：Springer，2008.

[36]DANESI M. Encyclopedia of media and communication[M]. Toronto：University of Toronto Press，2013.

[37]DICKINSON J. Interpreting in the workplace[M]. Coleford，UK：Douglas McLean，2014.

[38]DIMITROVA B E. Degree of interpreter responsibility in the interaction process in community interpreting[M]// The critical link：Interpreters in the community. Amsterdam：John Benjamins，1997：147.

[39]ERICSSON K A. Attaining excellence through deliberate practice：Insights from the study of expert performance[M]//The pursuit of excellence through education. London/NewYork：Routledge，2001：21-56.

[40]GARZONE G，VIEZZI M. Interpreting in the 21st century：Challenges and opportunities[M]. Amsterdam：John Benjamins，2002.

[41] GERVER D. The effect of source language presentation on the

performance of simultaneous conference interpreters[M]. London/New York: Routledge, 1969: 52-66.

[42] GERVER D, WALLACE H S. Language interpretation and communication[M]. New York/London: Plenum Press, 1978.

[43] GARCIA-LANDA M. A theoretical framework for oral and written translation research[M]. Trieste: EUT - Edizioni Università di Trieste, 1998.

[44] GILE D. Basic concepts and models for interpreter and translator training[M]. Amsterdam, Netherlands: John Benjamins Publishing, 2009.

[45] GOFFMAN E. Forms of talk[M]. Philadelphia: Pennsylvania Press, 1981.

[46] GOFFMAN E. The presentation of self in everyday life[M]. London: Penguin, 1990.

[47] GOODWIN C. Conversational organization: Interaction between speakers and hearers[M]. New York: Academic Press, 1981.

[48] GUMPERZ J J. Discourse strategies [M]. Cambridge: Cambridge University Press, 1982.

[49] HATIM, BASEL, IAN M. Discourse and the translator[M]. London/New York: Longman, 1990.

[50] HERBERT J. The interpreter's handbook: How to become a conference interpreter[M]. Lausanne: Librairie de l'Universitei, 1952.

[51] HERITAGE J, DOUGLAS M. Communication in medical care: Interaction between primary care physicians and patients [M]. Cambridge: Cambridge University Press, 2006.

[52] JEWITT C. The Routledge handbook of multimodal analysis[M]. 2nd edition. London/New York: Routledge, 2014.

[53] JOHNSTON D H. Encyclopedia of international media and communications [M]. Amsterdam: Elsevier, 2003.

[54] KAHNEMAN D. Attention and effort[M]. Englewood Cliffs, NJ: Prentice-Hall, 1973.

[55] KEISER W. Selection and training of conference interpreters[M]. New York: Springer US, 1978.

[56] KELLY N. Telephone interpreting: A comprehensive guide to the profession[M]. Victoria, BC: Traford Publishing, 2008.

[57] KENDON A. Gesture: Visible action as utterance[M]. Cambridge: Cambridge University Press, 2004.

[58] KIERKEGAARD S. The concept of anxiety: A simple psychologically oriented deliberation in view of the dogmatic problem of hereditary sin [M]. New York: WW Norton & Company, 2014.

[59] KOPCZYNSKI A. Conference interpreting: Some linguistic and communicative problems [M]. Poznan, Poland: Adam Mickiewicz University Press, 1980.

[60] KORAK C. Remote interpreting via skype. Anwendungsmöglichkeiten von voipsofware im bereich community interpreting-communicate everywhere? [M]Berlin: Frank & Timme, 2010.

[61] KRESS G. Multimodality: A social semiotic approach to contemporary communication[M]. London/New York: Routledge, 2010.

[62] KRESS G, TEO V L. Multimodal discourse: The modes and media of contemporary communication[M]. London: Arnold, 2001.

[63] KUHN T S. The structure of scientific revolutions[M]. Chicago: University of Chicago Press, 1962.

[64] LABOV W. A study of non-standard English[M]. Natl Council of Teachers, 1969.

[65] LAMBERT, S, MOSER-MERCER B. Bridging the gap: Empirical research in simultaneous interpretation[M]. Amsterdam: John Benjamins Publishing, 1994.

[66] LEDERER M. Simultaneous interpretation—units of meaning and other features[M]// Language interpretation and communication. Boston, MA: Springer US, 1978.

[67] LEEDS R. Who do they think we are? The view of the interpreter, as seen by medical practitioners[M]. Leeds: University of Leeds, 2009.

[68] LINELL P. The written language bias in linguistics: Its nature, origins and transformations[M]. London: Routledge, 2005.

[69] LLEWELLYN-JONES P. Te impact of monological interpreting models when applied to remote interpretation[M]// FIŠER J P. Technology vs

interpreter: Support or replacement? Proceedings of the 2013 efsli Conference, Brussels: European Forum of Sign Lan guage Interpreters, 2014.

[70] LLEWELLYN-JONES P, ROBERT G L. Redefining the role of the community interpreter: The concept of role-space[M]. Lincoln: SLI Press, 2014.

[71] MALONE M. Worlds of talk: The presentation of self in everyday conversation[M]. Cambridge and Malden, MA: Polity Press, 1997.

[72] MASON I, STEWART M. Interactional pragmatics, face and the dialogue interpreter[M]// Manchester: St. Jerome Publishing, 2001.

[73] MASSARO D W. An information-processing model of understanding speech[M]. New York: Springer US, 1978.

[74] METZGER M. Sign language interpreting: Deconstructing the myth of neutrality[M]. Washington, DC: Gallaudet University Press, 1999.

[75] MOSER B. Simultaneous interpretation: A hypothetical model and its practical application[M]// Language interpretation and communication. Boston, MA: Springer US, 1978.

[76] MÜLLER C, ALAN C, ELLEN F, SILVA H L, DAVID M, SEDINHA T. Body-language-communication: An international handbook on multimodality in human interaction [M]. Berlin: De Gruyter Mouton, 2014.

[77] O'HAGAN M. The coming industry of teletranslation[M]. Bristol: Multilingual Matters, 1996.

[78] O'HAGAN M, ASHWORTH D. Translation-mediated communication in a digital world[M]. Bristol: Multilingual Matters, 2002.

[79] OVIATT S L. Discourse structure and performance efficiency in interactive and noninteractive spoken modalities[M]. New York: CSLI/ Stanford, 1990.

[80] PÖCHHACKER F. Introducing interpreting studies[M]. London/New York: Routledge, 2004.

[81] PÖCHHACKER F. Introducing interpreting studies [M]. London: Routledge, 2016.

[82] PÖCHHACKER F, SHLESINGER M. The interpreting studies reader

[M]. London，UK：Routledge，2002.

［83］PÖCHHACKER F，SCHLESINGER M. Healthcareinterpreting：Discourse and interaction ［M］. Amsterdam/Philadelphia：John Benjamins Publishing Company，2007.

［84］POYATOS F. Paralanguage：A linguistic and interdisciplinary approach to interactive speech and sounds［M］. Amsterdam：John Benjamins. 1993.

［85］POYATOS F. Nonverbal communication across disciplines. Volume II：Paralanguage，kinesics，silence，personal and environmental interaction ［M］. Amsterdam：John Benjamins，2002.

［86］RICCARDI A. The relevance of interpreting strategies for defining quality in simultaneous interpreting［M］// La evaluación de la calidad en interpretación：investigación. Madrid：Editorial Comares，2003：257-265.

［87］ROY C. Interpreting as a discourse process［M］. New York and Oxford：Oxford University Press，2000.

［88］SACKS H. Lectures on conversation. Vol. 2.［M］. New Jersey：Wiley-Blackwell，1968

［89］SAINT-LOUIS L et al. Testing new technologies in medical interpreting ［M］. Somerville，Massachusetts：Cambridge Health Alliance，2003.

［90］SAWYER D B. Fundamental aspects of interpreter education：Curriculum and assessment ［M］. Amsterdam，Netherlands：John Benjamins，2004.

［91］SCHIFRIN D. Approaches to discourse［M］. Cambridge，MA & Oxford：Blackwell，1994.

［92］SETTON R. Simultaneous interpretation：A cognitive-pragmatic analysis［M］. Amsterdam，Netherlands：John Benjamins Publishing，1999.

［93］SHORT J，WILLIAMS E，CHRISTIE B. The social psychology of telecommunications［M］. London：Wiley，1976.

［94］SOLOW S N. Sign language interpreting：A basic resource book［M］. Silver Spring，Maryland：National Association of the deaf，1981.

［95］STÖCKL H. In between modes：Language and image in printed media

［M］// EIJA V，CASSILY C，MARTIN K. Perspectives on multimodality. Amsterdam：John Benjamins，2014：9-30.

［96］TIFFIN J，RAJASINGHAM L. In search of the virtual class：Education in an information society［M］. New York：Psychology Press，1995.

［97］TOURY G. Descriptive translation studies-and beyond［M］. Amsterdam：John Benjamins，1995.

［98］TYER T. Don't leave me hanging on the telephone：Telework, professional isolation，and the work of video remote British sign language English interpreters［M］// NAPIER J，SKINNER R，BRAUN S. Here or there：Research on interpreting via video link. Washington，DC：Gallaudet University Press，2018：61-88.

［99］VAN DIJK T A，KINTSCH W. Strategies of discourse comprehension［M］. Academic Pr，New York：1983.

［100］VAN DIJK T. Discourse as social interaction［Discourse Studies：a multidisciplinary introduction II］［M］. London：Sage，1997.

［101］VAN HOOF H. Théorie et pratique de l'interprétation［M］. Munich：Hueber，1962.

［102］VENTOLA E，CHARLES C，MARTIN K. Perspectives on multimodality［M］. Amsterdam：John Benjamins，2004.

［103］VERMEER H J. A skopos theory of translation：(some arguments for and against)［M］. Heidelberg：TEXTconTEXT-Verlag，1996

［104］WADENSJÖ C. Recycled information as a questioning strategy：Pitfalls in interpreted-mediated talk［M］// The critical link：Interpreters in the community. Amsterdam：John Benjamins，1997：35.

［105］WADENSJÖ C，DIMITROVA B E，NILSSON A L. The critical link 4：professionalisation of interpreting in the community：selected papers from the 4th International Conference on Interpreting in Legal，Health and Social Service Settings，Stockholm，Sweden，May 2004［M］. Amsterdam：John Benjamins，2007：20-23.

［106］WADENSJÖ C. Interpreting as interaction［M］. London/New York：Longman，1998.

二、论文集、会议录

［1］BALOGH K，HERTOG E，BRAUN S. Avidicus comparative studies-part II: Traditional, video- conference and remote interpreting in police interviews[C]// BRAUN S, TAYLOR J. Video- conference and remote interpreting in criminal proceedings. Guildford: University of Surrey, 2012: 99-117.

[2] BALOGH K, SALAETS H. Videoconferencing in legal context: A comparative study of simulated and real-life settings[C]//NAPIER J, SKINNER R, BRAUN S. Here or there: Research on interpreting via video link. Washington, DC: Gallaudet University Press, 2018: 264-298.

[3] BALZANI M. Le contact visuel en interprétation simultanée: résultats d'une expérience (Français-Italien)[C]// LAURA G., CHRISTOPHER T. Aspects of applied and experimental research on simultaneous interpretation. Udine: Campanott, 1990: 93-100.

[4] BARIK H C. A description of various types of omissions, additions and errors of translation encountered in simultaneous interpretation[C]// SOPHIE L, MOSER-MERCER B. Bridging the Gap. Empirical research in simultaneous interpretation. Amsterdam/Philadelphia: John Benjamins, 1994: 124-138.

[5] BARIK H C. Simultaneous interpretation: Qualitative and linguistic data [C]// PÖCHHACKER F, SHLESINGER M. The interpreting studies reader. London, UK: Routledge, 2002: 78-91.

[6] BATES C. Introduction: Putting things in motion[C]// BATES C. Video methods: Social science research in motion. New York/London: Routledge, 2015: 1-9.

[7] BÖCKER M, ANDERSON D. Remote conference interpreting using ISDN videotelephone: a requirements analysis and feasibility study[C]// Proceedings of the human factors and ergonomics society annual meeting. Sage CA. Los Angeles, CA: SAGE Publications, 1993, 37(3): 235-239. .

[8] BRAUN S. ViKiS-Videokonferenz mit integriertemsimultandolmetschen für kleinere und mittlere unternehmen[C]// BECK U, SOMMER W. Europäischer kongreß und fachmesse für bildungs- und informationstechnologie. Karlsruhe: Schriftenreihe der karlsruher kongreß- und ausstellungs gmbH, 2001: 263-273.

［9］BRAUN S. Kommunikation unter widrigenumständen? —optimierungsstrategien in zweisprachigen videokonferenz-gesprächen ［C］// DÖRING J, SCHMITZ W H, SCHULTE O A. Connecting perspectives. Videokonferenz: Beiträge zu ihrer erforschung und anwendung. Aachen: Shaker, 2003: 167-185.

［10］BRAUN S. Remote interpreting[C]// MIKKELSON H, JOURDENAIS R. Routledge handbook on interpreting. London, UK: Routledge, 2015: 352-367.

［11］BRAUN S. Videoconferencing as a tool for bilingual mediation[C]// TOWNSLEY B. Understanding justice: An enquiry into interpreting in civil justice and mediation. London: Middlesex University, 2016: 194-227.

［12］BRAUN S, TAYLOR J L. AVIDICUS comparative studies—Part I: Traditional interpreting and remote interpreting in police interviews ［C］// BRAUN S, TAYLOR J L. Videoconferencing and remote interpreting in criminal proceedings. Antwerp, Belgium: Intersentia Publishing Ltd. , 2012a: 99-117.

［13］BRAUN S, TAYLOR J L. Video-mediated interpreting in criminal proceedings: Two European surveys[C]// BRAUN S, TAYLOR J L. Videoconferencing and remote interpreting in criminal proceedings. Antwerp, Belgium: Intersentia Publishing Ltd. , 2012b: 69-98.

［14］BRAUN S, DAVITTI E, DICERTO S. Video-mediated interpreting in legal settings: Assessing the implementation ［C］// NAPIER J, SKINNER R, BRAUN R. Here or there: Research on interpreting via video link. Washington, DC: Gallaudet University Press, 2018: 144-179.

［15］BRUNSON J L. The irrational component in the rational system: Interpreters talk about their motivation to work in relay services[C]// NAPIER J, SKINNER R, BRAUN R. Here or there: Research on interpreting via video link. Washington, DC: Gallaudet University Press, 2018: 39-60.

［16］BRAUN S, TAYLOR J L. Video-mediated interpreting: an overview of current practice and research ［C］// BRAUN S, TAYLOR J L.

Videoconference and remote interpreting in criminal proceedings. Antwerp，Belgium：Intersentia Publishing Ltd.，2012：33-68.

［17］BÜHLER H. Translation und nonverbalekommunikation［C］// WOLFRAM W. Semiotik und übersetzen. Tübingen：Gunter Narr Verlag，1980：43-53.

［18］CAUSO J E. Conference interpreting with information and communication technologies. Experiences from the European commission DG interpretation［C］// BRAUN S，TAYLOR J L. Videoconference and remote interpreting in criminal proceedings. Guildford：University of Surrey，2011：199-203.

［19］DENG X D. Listener response［C］// SIGURD D，JAN-OLA Ö，JEF V. The pragmatics of interaction. Amsterdam/Philadelphia：John Benjamins，2009：104-124.

［20］FOWLER Y. Interpreting into the ether：Interpreting for prison/court video link hearings［C］. Sydney：Proceedings of the Critical Link 5 conference，2007：11-15，.

［21］FOWLER Y. Interpreted prison video link：The prisoner's eye view ［C］// NAPIER J，SKINNER R，BRAUN S. Here or there：Research on interpreting via video link. Washington，DC：Gallaudet University Press，2018：183-209.

［22］GARZONE G E. Quality and norms in interpretation［C］// Interpreting in the 21st century：challenges and opportunities. Selected papers from the first forlì conference on interpreting studies，November，9-11，2000. Amsterdam：John Benjamins Publishing Company，2002：107-119.

［23］GIAMBRUNO C. The current state of affairs in the UE：Member state profiles［C］// GIAMBRUNO C. Assessing legal interpreter quality through testing and certification：The qualities project. Alicante，Spain：Universidad de Alicante，2014：149-190.

［24］GILE D. Conferenceinterpreting as a cognitive management problem ［C］// JOSEPH H D，GREGORY M S，STEPHEN B F，MICHAEL K M. Cognitive processes in translation and interpreting. London and New Delhi：Sage Publications，1997：196-214.

［25］GILE D. Scientific research vs. personal theories in the investigation of interpretation[C]// Aspects of applied and experimental research on conference interpretation. Udine: Campanotto, 1990(28): 41.

[26] GOODWIN C. Interactive construction of a sentence in natural conversation [C]// GEORGE P. Everyday language: Studies in ethnomethodology. New York: Irvington Publishers, 1979: 97-121.

[27] GRACIA-GARCÍA R A. Telephone interpreting: A review of pros and cons[C]// BRENNAN S. Proceedings of the 43rd annual conference. Alexandria, VA: American Translators Association, 2002: 195-216.

[28] GRBIĆ N. Quality[C]// PÖCHHACKER F. Routledge encyclopedia of interpreting studies. London, UK: Routledge, Taylor & Francis Group, 2015: 333-336.

[29] GRICE H P. Logic and conversation[C]// PETER C, JEREMY L M. Syntax and semantics. New York: Academic Press, 1975: 41-58.

[30] GUMPERZ J J. The communicative bases of social inequality[C]// Minorities: Community and identity: Report of the dahlem workshop on minorities: Community and identity Berlin 1982, Nov. 28-Dec. 3. Springer Berlin Heidelberg, 1983: 109-118.

[31] GUMPERZ J J. Contextualization and understanding [C]// ALESSANDRO D, CHARLES G. Rethinking context: Language as an interactive phenomenon. Cambridge: Cambridge University Press, 1992: 229-252.

[32] HAY D, PABSCH A. Act. React. Impact: 2014 EUD election manifesto[C]// PABSCH A. UNCRPD implementation in Europe—A deaf perspective: Article 29, participation in political and public life. Brussels, Belgium: European Union of the Deaf, 2014: 97-102.

[33] HERITAGE J. Analyzing news interviews: Aspects of production of talk for an overhearing audience[C]// TEUNV D. Handbook of discourse analysis, Vol. 3. Discourse and dialogue. London: Academic Press, 1985: 95-117.

[34] HERTOG E. Legal interpreting[C]// PÖCHHACKER F. Routledge encyclopedia of interpreting studies. London, UK: Routledge, Taylor & Francis Group, 2015: 230-235.

[35] HSIEH E. Conceptualizing bilingual health communication: a theory-

based approach to interpreter-mediated medical encounters［C］// ELIZABETH J，LISA D. Providing health care in the context of language barriers. International perspectives. Bristol UK：Multilingual Matters，2017：35-55.

[36]JAKOBSONR. On linguistic aspects of translation[C]// LAWRENCE V. The translation studies reader. London/New York：Routledge，1959/2000：113-118.

[37] KIRCHHOFF K，PARANDEKAR S，BILMES J. Mixed-memory markov models for automatic language identification[C]// 2002 IEEE International Conference on Acoustics，Speech，and Signal Processing，IEEE，2002(1)：761-764.

[38]KITANO H. Challenges of massive parallelism[C]// Proceedings of the 13th international joint conference on artifical intelligence-volume 1，1993：813-834.

[39]KO L. The need for long-term empirical studies in remote interpreting research：A case study of telephone interpreting[C]// ERIK H，BART V D V. Taking stock：Research and methodology in community interpreting. Antwerpen：Linguistica Antverpiensia，2006：325-338.

[40]KRESS G. What is a mode? In the routledge handbook of multimodal analysis[C]. 2nd ed. London/New York：Routledge，2014：60-75.

[41]KURZ I. Mediendolmetschen undvideokonferenzen[C]// KALINA B. Gerzymisch-arbogast. Dolmetschen：Theorie-praxis-didaktik； mit ausgewählten beiträgen der saarbrücker symposien. St. Ingbert：Röhrig Universitätsverlag，2000a：89-106.

[42] KURZ I. Tagungsort Genf/Nairobi/Wien：Zu einigenaspekten des teledolmetschens[C]// KADRIC M，KAINDL K，PÖCHHACKER F. Festschrift für Mary Snell-Hornby zum 60. Geburtstag. Tübingen：Stauffenburg，2000b：291-302.

[43]KURZ I. Conference interpreting：User expectations[C]// Coming of age：Proceedings of the 30th annual conference of the American Translators Association. Medford，NJ：Learned Information，1989：143-148.

[44] LANG R. Behavioural aspects of liaison interpreters in Papua New

Guinea：Some preliminary observations[C]// DAVID G，WALLACE S. Languageinterpretation and communication. New York/London：Plenum Press，1978：231-244.

[45]LEE R G. From theory to practice：Making the interpreting process come alive in the classroom[C]// CYNTHIA R. Advances in teaching sign language interpreters. Washington，DC Gallaudet University Press，2005：138-150.

[46]LLEWELLYN-JONES P，ROBERT G L. Te "role" of the community/public service interpreter [C/OL]. Online：Paper presented at the Supporting Deaf People online conference，January，2009.

[47]MARTINSEN B，MIZUNO A，RUSSO M C et al. On media and court interpreting[C]// Conference interpreting：Current trends in research：Proceedings of the international conference on Interpreting—What do we know and how? John Benjamins Publishing，1997(23)：187.

[48] MASON I. Gaze，positioning and identity in interpreter-mediated dialogues[C]// CLAUDIA B，LAURA G. Coordinating participation in dialogue interpreting. Amsterdam/Philadelphia：John Benjamins，2012：177-200.

[49]MCNEILL D. Introduction[C]// DAVIDM. Language and Gesture. Cambridge：Cambridge University Press，2000：1-10.

[50]MERLINI R，ROBERTA F. Examining the voice of interpreting in speech pathology[C]// FRANZ P，MIRIAM S. Healthcareinterpreting. Amsterdam/Philadelphia：John Benjamins，2007：101-137.

[51]MIKKELSON H. Telephone interpreting：Boon or bane? [C]// PÉREZ G. Speaking intongues：Language across contexts and users. València，Spain：Universitat de València，2003：251-269.

[52]MILER-CASSINO J，RYBINSKA Z. Avidicus comparative studies—Part III：Traditional interpreting and videoconferencing interpreting in prosecution interviews [C]// BRAUN S，TAYLOR J L. Videoconference and remote interpreting in criminal proceedings，Antwerp. Belgium：Intersentia Publishing Ltd.，2012：99-117.

[53]MONDADA L. Video as a tool in the social sciences[C]//MÜLLER C，ALAN C，ELLEN F，SILVA H L，DAVID M，SEDINHA T. Body-

language-communication：An international handbook on multimodality in human interaction，Vol. 1. Berlin：De Gruyter Mouton，2013：982-992.

［54］MÜLLER C. Introduction［C］//MÜLLER C，ALAN C，ELLEN F，SILVA H L，DAVID M，SEDINHA T. Body-language-communication：An international handbook on multimodality in human interaction，Vol. 1. Berlin：De Gruyter Mouton，2013：1-6.

［55］NAPIER J. Omissions［C］// FRANZ P. Routledge encyclopedia of interpreting studies. London，UK：Routledge，Taylor & Francis Group，2015：289-291

［56］NAPIER J. Here or there? An assessment of video remote signed language interpreter-mediated interaction in court［C］// BRAUN S，TAYLOR J L. Videoconference and remote interpreting in criminal proceedings. Antwerp，Belgium：Intersentia Publishing Ltd. ，2012a：167-214.

［57］NAPIER J. Exploring themes in stakeholder perspectives of video remote interpreting in court［C］// KELLETT C J. Interpreting across genres：Multiple research perspectives. Trieste，Italy：EUT Edizioni Universtà di Trieste，2012b：219-254.

［58］NAPIER J. You get that vibe：A pragmatic analysis of clarification and communicative accommodation in legal video remote interpreting［C］// MEURANT L，SINTE A，HERREWEGHE M，VERMEERBERGEN M. Sign language research uses and practices：Crossing views on theoretical and applied sign language linguistics. Nijmegen，The Netherlands：De Gruyter Mouton and Ishara Press，2013：85-110.

［59］NAPIER J，SKINNER R，TURNER G H. Enabling political participation through remote interpreting：A case study［C］// NAPIER J，SKINNER R，BRAUN S. Here or there：Research on interpreting via video link. Washington，DC：Gallaudet University Press，2018：230-263.

［60］NISKA H. Quality issues en remote interpreting［C］// Anovar-anosar：Estudios de traducción e interpretación. Servizo de Publicacións，1999：109-122.

［61］NISKA H. Community interpreter training：past，present，future［C］//

GARZONE G, VIEZZI M. Interpreting in the 21st Century. Amsterdam: Benjamins, 2002: 133-144.

[62]PARAS M et al. Videoconferencing medical interpretation. The results of clinical trials[C]. Oakland: Health Access Foundation, 2002.

[63] PETERSON R. Profession in pentimento: A narrative inquiry into interpreting in video settings[C]// LAURA S, BRENDA N. Advances in interpreting research. Amsterdam, Netherlands: John Benjamins, 2011: 199-223.

[64]PÖCHHACKER F. Media interpreting[C]// YVES G, LUC VAN D. Handbook of translation studies, Vol. 1, ed. John Benjamins: Amsterdam, 2010: 224-226.

[65]PÖCHHACKER F. Remote possibilities: Training simultaneous video interpreting for Austrian hospitals[C]// BRENDA N, MELANIE M. Investigations in healthcare interpreting. Washington, DC: Gallaudet University Press, 2014: 302-325.

[66]PORRERO P, GUNNAR H. The public Swedish video relay service [C]// PLACENCIA P. Improving the quality of life for the European citizen: Technology for inclusive design and equality (volume 4). IOS Press, 1998: 267-270.

[67] POYATOS F. Nonverbal communication in simultaneous and consecutive interpretation: A theoretical model and new perspectives [C]// PÖCHHACKER F, MIRIAM S. Te interpreting studies reader. London/New York: Routledge, 1987/2002: 235-246.

[68] POYATOS F. The reality of multichannel verbal-nonverbal communication in simultaneous and consecutive interpretation [C]// POYATOS F. Nonverbal communication and translation: New perspectives and challenges in literature, interpretation and the media. Amsterdam: John Benjamins, 1997: 249-282.

[69]PYM A. On omission in simultaneous interpreting: Risk analysis of a hidden effort[C]// GUY H, ANDREW C, HEIDRUN G. Efforts and models in interpreting and translation research: A tribute to Daniel Gile. Amsterdam, The Netherlands: John Benjamins, 2008: 83-105.

[70] RENNERT S. Visual access [C]// PÖCHHACKER F. Routledge

encyclopedia of interpreting studies. London/New York：Routledge，2015：439-440.

[71]RICARDI A. Dierolle des dolmetschens in der globalisierten gesellschaft [C]// KALINA B. Gerzymisch-arbogast，dolmetschen：Theorie - praxis - didaktik；mit ausgewählten Beiträgen der saarbrücker symposien. St. Ingbert：Röhrig Universitätsverlag，2000：75-89.

[72]ROSENBERG B A. A quantitative analysis of telephone interpreting [C]// I KEMBLE. Using corpora and databases in translation. University of Portsmouth，2004：156-165.

[73]ROSENBERG B A. A data driven analysis of telephone Interpreting [C]// WADENSJÖ C，ENGLUND D B，NILSSON A L. The critical link 4. Professionalisation of interpreting in the community. Benjamins，2007：65-76.

[74]ROMBOUTS D. The police interview using videoconferencing with a legal interpreter：A critical view from the perspective of interview techniques[C]// BRAUN S，JUDITH T. Videoconference and remote interpreting in criminal proceedings. Cambridge，UK：Intersentia Publishing Ltd.，2012：159-166.

[75]SALAETS H，KATALIN B. Participants' and interpreters' perception of the interpreter's role in interpreter-mediated investigative interviews of minors：Belgium and Italy as a case study[C]// TIPTON R，VALERO-GARCES C. Ethics，ideology and policy development in public service interpreting and translating. Clevedon：Multilingual Matters，2017：151-178.

[76]SCHEGLOF E A. Discourse as an interactional achievement：Some uses of "uhhuh" and other things that come between sentences [C]// DEBORAH T. Analyzing discourse：text and talk. Georgetown：Georgetown University Press，1982：71-93.

[77]SCHMITZ U. Multimodale Texttypologie[C]// NINA-MARIA K，HARTMUT S. Handbuch Sprache im multimodalen Kontext. Berlin：De Gruyter，2016：327-347.

[78]SCHÖNHERR B. Categories and functions of posture，gaze，face，and body movements[C]// CORNELIA M，ALAN C，ELLEN F，SILVA H

L, DAVID M, SEDINHA T. Body-language-communication: An international handbook on multimodality in human interaction. Berlin: De Gruyter Mouton, 2014: 1333-1341.

[79]SHAW S. Interpreting for deaf blind persons[C]//PÖCHHACKER F. Routledge encyclopedia of interpreting studies. London/New York: Routledge, 2015: 200-201.

[80]SHLESINGER M. Quality in simultaneous interpreting[C]// YVES G, DANIEL G, CHRISTOPHER T. Conference Interpreting: Current trends in research. Amsterdam/Philadelphia: Benjamins, 2007: 123-131.

[81]SHLESINGER M. Norms, strategies and constraints: How do ve tell them apart? [C]// Anovar-anosar: Estudios de traducción e interpretación. Servizo de Publicacións, 1999: 65-78.

[82]STENZL C. From theory to practice and from practice to theory[C]// The theoretical and practical aspects of teaching conference interpretation. Udine: Campanotto, 1989: 26.

[83]STÖCKL H. In between modes: Language and image in printed media [C]// EIJA V, CHARLES C, MARTIN K. Perspectives on multimodality. Amsterdam: John Benjamins, 2004: 9-30.

[84]SUNNARI M, HILD A. A multi-factorial approach to the development and analysis of professional expertise in SI[C]. Trieste: EUT Edizioni Università di Trieste, 2010.

[85]TEBBLE H. A discourse model for dialogue interpreting in Australian institute of interpreters and translators (AUSIT) [C]// Canberra: NAATI: Proceedings of the first practitioners. Seminar of AUSIT, November 1992: 1-26. .

[86]TEBBLE H. Interpreting of interfering? [C]// CLAUDIA B, LAURA G. Coordinating participation in dialogue interpreting. Amsterdam/ Philadelphia: John Benjamins, 2012: 23-44.

[87] TOMMOLA J, JOHAN L. Experimentalresearch on interpreting: Which dependent variable? [C]// JORMA T. Topics in interpreting research. Turku: University of Turku Press, 1995: 121-133.

[88] VAN R P, RONALD V D H. True-to-life requirements for using

videoconferencing in legal proceedings[C]// BRAUN S, TAYLOR J L. Videoconference and remote interpreting in criminal proceeding. Guildford: University of Surrey，2011：187-197.

[89]VERREPT H. Intercultural mediation through the Internet in Belgian hospitals［C］// 4th International Conference on Public Service Interpreting and Translation，April，13-15，2011：13-15.

[90]WARNICKE C. Co-creating communicative projects within the Swedish video-relay service[C]// NAPIER J，SKINNER R，BRAUN S. Here or there：Research on interpreting via video link. Washington，DC：Gallaudet University Press，2018：210-229.

[91]WHITTAKER S, BRID O'C. The role of vision in face-to-face and mediated communication[C]// KATHLEEN E F et al. Video-mediated communication. Amsterdam/Philadelphia：John Benjamins，1997：104-124.

[92]ZAGAR GALVÃO E, ISABEL GALHANO R. Nonverbal communication ［C］//PÖCHHACKER F. Routledge encyclopedia of interpreting studies. London：Routledge，2015：280-281.

三、论文类

[1]陈顺森,唐丹虹.考试焦虑对错误记忆的影响[J].心理发展教育,2009(1)：46-53.

[2]邓愉联.外语学习焦虑感研究[J].当代教育论坛(学科教育研究),2008(12)：81-82.

[3]方琪.电话口译在中国的职业现状[J].湖北第二师范学院学报,2014(4)：123-125.

[4]葛明贵,鲍奇.考试焦虑与智力水平、人格类型的关系[J].中国心理卫生杂志,1995(3)：105-106.

[5]郝玫,郝君平.英语成绩与成就动机、状态焦虑的相关研究[J].外语教学与研究,2001(2)：111-115.

[6]贾飞.私立大学非英语专业大学生英语学习焦虑调查研究[J].中外教育研究,2020(11)：72.

[7]康志峰.口译焦虑的动因、级度及其影响[J].外语研究,2011(4)：81-85.

[8]康志峰.多模态口译焦虑的级度溯源[J].外语教学,2012(3)：106-109.

［9］康志峰. 现代信息技术下口译多模态听焦虑探析［J］. 外语电化教学，2012
　　（3）：42-45.

［10］康志峰. 立体论与多模态口译教学［J］. 外语界，2012（5）：34-41.

［11］康志峰. 模因论·整体论·级度论——多模态口译焦虑的模因建构［J］. 外
　　语教学理论与实践，2013（3）：76-81.

［12］李炯英. 外语学习焦虑的心理学和神经生物学分析［J］. 天津外国语学院学
　　报，2004（4）：46-51.

［13］刘和平. 口译理论研究成果与趋势浅析［J］. 中国翻译，2005（4）：21-24.

［14］刘和平. 职业口译新形势与口译教学［J］. 中国翻译，2003（3）：34-38.

［15］刘绍龙，王柳琪. 对近十年中国口译研究现状的调查与分析［J］. 广东外语
　　外贸大学学报，2007（1）：37-40.

［16］罗海峰. 电话口译的特点及应对策略［J］. 湖南工业职业技术学院学报，
　　2010（2）：86-88.

［17］王湘玲，胡珍铭，邹玉屏. 认知心理因素对口译策略的影响——职业译员与
　　学生译员交替传译之实证研究［J］. 外国语，2013（1）：73-81.

［18］王银泉，万玉书. 外语学习焦虑及其对外语学习的影响——国外相关研究
　　概述［J］. 外语教学与研究，2001（4）：122.

［19］王斌华. "口译能力"评估和"译员能力"评估——口译的客观评估模式初探
　　［J］. 外语界，2007（3）：44-50.

［20］韦琴红. 论多模态话语中的模态、媒介与情态［J］. 外语教学，2009（4）：54.

［21］肖晓燕，郁锐玲. 社区口译新趋势——电话口译［J］. 中国翻译，2009（2）：
　　22-27.

［22］肖晓燕，张梅. 美国电话口译的职业现状及理论分析［J］. 上海翻译，2009
　　（2）：22-27.

［23］许明. 口译认知研究的心理学基础［J］. 天津外国语学院学报，2007（6）：69-
　　72.

［24］叶仁敏，HAGTVET K A. 中学生的成就动机、测验焦虑、智力水平与学业
　　成绩关系的探讨［J］. 应用心理学，1989（3）：52-56.

［25］姚斌. 远程会议口译——回顾与前瞻［J］. 上海翻译，2011（1）：32-37.

［26］张承芳，毛伟宾. 考试焦虑、能力自我知觉与学生成就归因关系初探［J］. 心
　　理科学，1992（6）：54-56.

［27］张威. 口译研究的跨学科探索：困惑与出路［J］. 中国翻译，2012（3）：13-19.

［28］周统权，徐晶晶. 心智哲学的神经、心理学基础：以心智理论研究为例［J］.

外语教学,2011(1):8.

[29]詹成,索若楠.电话口译在我国的一次重要实践——广州亚运会、残运会多语言服务中心的电话口译.中国翻译,2012(1):107-110.

[30]张威,柯飞.从口译用户看口译质量评估[J].外语学刊,2008(3):114-118.

[31]仲伟合.英汉同声传译技巧与训练[J].中国翻译,2001(5):40-44.

[32]康志峰.口译中听、译两种焦虑模态的认知心理管窥[D].复旦大学,2011.

[33]张威.同声传译与工作记忆的关系研究[D].北京:北京外国语大学,2007.

[34] Aís Á C. Quality assessment and intonation in simultaneous interpreting:Evaluation patterns[J]. MonTI. monografías de traducción e interpretación,2016:213-238.

[35] ALEXIEVA B. A typology of interpreter-mediated events[J]. The translator,1997(2):153-174.

[36] ALLEY E. Exploring remote interpretation[J]. International journal of interpreter education,2012(1):111-119.

[37] ALLEY E. Who makes the rules anyway? Reality and perception of guidelines in video relay service interpreting[J]. The interpreter's newsletter,2014(19):13-26.

[38] ALTMAN J. What helps effective communication? Some interpreters' view[J]. The interpreters' newsletter,1990(3):23-32.

[39] ANDRES D, FALK S. Information and communication technologies (ICT) in interpreting-remote and telephone interpreting[J]. Spürst du, wie der bauch rauf-runter,2009:9-27.

[40] ANGELELLI C. Interpretation as a communicative event:A look through Hymes' lenses[J]. Meta,2000,45(4):580-592.

[41] AZARMINA P, WALLACE P. Remote interpretation in medical encounters:A systematic review[J]. Journal of telemedicine and telecare, 2005,11(3):140-145.

[42] BAKER, MONA. Contextualization in translator and interpreter-mediated events[J]. Journal of pragmatics,2006,38(3):321-337.

[43] BARALDI C, GAVIOLI L. Are close renditions the golden standard? Some thoughts on translating accurately in healthcare interpreter-mediated interaction[J]. The interpreter and translator trainer,2014, 8 (3):336-353.

[44]BARIK H C. Simultaneous interpretation: Qualitative and linguistic data [J]. Language and speech, 1975, 18(3): 272-297.

[45]BARIK H C. Simultaneous interpretation: Temporal and quantitative data[J]. Language and speech, 1973, 16(3): 237-270.

[46]BARTŁOMIEJCZYK M. Strategies of simultaneous interpreting and directionality[J]. Interpreting, 2006, 8(2): 149-174.

[47]BERGE S S. Sign language interpreters' embodied action of coordinating turn-taking in group work between deaf and hearing high-school students [J]. Interpreting, 2018(1): 97-126.

[48]BERK-SELIGSON S. The impact of politeness in witness testimony: The influence of the court interpreter[J]. Multilingua, 1988(4): 411-439.

[49]BÉLANGER D. Interactional patterns in dialogue interpreting[J]. Journal of interpretation, 2004(17): 1-18.

[50]BLACK P, WILIAM D. Assessment and classroom learning[J]. Assessment ineducation: Principles, policy & practice, 1998, 5(1): 7-74.

[51]BOHLE U. Contemporary classification systems[J]. Ac müller cüller, body-language-communication: An international handbook on multimodality in human interaction, 2014: 1453-1461.

[52]BONTEMPO K, NAPIER J. Mind the gap! A skills gap analysis of sign language interpreters[J]. The sign language translator & interpreter, 2017, 1(2): 275-299.

[53]BONTEMPO K, NAPIER J. Evaluating emotional stability as a predictor of interpreter competence and aptitude for interpreting[J]. Interpreting, 2011, 13(1): 85-105.

[54]BOWER K. Stress and burnout in video relay service (VRS) interpreting [J]. Journal of interpretation, 2015, 24(1): 2.

[55]BRINKMAN W B, GERAGHTY S R, LANPHEAR B P, et al. Effect of multisource feedback on resident communication skills and professionalism: a randomized controlled trial[J]. Archives of pediatrics & adolescent medicine, 2007, 161(1): 44-49..

[56]BRAUN S. Interpreting in small-group bilingual video conferences:

challenges and adaptation processes[J]. Interpreting, 2007, 9(1): 21-46.

[57]BRAUN S. Keep your distance? Remote interpreting in legal proceedings: A critical assessment of a growing practice[J]. Interpreting, 2013, 15(2): 200-228.

[58] BRAUN S. What a micro-analytical investigation of additions and expansions in remote interpreting can tell us about interpreters' participation in a shared virtual space[J]. Journal of pragmatics, 2017 (107): 165-177.

[59]BRAUN S, KOHN K. Dolmetschen in dervideokonferenz. Kommunikative kompetenz und monitoringstrategien [J]. Kultur und translation: Methodologische probleme des kulturtransfers, 2001: 3-32.

[60] BRENNER C. Depression, anxiety and affect theory [J]. The international journal of psycho-analysis, 1997(55): 25.

[61]BROS-BRANN E. L'interprétation en direct pour la télévision[J]. Lestransferts linguistiques dans les médias audiovisuels, paris, presses universitaires du septentrion, 1996: 207-216.

[62]BUCKETT J, STRINGER G, DATTA J. Life after relate: Internet videoconferencing's growing pains[J]. Call and the learning community, 1999: 31-38.

[63]BÜHLER H. Linguistic (semantic) and extra-linguistic (pragmatic) criteria for the evaluation of conference interpretation and interpreters [J]. Multilingua, 1986, 5(4): 231-235.

[64]BÜHLER H. Conference interpreting- a multichannel communication phenomenon[J]. Meta, 1985, 30(1): 49-54.

[65]CAO D. Towards a model of translation proficiency[J]. International journal of translation studies, 1996, 8(2): 325-340.

[66]CALVO M G, CARREIRAS M. Selective influence of test anxiety on reading processes[J]. British journal of psychology, 1993, 84(3): 375-388.

[67]CASSADY J C, JOHNSON R E. Cognitive test anxiety and academic performance[J]. Contemporaryeducational psychology, 2002, 27(2): 270-295.

［68］CHEN N S, KO L. An online synchronous test for professional interpreters[J]. Journal of educational technology & society, 2010, 13 (2): 153-165.

［69］CHERNOV G V. Towards a psycholinguistic model of simultaneous interpretation[J]. Linguistischearbeitsberichte, 1973, 7: 225-260.

［70］CHERNOV G V. Semantic aspects of psycholinguistic research in simultaneous interpretation[J]. Language and speech, 1979, 22 (3): 277-295.

［71］CHERNOV G V. Conference interpreting in the USSR: History, theory, new frontiers[J]. Meta, 1992, 37(1): 149-162.

［72］CHERNOV G V. Message redundancy and message anticipation in simultaneous interpretation[J]. Bridging the gap: Empirical research in simultaneous interpretation, 1994(3): 139-153.

［73］CHESTERMAN A. From "is" to "ought" laws, norms and strategies in translation studies[J]. Target, 1993, 5(1): 1-20.

［74］CHOU C C. Formative evaluation of synchronous CMC systems for a learner-centered online course [J]. Journal of interactive learning research, 2001, 12(2): 173-192.

［75］CIRILLO L. Managing affect in interpreter-mediated institutional talk: Examples from the medical setting [J]. The journal of specialised translation, 2010(14): 55-79.

［76］CLANCY P, TOMPSON S, SUZUKIA R, TAOB H. Te conversational use of reactive tokens in English, Japanese, and Mandarin[J]. Journal of pragmatics, 1996(3): 355-387.

［77］COLLADOS AÍS Á. Quality assessment in simultaneous interpreting: The importance of nonverbal communication[J]. The interpreting studies reader, 2002: 327-336..

［78］COLLADOS AÍS Á, GARCÍA BECERRA O. Quality criteria [J]. Routledgeencyclopedia of interpreting studies, 2015: 337-338.

［79］CONNELL T. The application of new technologies to remote interpreting[J]. Linguisticaantverpiensia ns, 2006(5): 311-324.

［80］CROSSMAN K L et al. Interpreters: Telephonic, in-person interpretation and bilingual providers[J]. Pediatrics, 2010, 125(3): 631-

638.

[81]CURREN L，HUZ I，MCKEE M et al. Patient primary language in a culturally focused intervention for Latino Americans with depression[J]. Annals of clinical psychiatry：Official journal of the American academy of clinical psychiatrists，2018，30(2)：84.

[82] DAVITTIE. Dialogue interpreting as intercultural mediation： Interpreters' use of upgrading moves in parent-teacher meetings[J]. Interpreting，2013，15(2)：168-199.

[83]DAM H V. On the option between form-based and meaning-based interpreting：The effect of source text difficulty on lexical target text form in simultaneous interpreting[J]. The interpreters' newsletter，2001 (11)：27-55.

[84] DONATO V. Strategies adopted by student interpreters in SI：A comparison between the English-Italian and the German-Italian language-pairs[J]. Interpreters' newsletter，2003(12)：101-134.

[85] DUNCAN S J R. Toward a grammar for dyadic conversation[J]. Semiotica，1973，9(1)：29-46.

[86]ERICSSON K A，CHARNESS N. Cognitive and developmental factors in expert performance[J]. Expertise in context：Human and machine，1997：3-41.

[87]FABBRO F. The bilingual brain：Cerebral representation of languages [J]. Brain and language，2001，79(2)：211-222.

[88]FIRTH J R. Descriptive linguistics and the study of English[J]. World Englishes：Critical concepts in linguistics，1968(3)：203-217.

[89]FLORES D'ARCAIS G B. The contribution of cognitive psychology to the study of interpretation [J]. Language interpretation and communication，1978(6)：385-402.

[90]FLORES G et al. Errors in medical interpretation and their potential clinical consequences in pediatric encounters[J]. Pediatrics，2003(111)：6-14.

[91]FLORES G et al. Errors of medical interpretation and their potential clinical consequences：a comparison of professional versus ad hoc versus no interpreters[J]. Annals of emergency medicine，2012(5)：545-553.

［92］FOLSTEIN M F, LURIA R. Reliability, validity, and clinical application of the visual analogue mood scale［J］. Psychological medicine, 1973, 3(4): 479-486.

［93］SEEBER K, ZELGER C. Betrayal-vice or virtue? An ethical perspective on accuracy in simultaneous interpreting［J］. Meta, 2007, 52(2): 290-298.

［94］GARDNER M R, SARAH M J, DANIEL A O, DOUGLAS L W, BARBARA R S, SANDHYA P. Perceptions of video-based appointments from the patient's home: A patient survey［J］. Telemedicine journal and e-health, 2015(4): 281-285.

［95］GANY F et al. Patient satisfaction with different interpreting methods: A randomized controlled trial［J］. Journal of general internal medicine, 2007a(2): 312-318.

［96］GANY F et al. The impact of medical interpretation method on time and errors［J］. Journal of general internal medicine, 2007b(2): 319-323.

［97］GERVER D, DINELEY G. Aspa: Automatic speech-pause analyzer［J］. Behavior research methods & instrumentation, 1972, 4(5): 265-270.

［98］GILE D. Le modèle d'efforts et l'équilibre d'interprétation en interprétation simultanée［J］. Meta, 1985, 30(1): 44-48.

［99］GILE D. Testing the effort models' tightrope hypothesis in simultaneous interpreting—A contribution［J］. Hermes: Journal of linguistics, 1999 (23): 153-172.

［100］GILE D. The coming of age of a learned society in translation studies: EST, a case study［J］. International journal of translation studies, 2014, 26(2): 247-258.

［101］GLEMET, R. Conference interpreting［J］. Aspects of translation. London: Studies in communication 2, communication research centre, University College, 1958: 105.

［102］GOLDMAN-EISLER F. Segmentation of input in simultaneous translation［J］. Journal of psycholinguisticresearch, 1972, 1(2): 127-140.

［103］GRAN L, TAYLOR C. Aspects of applied and experimental research on conference interpretation［J］. SSLM, university of trieste, Udine:

Campanotto，1989：11.

[104]HAUALAND H. Video interpreting services：Calls for inclusion or redialing exclusion[J]. Ethnos, 2014(2)：287-305.

[105]HENRDON J et al. Continuing concerns, new challenges, and next steps in physician-patient communication[J]. The journal of bone and joint surgery, 2002(2)：309-315.

[106]HORNBERGER J et al. Eliminating language barriers for non-English-speaking patients[J]. Medical care,1996(8)：845-856.

[107]HUMPHRIES T, POORNA K, GAURAV M, DONNA J N, CAROL P, CHRISTIAN R. Ensuring language acquisition for deaf children：What linguists can do[J]. Language, 2014, 90(2)：31-52.

[108] INGRAM R M. Simultaneous interpretation of sign languages：Semiotic and psycholinguistic perspectives[J]. Multilingua, 1985, 4 (2)：91-102.

[109] ISHAM W P. Memory for sentence form after simultaneous interpretation：Evidence both for and against deverbalization [J]. Bridging the gap：Empirical research in simultaneous interpretation, 1994：191-211.

[110]JÖRG U. Bridging the gap：Verb anticipation in German-English simultaneous interpreting[J]. Benjaminstranslation library, 1997(20)：217-228.

[111]JONES D et al. An exploratory study of language interpretation services provided by videoconferencing[J]. Journal of telemedicine and telecare, 2003(9)：51-56.

[112]JONES D, GILL P. Breaking down language barriers[J]. British medical journal, 1998, 316(7143)：1476.

[113]JOSEPH C, GARRUBA M, MELDER A. Patient satisfaction of telephone or video interpreter services compared with in-person services：A systematic review[J]. Australian health review, 2017(2)：168-177.

[114] JUMPELT R, WALTER. The conference interpreter's working environment under the new ISO and IEC standards[J]. Meta, 1985, 30 (1)：82-90.

［115］ KADE O, CARTELLIERI C. Some methodological aspects of simultaneous interpreting［J］. Babel, 1971, 17(2): 12-16.

［116］KALINA S. Interpreters as professionals［J］. Across languages and cultures, 2002, 3(2): 169-187.

［117］KEATING E, MIRUS G. American sign language in virtual space: Interactions between deaf users of computer-mediated video communication and the impact of technology on language practices［J］. Language in society, 2003, 32(5): 693-714.

［118］KENDON A. Some function of gaze direction in social interaction［J］. Actapsychologica, 1967(26): 22-63.

［119］KENT S J. Deaf voice and the invention of community interpreting［J］. Journal of interpretation, 2012, 22(1): 3.

［120］KO L. The need for long-term empirical studies in remote interpreting research: A case study of telephone interpreting ［J］. Linguisticaantverpiensia, new series: Themes in translation studies, 2006(5): 325-338.

［121］KO L. Teaching interpreting by distance mode［J］. Interpreting, 2006, 8(1): 67-96.

［122］ KO L, CHEN N S. Online-interpreting in synchronous cyber classrooms［J］. Babel, 2011, 57(2): 123-143.

［123］KOHN K, KALINA S. The strategic dimension of interpreting［J］. Meta, 1996, 41(1): 118-138.

［124］KÖTTER M, SHIELD L, STEVENS A. Real-time audio and email for fluency: Promoting distance language learners' aural and oral skills via the Internet［J］. Recall, 1999, 11(2): 55-60.

［125］KRYSTALLIDOU D. Gaze and body orientation as an apparatus for patient inclusion into/ exclusion from a patient-centred framework of communication［J］. The interpreter and translator trainer, 2014, 8(3): 399-417.

［126］KRYSTALLIDOU D. Investigating the interpreter's role(s). The A. R. T. framework［J］. Interpreting, 2016, 18(2): 172-197.

［127］ KUO D, MARK J F. Satisfaction with methods of Spanish interpretation in an ambulatory care clinic ［J］. Journal of general internal medicine，1999(14)：547-550.

[128] KURZ I. Conference interpretation：Expectations of different user groups[J]. The interpreters' newsletter，1993(5)：13-21.

[129] KURZ I. Interpreting：Sound vs. sound and picture[J]. The jerome quarterly，1996(1)：5-14.

[130] KURZ I. Getting the message across-simultaneous interpreting for the media[J]. Benjamins translation library，1997(20)：195-206.

[131] KURZ I. Interpreting training programmes[J]. Teaching translation and interpreting 4：Building bridges，2002：65-72.

[132] KURZ I. Physiological stress during simultaneous interpreting：A comparison of experts and novices[J]. The interpreters' newsletter，2003(12)：51-67.

[133] LA BELLE T J，WHITE P S. Education and colonial language policies in Latin America and the Caribbean [J]. International review of education，1978(24)：243-261.

[134] LAMBERT W E. Psychological approaches to bilingualism，translation and interpretation [J]. Languageinterpretation and communication，1978：131-143.

[135] LARSEN S. Videoconferencing in business meetings：An affordance perspective[J]. Internationaljournal of e-collaboration，2015(4)：64-79.

[136] LE FÉAL D. Some thoughts on the evaluation of simultaneous interpretation[J]. Interpreting-yesterday，today and tomorrow，1990：154-60.

[137] LEE J. Telephoneinterpreting-seen from the interpreter's perspective [J]. Interpreting，2007，9(2)：231-252.

[138] LEE L J et al. Effect of Spanish interpretation method on patient satisfaction in an urban walk-in clinic[J]. Journal of general internal medicine，2002，17(8)：641-645.

[139] LEEMANN P E et al. Interpreter perspectives of in-person，telephonic，and video-conferencing medical[J]. Patient education and counseling，2012(87)：226-232.

[140] LIM L. Examining students' perceptions of computer-assisted

interpreter training[J]. The interpreter and translator trainer, 2013, 7 (1): 71-89.

[141]LLEWELLYN-JONES P, ROBERT G L. Getting to the core of role: Defining the role-space of interpreters [J]. Internationaljournal of interpreter education, 2013, 5(2): 54-72.

[142]LOCATIS C et al. Comparing in-person, video, and telephonic medical interpretation[J]. Journal of general internal medicine, 2010, 25(4): 345-350.

[143] LOCATIS C et al. Video medical interpretation over 3G cellular networks:A feasibility study[J]. Telemedicine and e-health, 2011, 17 (10): 809-813.

[144]MACKINTOSH J. Interpreters are made not born[J]. Interpreting, 1999, 4(1): 67-80.

[145] MASLAND M, LOU C, SNOWDON L. Use of communication technologies to cost-effectively increase the availability of interpretation services in healthcare settings[J]. Telemedicine and e-health, 2010, 16 (6): 739-745.

[146]MCANDREW P, FOUBISTER S P, MAYES T. Videoconferencing in a language learning application[J]. Interacting with computers, 1996, 8 (2): 207-217.

[147]MEAK L. Interprétation simultanée et congrès médical:Attentes et commentaires[J]. Psychology, 1990(3): 8-13.

[148]MOEKETSI R, WALLMACH K. From sphaza to makoya!: A BA degree for court interpreters in South Africa[J]. Journal for speech, language and the law: Forensic linguistics, 2005(12): 77-108.

[149]MOSER-MERCER B. The expert-novice paradigm in interpreting research[J]. Translationsdidaktik: Grundfragen der übersetzungswissenschaft, 1997: 255-261.

[150] MOSER-MERCER B. Remote interpreting: assessment of human factors and performance parameters [J]. Joint projectinternational, 2003: 1-17.

[151] MOSER-MERCER B. Skill acquisition in interpreting: A human performance perspective [J]. The interpreter and translator trainer,

2008, 2(1): 1-28.

[152]MOSER-MERCER B. Simultaneous interpreting: Cognitive potential and limitations[J]. Interpreting, 2000(2): 83-94.

[153]MOSER-MERCER B. Remote interpreting: Issues of multi-sensory integration in a multilingual task[J]. Meta, 2005a(2): 727-738.

[154]MOSER-MERCER B. Remote interpreting: The crucial role of presence [J]. Bulletinsuisse de linguistique appliqué, 2005b(81): 73-97.

[155]MOSER-MERCER B, KÜNZLI A, KORAC M. Prolonged turns in interpreting: Effects on quality, physiological and psychological stress (pilot study)[J]. Interpreting, 1998, 3(1): 47-64.

[156]MOSER P. Expectations of users of conference interpretation[J]. Interpreting, 1996(2): 145-178.

[157]MOUZOURAKIS P. That feeling of being there: Vision and presence in remote interpreting[J]. The AIIC webzine, 2003: 23.

[158]MOWRER O H. A stimulus-response analysis of anxiety and its role as a reinforcing agent[J]. Psychological review, 1939, 46(6): 553.

[159]MOUZOURAKIS P. Videoconferencing: Techniques and challenges[J]. Interpreting, 1996, 1(1): 21-38.

[160]MOUZOURAKIS P. Remote interpreting: A technical perspective on recent experiments[J]. Interpreting, 2006, 8(1): 45-66.

[161] NAPIER J. Interpretingomissions: A new perspective [J]. Interpreting, 2004, 6(2): 117-142.

[162] NAPIER J, LENEHAM M. It was difficult to manage the communication: Testing the feasibility of video remote signed language interpreting in court[J]. Journal of interpretation, 2011, 21(1): 5.

[163]NAPIER J, SKINNER R, TURNER G H. "It's good for them but not so for me": Inside the sign language interpreting call centre[J]. Translation &interpreting, 2017, 9(2): 1-23.

[164]NÁPOLES A M et al. Clinician ratings of interpreter mediated visits in underserved primary care settings with ad hoc, in-person professional, and video conferencing modes[J]. Journal of health care for the poor and underserved, 2010, 21(1): 301-317.

[165] NISKA H. Explorations in translational creativity: Strategies for

interpreting neologisms[J]. Interpreting, 1998, 2(1): 375-402.

[166]NISHIYAMA S. Simultaneous interpreting in Japan and the role of television: A personal narration[J]. Meta, 1988(1): 64-69.

[167]NORRIS S. Editor's introduction[J]. Multimodalcommunication, 2012 (1): 3-4.

[168]OVIATT S, COHEN P. Spoken language in interpreted telephone dialogues[J]. Computer speech and language, 1992, 6(3): 277-302.

[169]OZOLINS U. The myth of the myth of invisibility? [J]. Interpreting, 2016(2): 273-284.

[170]OZOLINS U. Telephone interpreting: Understanding practice and identifying research needs[J]. Translation &interpreting, 2011, 3(2): 33-47.

[171]PASQUANDREA S. Co-constructing dyadic sequences in healthcare interpreting: A multimodal account [J]. New voices in translation studies, 2012, 8(1): 132-157.

[172]PÖCHHACKER F. Quality assessment in conference and community interpreting[J]. Meta, 2001, 46(2): 410-425.

[173] PÖCHHACKER F. Research and methodology in healthcare interpreting [J]. Linguisticaantverpiensia, new series-themes in translation studies, 2006(5): 135-159.

[174]POTTER J. Discourse analysis[J]. Handbook of data analysis, 2004: 607-624.

[175]PARTON S. Distance education brings deaf students, instructors, and interpreters closer together: a review of prevailing practices, projects, and perceptions[J]. Internationaljournal of instructional technology and distance learning, 2005, 2(1): 65-75.

[176]POYATOS F. Language and nonverbal systems in the structure of face-to-face interaction[J]. Language &communication, 1983, 3(2): 129-140.

[177]PRICE E L, PÉREZ-STABLE E J, NICKLEACH D, LÓPEZ M, KARLINER L S. Interpreter perspectives of in-person, telephonic, and videoconferencing medical interpretation in clinical encounters [J]. Patient education and counseling, 2012, 87(2), 226-232.

[178] RICCARDI A. On the evolution of interpreting strategies in simultaneous interpreting[J]. Meta, 2005, 50(2): 753-767.

[179] ROZINER I, SHLESINGER M. Much ado about something remote: stress and performance in remote interpreting[J]. Interpreting, 2010, 12(2): 214-247.

[180] ROY C. The problem with definitions, descriptions and the role metaphor of interpreters[J]. Journal of interpretation, 1993, 6(1):127-153

[181] SACKS H. An analysis of the course of a joke's telling in conversation [J]. Explorations in the ethnography of speaking, 1974(8): 337-353.

[182] SADLER D R. Formative assessment and the design of instructional systems[J]. Instructional science, 1989, 18(2): 119-144.

[183] SACKS H et al. A simplest systematics for the organization of turn-taking in conversation[J]. Language, 1974(50): 696-736.

[184] SCHJOLDAGER A. Interpreting research and the "manipulation school" of translation studies[J]. International journal of translation studies, 1995, 7(1): 29-45.

[185] SEEBER K G, KERZEL D. Cognitive load in simultaneous interpreting: Model meets data [J]. Internationaljournal of bilingualism, 2012, 16(2): 228-242.

[186] SELHI T. Interpretation on the Internet[J]. Aiic communicate, 2000 (10): 2000.

[187] SELESKOVITCH D. L'interprétation de conférence[J]. Babel, 1962, 8(1): 13-18.

[188] SELESKOVITCH D. Language and cognition [J]. Language interpretation and communication, 1978: 333-341.

[189] SELLERS R. Video interviewing and its impact on recruitment[J]. Strategic interview, 2014, 13(3).

[190] SHLESINGER M. Shifts in cohesion in simultaneous interpreting[J]. The translator, 1995, 1(2): 193-214.

[191] SHLESINGER M. Interpreting as a Cognitive Process: How can we know what really happens? [J]. Benjamins translation library, 2000 (37): 3-16.

[192]SPIELBERGER C D. Anxiety, drive theory, and computer-assisted learning[J]. Progexp pers res, 1972(6): 109-148.

[193]SPIELBERGER C D. State-trait anxiety inventory for adults[J]. Psyctests, 1983.

[194]SQUARE R L, GERVER D. Language and language teaching:Current research in Europe: Britain[J]. Language teaching, 1979, 12(1): 59-65.

[195]STEINER B. Signs from the void: Te comprehension and production of sign language on television[J]. Interpreting, 1998, 3(2): 99-146.

[196]STOWE S, HARDING S. Technology applied to geriatric medicine. Telecare, telehealth and telemedicine[J]. European geriatric medicine, 2010(1): 193-197.

[197] STOLL K H. Zukunftsperspektiven der Translation [J]. Lebendesprachen, 2000, 45(2): 49-59.

[198]STRONG M, RUDSER S F. An assessment instrument for sign language interpreters[J]. Sign language studies, 1985: 343-362.

[199] SUMBY W H, POLLACK I. Visual contribution to speech intelligibility in noise[J]. The journal of the acoustical society of america, 1954, 26(2): 212-215.

[200]TANNEN D. Discourse analysis: The excitement of diversity[J]. Text-interdisciplinary journal for the study of discourse, 1990, 10(1-2): 109-112.

[201]TEBBLE H. Te tenor of consultant physicians. Implications for medical interpreting[J]. Thc Translator, 1999(5): 179-200.

[202]TURNER R H. Role-taking, role standpoint, and reference-group behaviour[J]. American journal of sociology, 1956, 61(4):316-328.

[203]TURNER G H, MERRISON A J. Doing "understanding" in dialogue interpreting: Advancing theory and method[J]. International journal of research and practice in interpreting, 2016, 18(2): 137-171.

[204]TURNER G H, NAPIER J, SKINNER R, et al. Telecommunication relay services as a tool for deaf political participation and citizenship[J]. Information,communication & society, 2017, 20(10): 1521-1538.

[205]VERREPT H, COUNE I. Guide for intercultural mediation in health

care[J]. Brussels: Federal public service public health, food chain safety and environment, 2016: 1-33.

[206]VIAGGIO S. Towards a more precise distinction between context and situation, intention and sense[J]. Review of general psychology, 1999, 24(3): 268-283. .

[207] WANG Y. Supportingsynchronous distance language learning with desktop videoconferencing[J]. Language learning & technology, 2004, 8(3): 90-121.

[208]WADENSJÖ C. Telephone interpreting and the synchronisation of talk in social interaction[J]. The translator, 1999(2): 301-318.

[209] WANG J H. Telephone interpreting should be used only as a last resort. Interpreters perceptions of the suitability, remuneration and quality of telephone interpreting [J]. Perspectives: Studies in translation theory and practice, 2017: 100-116.

[210]WANG J H. I only interpret the content and ask practical questions when necessary[J]. Perspectives, 2021, 29(4): 625-642.

[211]WESSLING D M, SHAW S. Persistent emotional extremes and video relay service interpreters[J]. Journal of interpretation, 2014, 23(1): 6.

[212]WIDDOWSON H G. Rules and procedures in discourse analysis[J]. Explorations in applied linguistics, 1979: 138-146.

[213] WILSS W. Syntactic anticipation in German-English simultaneous interpreting[J]. Language interpretation and communication, 1978: 343-352.

[214]WONG J, FAUVERGE A. Leverage: Reciprocal peer tutoring over broadband networks[J]. Recall, 1999, 11(1): 133-142.

[215]YOUNG R, LEE J. Identifying units in interaction: Reactive tokens in Korean and English conversations [J]. Journal of sociolinguistics (Special issue: Acquisition of sociolinguistic competence), 2004: 380-407.

[216]ZAUBERGA I. Variables in quality assessment in interpreting[J]. Dolmetschen: Beiträge ausforschung, lehre und praxis, 2001(30): 279.

[217] ANDERSON L. Simultaneous interpretation: Contextual and translation aspects[D]. Montreal: Concordia University, 1979.

［218］BRUNSON J L. The practice and organization of sign language interpreting in video relay service: An institutional ethnography of access［D］. Syracuse: Syracuse University, 2008.

［219］Chernov G V. Theory and practice of simultaneous interpretation (in Russian). Translated by JR Myers［D］. Monterey: Monterey Institute of International Studies, 1978.

［220］DE BOE E. Remote interpreting in healthcare settings: A comparative study on the influence of telephone and video link use on the quality of interpreter-mediated communication［D］. Antwerp: University of Antwerp, 2020.

［221］DEVAUX J. Technologies ininterpreter-medicated criminal court hearings: An actor-network account on the interpreter's perception of her role-space［D］. Manchester: University of Salford, 2017.

［222］GERVER D. Aspects of simultaneous interpretation and human information processing［D］. Oxford: Oxford University. 1971.

［223］LIONTOU K. Anticipation in german to greek simultaneous interpreting: A corpus-based approach［D］. Wien: Universitat Wien, 2012.

［224］MOSER-MERCER B. Simultaneous translation: Linguistic, psycholinguistic, and human information processing aspects: dissertation［D］. Nairobi: University of Nairobi, 1976.

［225］REINHARDT L R. Deaf-hearing interpreter teams: Navigating trust in shared space［D］. Monmouth: University of Western Oregon, 2015.

［226］STENZL C. Simultancous interpretation groundwork towards a comprehensive model［D］. London: University of London, 1983.

附录
双语庭审远程视频口译手册

This handbook is designed to be a comprehensive guide to the use of videoconference (VC) in legal proceedings where such proceedings are conducted with the assistance of an interpreter, leading to situations of bilingual (or multilingual) videoconferencing. The handbook applies to the use of VC in judicial and law enforcement proceedings at national level and to cases of mutual legal assistance, which entail cross-border videoconferencing.

The use of a VC creates a specific type of communication. It comes with its own challenges and opportunities, which need to be thoroughly understood to guarantee its efficient use. Despite their many technical, logistical, organisational and communicative complexities, video links are often seen as an "on-demand" service that can be used without prior induction and training. However, the research into bilingual videoconferencing in legal proceedings conducted in the European AVIDICUS projects (2008-16) has shown that VC communication can be challenging, especially when it is combined with interpreting services. This handbook offers guidance for the effective and efficient use of VCs in bilingual legal proceedings. It promotes awareness of the basic training requirements for all parties involved and provides indications on how this training should be organised and delivered.

This guide is designed for the following user groups:

—Policy makers interested in learning more about good practices in order to develop or improve the procedures of procuring and implementing VC at institutional level;

—Legal professionals (e. g. judges, lawyers, prosecutors, court clerks, police officers) using VC in their everyday work at different levels, from organising VCs to handling or chairing them, or even "just" VC participation;

—Legal interpreters wishing to expand their knowledge about VC communication for their continuous professional development;

—Technicians tasked with installing, maintaining and managing VC equipment, setting up and operating VC sessions.

The handbook may also serve as a resource for eliciting guidance for speakers of another language who take part in video links as litigants, witnesses, victims, accused persons, suspects or defendants and require the assistance of an interpreter.

This introduction will outline the structure of the handbook, explain how to consult this resource, and present an overview of the potential settings and configurations of bilingual legal VCs, and cover the main concepts and relevant terminology linked to this practice.

1.1 Structure of the handbook

The handbook is organised around themes. Each theme is covered in a different section. Users can choose to consult one, more or all the sections depending on their level of involvement with VC, their (potential) role in video links, their previous knowledge of the subject and individual interests. The following themes are covered:

—*Uses of Bilingual Videoconferencing* (legal settings in which VCs are used)

—*Procurement and Implementation* (choice of equipment appropriate for bilingual VCs)

—*VC Connection and Equipment* (technical requirements and support for bilingual VCs)

—*Participant Distribution* (location of the parties and the interpreter during bilingual VCs)

—*Pre-VC/Post-VC* (preparation of VCs and debriefing of participants after conclusion of the VC)

—*Mode of Interpreting* (method used by interpreters to relay questions and answers)

—*VC Management* (effective management of bilingual VCs)

—*Communication Management* （maintaining communication flow and interaction）

—*Further Support and Training* （features and organisation of training for all VC participants）

Each theme-related section includes

—A *highlight* box at the beginning，presenting the most important points to consider for VC practice；

—The main body of the text，which moves from a general overview relevant to all stakeholders to specific VC issues and opportunities；

—A *summary* box at the end，containing the main relevant points for each user group.

The final section of this handbook provides suggestions on how to organise and deliver training in VC for bilingual legal proceedings.

1. 2　Using this resource

As outlined above，the sections of this handbook can be consulted individually as stand-alone units. However，users are strongly advised to read the entire handbook，as the themes covered in the individual sections are often intertwined. Users who access this resource because they are tasked with designing/updating a VC system may find a thorough reading of all sections particularly helpful in order to gain extensive knowledge of VC issues. A VC solution that is well designed not only from the point of view of technical equipment，but also from the point of view of the organisation of human resources is an important step towards offering a VC service that meets the needs of all participants. This is all the more important as judicial and law enforcement authorities are increasingly turning towards videoconferencing an alternative solution for logistically complex proceedings involving courts，prisons and police stations. VC solutions must therefore take account of the needs of all participants.

As the factors influencing the decisions about VC solutions at national level will be different for individual countries and institutions，different VC solutions may be more or less appropriate for responding to local needs. Therefore，this handbook does not advocate the use of specific systems， setups or solutions. Rather, it proposes guidelines that should be considered along with knowledge of local procedures, needs and states of affairs for the creation of tailored solutions. Where good practices regarding the use of VC have been identified (irrespective of a country's individual circumstances), these are included in this handbook and supported by examples.

Links between sections have been made explicit in this handbook by means of cross-references to other sections placed next to the relevant paragraph.

1. 3　Bilingual VC illegal proceedings: Key concepts, definitions, configurations

This section outlines key concepts and definitions that will be used throughout the document. This handbook refers to proceedings that include *bilingual videoconferencing*, i. e. proceedings involving all of the following:

a. at least one party or witness who is not (sufficiently) proficient in the official language

b. an interpreter

c. a video link

and where the video link is used in one or more of the following ways:

i. To connect the party or witness who requires an interpreter to the proceedings;

ii. To connect a legal professional or expert from their location (e. g. office) to the proceedings;

iii. To connect a lawyer with a client who requires an interpreter to communicate with the lawyer;

iv. To connect the interpreter to the proceedings (including investigative interviews) or to the lawyer-client communication ("remote interpreting").

These settings are not interchangeable, as they respond to different communication needs. Settings i to iii refer to settings in which those who need to communicate with each other, e. g. a court and a witness or a lawyer and a client, are in different locations. By contrast, setting iv refers to a setting in which the interpreter is separated from the other participants. Some of the settings can be combined, leading to videoconferences with more than two sites.

The common denominator of these settings is that they involve a combination of videoconferencing with bilingual, interpreter-mediated communication. From an interpreter's perspective, the settings require different methods of *video-mediated interpreting* (*VMI*).

Each setting can have different configurations regarding the geographical/physical distribution of the participants, including the location of the interpreter. In the remainder of this section, each setting and its configurations will be briefly explained. Sections 2 and 5 of this handbook (Uses of bilingual videoconferencing; Participant distribution) will distinguish the different settings and configurations in more detail.

i. The VC is used to connect a party or witness who requires an interpreter to the proceedings

This setting refers to the use of a video link between the site of a judicial or law enforcement authority (the "main site"), e. g. a court or police station, and a person at a different site (the "remote site") who requires the services of an interpreter. Although legislation about who can participate in legal proceedings via video link differs between countries, the person at the remote site can, in principle, be a person accused or suspected of a crime, a defendant, witness or victim in criminal proceedings; an asylum seeker in asylum/immigration proceedings; or a litigant or witness in civil proceedings. Typical examples of this setting are video links between a court and a defendant in prison for different types of pre-trial hearings or links between a court and a witness who testifies from a separate room (e. g. a vulnerable witness) or another court house (e. g. a witness in another country).

In cross-border proceedings, where video links are most commonly used for witness testimony, the court or authority who needs to hear the witness is the "requesting court" or "requesting authority", and the witness is located at the "requested court" or with the "requested authority".

Different configurations are possible with regard to the interpreter's location. S/he can be co-located with those speaking the official language of the proceedings or with the party who does not speak the official language. These configurations are illustrated in Figures 1 and 2 below respectively.

Each figure shows an investigative interview, i. e. a small-group setting, and a court hearing. A third option is for the interpreter to be located at a third site, leading to a three-way video link.

ii. The VC is used to connect a legal professional or expert from their location (e. g. office) to the proceedings

This refers to a range of settings that are still infrequent, but that may play a more important role in the near future. For example, it is possible that a defence lawyer, prosecutor, investigating judge or other legal professional participates in a court hearing by video link from his or her own office. Similarly, an expert witness can attend court by video link.

All of these settings have a bilingual element if they involve a party or witness who requires interpretation. For example, when the defendant is physically present in the courtroom but the prosecutor attends by video link, the interpreter will relay to the defendant not only what those present in the courtroom say but also what the remote prosecutor says; the defendant's utterances will have to be relayed to those present in court and to the remote prosecutor. The interpreter would typically be in court in this setting, but it is also possible that s/he works from another location. The latter would be a combination of settings i and iv.

Furthermore, a combination of settings i and ii is possible. A court may connect to a remote defendant in prison and a remote prosecutor in his/her own office. Such settings are largely unexplored with regard to the most appropriate location for the interpreter.

iii. The VC is used to connect a lawyer with a client who requires an interpreter to communicate with the lawyer

This setting involves the private communication between lawyers and their clients before, during or after law enforcement or judicial proceedings. Possible configurations are for the lawyer to be in his/her firm or office, and the client to be in a police station or prison (in criminal proceedings), a detention centre (asylum/immigration proceedings) or in a place of his/her choice (in civil proceedings).

Another possible configuration in criminal proceedings is for the lawyer to be in a special room in court and to be linked to a client in prison, e. g. to prepare a pre-trial hearing, in which the client then appears by video link from prison while the lawyer attends in the courtroom.

Given the many variations of this setting, it is difficult to make generalisations about the location of the interpreter. It will often be determined by practical circumstances, but in principle the interpreter can be either co-located with the layer or with the client, or be in a third location.

iv. The VC is used to connect an interpreter to the proceedings (including investigative interviews) or to the lawyer-client communication

This setting is known as "remote interpreting". The interpreter works from a remote site (e. g. an interpreting hub), whilst all other participants are together in the location where the proceedings would traditionally take place, e. g. a courtroom or police custody suite.

The use of VC in legal proceedings is increasing and has many benefits, such as speeding up the proceedings, reducing travel costs and improving public security by avoiding prisoner transport to courts. However, the potential challenges of combining the technological mediation through VC and the lingua-cultural mediation through an interpreter are widely underestimated. The key questions revolve around the impact of combining VC and interpreting on the quality, fairness and efficiency of justice. In more detail, this concerns the effects of VC and interpreting on the quality of the interpretation and the communicative dynamics of the proceedings, how these are affected by the distribution of participants and the mode of interpreting, and whether video-mediated interpreting is sufficiently reliable for legal communication (for purposes such as evidence taking, information gathering, decision-making and delivering justice).

Potential concerns regarding the combination of VC and interpreting come from different sources. Previous studies have highlighted that video-mediated interpreting often magnifies known communication and interpreting problems. Remote participants, and in particular defendants, have reported difficulties in making themselves "heard" by the court and in understanding the content of their own trials. While such concerns do not mean that VC technology is unsuitable for legal proceedings, they point to the need for a greater understanding of the issues at stake from multiple points of view.

This handbook is designed to address this need.

2 Uses of Bilingual Videoconferencing Highlights

- The main motivations for the use of VC at national level are logistical difficulties, time efficiency, cost reduction, enhancement of public security and access to qualified interpreters.
- The same motivations may also play a role in the use of VC for cross-border hearings, along with the need to provide mutual legal assistance.
- Witnesses may appear remotely due to factors such as vulnerability and distance. The decision to have a person appear by VC should not undermine the fairness of the proceedings.
- VC is useful for brief events, especially with a small number of participants. Its use for long or complex proceedings with a larger number of participants is not advisable.
- The potential impact of VC technology on an interpreter's performance has to be taken into account to ensure that the VC does not jeopardise the quality of the communication and interpretation.

Bilingual VCs are currently used for both national and cross-border proceedings. The main motivations for the use of VC at national level include logistical difficulties, time efficiency, reduction of cost, and enhancement of public security. The need to access qualified legal interpreters and the potential to reduce travel costs associated with interpreting are further reasons for VC. Similar motivations also play a role in the use of VC for cross-border hearings. However, in this case an added rationale is the provision of mutual legal assistance and international cooperation with other countries.

Judicial and law enforcement institutions using VCs should agree procedures for deciding whether or not a video link is suitable for a particular situation. The use of video links in legal proceedings is increasingly becoming a default position in relevant legislation, although normally with some exceptions. Alternatively, the decision whether or not to use VC is at the discretion of a judge or other person responsible for the proceedings (e. g. a prosecutor). Where there is discretion, those in charge normally consider factors such as travel costs, seriousness of the crime and the general behaviour of a defendant. Regarding witnesses, issues of vulnerability and distance from the court play an important role. With regard to bilingual proceedings, judges and others making such decisions are advised to exercise caution. The additional layer of complexity that is introduced by linguistic and cultural barriers and by communicating through an interpreter needs to become a further factor in the decision-making process. It is imperative for judges and others to assure themselves that the combination of videoconferencing and interpreting does not undermine the fairness of the proceedings.

One of the factors to take into account is that the attendance of proceedings by video link can influence the participants' communicative behaviour and the participants' mutual perceptions of each other. This can skew the legal practitioner's assessment of a participant's credibility and engagement with the proceedings. For example, a remote participants' poor engagement with the authorities during a VC can normally be attributed to the "distance" created by the technology, which may give a remote participant the feeling of "not really" being before an authority. The video link can thus create a false impression of the remote participant. Linguistic and cultural barriers can magnify these problems.

There is also a risk that remote participants who require the services of an interpreter have difficulty following VC-based proceedings. This should be taken into account in the decision-making process, but it should also be monitored during the VC.

A further factor is the duration of the VC. Interpreters generally feel that interpreting in a VC is more stressful and tiring than working in the traditional settings. As a general principle, the use of VC involving an interpreter should therefore be reserved for brief hearings. If a planned VC is likely to last long (e. g. 2 hours or more), the interpreter should be consulted at the time of booking to find out whether this is manageable or whether two interpreters should be booked to work in a pair. For all VCs, it will be useful to discuss the interpreter's needs, e. g. for a break, before the VC begins.

2. 1 National proceedings

In national proceedings，there is currently a wide range of VC uses in the justice systems that potentially require the integration of an interpreter. Below gives an overview of the uses encountered in different countries.

Criminal Justice

■Links between courts and remote parties，i. e. ：

- Court/Prosecutor—accused at police station for first hearings
- Court—defendant in prison for pre-trial hearings and remote sentencing

■Links between courts and witnesses，i. e. ：

- Court—geographically remote witnesses
- Court—vulnerable witnesses

■Lawyer-client communication

- Lawyer from own office or from court—defendant in prison

■Court reports by probation

- Probation officer from own office—defendant in prison

■Police detention reviews

- Reviewing officer—detainee in custody

Civil Justice

- Links between courts and witnesses at home and overseas
- Lawyer-client communication
- Case management conferences
- Other uses by consent of the parties (e. g. remote lawyers)

Immigration and Asylum

- Links between immigration courts and immigration applicants in detention
- Lawyer-client communication

2. 2 Cross-border proceedings

In cross-border proceedings，the application of video links is more restricted. Although they are used in criminal and civil proceedings，they are primarily employed for witness testimony.

In Europe, cross-border videoconferencing in criminal proceedings has a legislative basis in the 2001 Second Additional Protocol of the 1959 European Convention on Mutual Assistance in Criminal Matters (Council of Europe) and the 2000 European Convention on Mutual Assistance in Criminal Matters between the Member States of the European Union (European Council). The legislation distinguishes between interpreting support for the judicial authority of the requested Member State, who is normally present during the proceedings (at least in criminal cases), and interpreting support for the person to be heard. A distinction therefore needs to be made between the following situations:

A. **The person to be heard speaks the language of the *requesting authority*, but resides permanently or temporarily in a different country.** For example, a Dutch court requests to hear a Dutch citizen who lives in Germany. In relation to this situation, the Conventions state that the judicial authority of the requested court (here: in Germany) shall where necessary be assisted by an interpreter. As the Dutch court would communicate with the Dutch witness in Dutch, an interpreter would be required to interpret from Dutch into German for the benefit of the German judge.

B. **The person to be heard speaks the language of the *requested authority* and resides permanently or temporarily in its territory.** For example, a Dutch court requests to hear a German citizen who lives in Germany. In relation to this, the Conventions state that *at the request of the requesting authority or the person to be heard the requested authority shall ensure that the person to be heard is assisted by an interpreter, if necessary.* An interpreter would be required to interpret between Dutch and German for the benefit of all parties involved.

Due to the presence of two judicial authorities in different jurisdictions, cross-border proceedings generally lead to greater complexity in terms of participant distribution than national proceedings. Given that cross-border hearings via VC often require a rather large amount of preparation, the best solution for handling the linguistic side may be to recruit two interpreters, i. e. one at each side. As an important point in this case, the interpreters should have an opportunity to communicate with each other in advance of the VC in order to agree on how they share the task and how they work together effectively. If only one interpreter is available, it is important to take into account whether the parties speaking the same language are all in one location (as in case B) or not (as in case A).

Other, more complex situations arise when the person to be heard speaks a third language (e. g. if a Dutch court hears a person who resides in Germany but does not speak sufficient German nor Dutch). Such situations may currently be rare, but they require well thought-through solutions designed for the specific circumstances. Two interpreters will normally be required here, i. e. one interpreter in the requesting Dutch court to translate between the third language and Dutch, and another interpreter in Germany to translate from the third language into German for the benefit of the requested German authority.

Summary

- **Policy makers:** While the main motivations for using VCs are multiple (logistics, economy, time-efficiency, public security and access to qualified legal interpreters), the Fair Trial principle should always be considered first. The legislation concerning VC should include recommendations on the typical features which make a proceeding suitable or unsuitable for VC. The need for interpreting services should be an important criterion. Appropriate training of legal professionals in the implementation of the decision for/against the use of VC needs to be developed. For cross-border proceedings, consider the use of two interpreters, one at each side.

- **Legal professionals:** When deciding whether to hold a hearing via VC, consult available guidelines, either through training or documentation. These should be able to guide you through the factors you need to consider to make sure that the proceeding you are about to hold is fair to all participants. Remind yourself that VC is particularly useful for brief events, especially with a contained number of participants. Its use for long or complex proceedings with a large number of participants is not advisable. If you will be using interpreting services, consider the potential impact of VC technology on an interpreter's performance. An interpreter is more likely to experience fatigue in a VC, so you will need to take measures to ensure an appropriate quality of the interpretation. For cross-border proceedings, it is advisable to work with two interpreters, one at each site, and to give the interpreters an opportunity to liaise with each other in advance in order to coordinate the interpreting task. This will provide enhanced interpretation quality, as the interpreters will be able to support each other in their work.

- **Interpreters**：Before attending a proceeding involving a VC, ask your client about the nature of the event if possible. Determine whether this is a national or a cross-border proceeding, and—especially in the latter case—whether there will be an interpreter at the other site. If this is the case, request to be able to contact, and coordinate the task with the other interpreter in advance, and propose arrangements which you believe are suitable for the communicative situation. Remember that you are more likely to experience fatigue when interpreting in VC. Find out the expected duration of the hearing. If you believe this may be too long for you, notify the authority that you will need a break and discuss when this is to take place. If a hearing is likely to be particularly long, discuss with the authority the possibility of pairing you up with a colleague.

- **Technicians**：Cross-border proceedings are often held with VC sites which may have equipment that is different from yours. Check their technical requirements, and test the connection beforehand to make sure there are no audio/video issues. In the case of hearings involving interpreters, check where they will be located, and verify that your network, along with the one at the other site, has the technical ability to deliver sustained high audio quality.

3 Procurement and Implementation Highlights

- A VC system used in legal proceedings needs to be designed or adjusted to accommodate video-mediated interpreting (VMI).
- The design and implementation or upgrade of the VC system should be overseen by an institutional task force including, and/or consulting with, legal, technological and linguistic experts, and representatives of all relevant stakeholder groups.
- Administrators looking to implement or upgrade VC systems should cooperate with other justice sector organisations which have already implemented VC equipment; they should also identify, and interact with, their counterparts in other countries to source relevant knowledge on the design of VC systems.
- It is strongly advisable to run suitable pilot projects as part of the first experimentation with VC. These should include instances of VMI.
- As part of the pilot project, protocols describing the procedure before, during and after a VC session including a VC session with an interpreter should be developed. Clear risk assessment procedures should also be agreed upon.

One very important point to consider in the process of implementing or upgrading a VC system are minimum standards. At present, there are recommendations for minimum standards for VC in cross-border legal proceedings, which were developed by the Informal Working Group (IWG) on Cross-border Videoconferencing in its 2015 report. Whilst these recommendations also provide a useful starting point for the implementation and upgrade of VC facilities used for national proceedings, there are no specific standards for bilingual videoconferences with interpreters yet. However, given current and expected future levels of multilingualism and migration in Europe, the demand for interpreting in VCs will increase. In the mid-term, the IWG recommendations should therefore be developed further at European level to cover the specifics of bilingual videoconferencing. In the absence of standards for bilingual videoconferencing, the specific requirements for bilingual videoconferencing, which have emerged from our research, should be given special consideration when VC facilities are implemented or updated in a justice sector institution.

Interpreting is much more than "replacing" words. Interpreters need to process what is said very thoroughly in order to identify the communicative message accurately and completely, and relay it in another language. This requires more concentration and cognitive effort than normal listening, and any disturbance such as muffled or tinny sound, breaking up of the sound or lack of lip and sound synchronisation will affect an interpreters' ability to concentrate and listen. Non-verbal clues also need to be readily available to facilitate comprehension. In light of this, the specific requirements for bilingual videoconferencing with an interpreter extend in the first place to the following aspects:

- The sound and image quality: Interpreters generally feel that their specific requirements for sound and image quality in VCs need to be taken into account better than is currently the case.

- The stability of the VC connection: Interpreters have drawn attention to the problems created by micro-breaks in the sound transmission, which can lead to part of a word being lost;

- Lip synchronisation: A lack of lip synchronisation is very distracting for interpreters trying to concentrate on identifying the communicative message from what is being said;

- The use of peripheral equipment: For example, the use of omni-directional microphones can create sound reverberation and lead to insufficient sound quality and comprehension problems on the part of interpreters.

These requirements apply to all VCs involving interpreters. A further set of requirements is influenced by the type of proceedings, the local situation and other variables, making it difficult to provide general guidelines. This set includes:

- The interpreter's geographical location in relation to the other participants;
- The interpreter's position in relation to the technical equipment;

- The visibility of the interpreter on screen;
- The mode of interpreting.

The remaining sections of this Handbook will discuss these requirements in more detail.

To ensure that a VC system is designed for, or adjusted to, the specific requirements of bilingual communication through an interpreter in the local context of the institution, the design of new VC systems and upgrade of existing systems should be carried out by an institutional task force that includes, and/or consults with, legal, technological and linguistic experts, and representatives of all relevant stakeholders.

The implementation should happen in stages, starting with a series of pilots in a small number of locations. The presence of cases requiring interpretation in the initial pilot should be carefully considered. A common pattern among institutions that have implemented VC facilities is to limit the number of variables in early pilot stages and to exclude cases requiring an interpreter. However, given the growing number of bilingual proceedings, it is important to design VC systems from the outset in such a way that they can accommodate VMI.

Furthermore, even if the use of VC for cases with interpreting is not planned at national level, a demand for interpreting is likely to arise in cross-border cases (both as requesting and requested authority). Therefore, provisions for VMI should always be made. A useful starting point for this can be the overview of main uses of VC shown in Table 1 (Section 2). An institution wishing to implement or upgrade their VC facilities can use this table to identify relevant uses and then explore which of them may require interpreters.

At its conclusion, the pilot should be evaluated against criteria established at its outset. A rigorous evaluation is crucial, including an open debate with all experts about the suitability of the solutions adopted. It is good practice to encourage consultation. In addition to economic and technical factors, the evaluation should embrace communicative factors including interpreting. The Fair Trial principle should be the overarching guideline. The remaining sections in this Handbook will highlight different aspects of bilingual videoconferencing which have been shown in our research to have an impact on the fairness of justice and should therefore be taken into account in the design of a VC system.

Professionals who have agreed to take part in the pilot should receive training through an early-stage induction on how to use the equipment and how to communicate in a VC. It is important to emphasise that, if the pilot includes provisions for the use of interpreting services, interpreters and legal staff should both be trained, if possible in joint training sessions.

If the implementation of VC facilities on a larger scale is decided, a consistent approach should be adopted across the estates of an institution. Technical and legal informants in our studies have pointed out that a consistent approach facilitates the use of the equipment and removes uncertainty about the technical specifications of remote VC sites. This will also be helpful for interpreters as they will know what to expect. More broadly, our research suggests that levels of satisfaction among users of VC systems are generally higher in countries which have piloted their equipment and taken care in ensuring consistency of the VC facilities and standards across their internal network.

Another important aspect in connection with implementing VC facilities is the development of local protocols and guidelines. The institutional task force should oversee this. Protocols need to specify who is responsible for the various tasks arising in connection with the use of VC, i. e.

—Decision on whether to use a VC when an interpreter is required in the proceedings (e. g. type of proceeding, risk assessment procedures);

—Preparation of the VC (e. g. booking, participant selection including interpreter, equipment testing);

—Management of the VC (starting and managing the connection, managing interaction);

—Management of technical problems or breakdowns;

—Closure of the VC (closing procedure, debriefing with participants for assessment).

Summary

• **Policy makers**: In the process of procuring and implementing VC equipment, it is important to take into account not only the standards and requirements for monolingual communication, but also the requirements for bilingual videoconferences involving interpreters. Running a pilot to test the VC facilities and their suitability for the purposes of interpreting is strongly advisable. It will be useful to form a task force that includes representatives from all categories and can act in an advisory capacity. It is pivotal that you include linguistic expertise in this task force. Participants in the pilot should receive basic training. A rigorous evaluation of the pilot is essential. Once the final setup has been agreed, a consistent approach across the estates of your institution is crucial to facilitate the use of the system. Local guidelines and protocol for the various aspects of VC should be developed, e. g. by the task force.

- **Legal professionals**: If you are asked to participate in discussions about the implementation of VC facilities, do not underestimate your role in shaping VC practice in your country. Your feedback will contribute to improving national and international practices. It will be useful to coordinate within your professional association, source feedback from your colleagues on what they believe is important in VCs, including colleagues who have experience in working with interpreters. Also, consult the relevant legislation and think of its possible interpretations.

- **Interpreters**: If you are a member of an interpreters' association and you know that the justice system in your country is looking to implement/upgrade a VC system, inquire with your association about whether your representatives are involved in the procurement/implementation. If this is not the case, encourage your association to start a dialogue on VMI requirements with the relevant authorities. If you are an expert legal interpreter, consider offering your personal expertise. Your presence at the discussion table is important—if no language professional points out the needs of interpreters, it is possible that this may be overlooked. This is likely to result in VC setups which are not suitable for interpreting, and which will make your work in legal settings more difficult.

- **Technicians**：If you are asked to contribute your point of view on VC procurement/implementation，make sure you are well informed not only on the technological state of the art but also on basic requirements for VC communication and interpreting，and that you have a basic understanding of the reasons for these requirements.

4　VC Connection and Equipment Highlights

- The VC connection and equipment must provide high sound and video quality，particularly when VC is used in conjunction with interpreting services.
- The sound transmission must support two-way communication，i. e. turn-taking and overlapping speech.
- Connection stability is fundamental，i. e. the system needs to deliver high sound and video quality continuously. Technical disruptions are likely to have a negative impact on the interpreter's rendition.
- The number and position of VC equipment items such as screens and cameras is crucial for effective
- VC communication and needs to be adjusted to the number and location of participants.
- Rooms designed for small groups may require only one VC screen，so long as this screen is clearly visible to all participants including the interpreter. Larger rooms will require multiple screens for good visibility.
- All participants who are expected to speak should be provided with individual microphones. Interpreters in particular should have a dedicated microphone. Headphones should be provided where applicable.
- All VC sessions should be set up and tested by a technician beforehand.
- Technical assistance should be generally available during a VC in case of a breakdown. Procedures for dealing with technological failure

should be set up by the managing authorities.

The VC connection, and the choice, arrangement and use of VC equipment are crucial for a good VC quality. While this handbook does not advocate the use of specific equipment or setups, this chapter outlines the factors that should inform the choice of connection and equipment in the context of bilingual videoconferencing.

In line with the requirements for interpreting set out in Section 3 above, VC connection and equipment used in bilingual settings must provide the highest possible sound and video quality. Interpreters need to pay attention not only to what is said but also to intonation, pauses in speech and the speaker's non-verbal clues in order to grasp the complete communicative message and provide a high-quality rendition. Audio and video signal need to deliver high quality both separately and together. It is also essential for audio and video to be synchronised to avoid distraction.

A case in point is sound transmission. As legal communication is often two-way communication (and, when interpreting is involved, three-way communication), the system needs to be designed with dialogue, i. e. turn-taking between speakers, and the possibility of overlapping speech in mind. Sound transmission should be full-duplex, with audio from both (or all) locations being transmitted at the same time without loss of information. Echo cancellation should also be used to minimise noise.

Connection stability is another essential factor, both for VCs in general and in particular for the use of VMI. While good equipment is crucial, it is also of the utmost importance that the equipment is connected to broadband networks that are capable of supporting high-quality streams of audio and video data without disruption. Legal informants as well as interpreters have reported a general "technological anxiety" when using systems that are not reliable, e. g. when the sound suddenly cuts out or the image quality drops, and that this impacts negatively on their inclination to use VC. Among interpreters, technical issues generate concerns about not being able to hear or be heard.

System quality and stability may be affected when a court connects to remote sites external to its network. This is typical of cross-border hearings, but in some countries VC is used at national level to connect to private network and devices, e. g. for the hearing of witnesses. While courts can determine their own technical standards and security requirements, external actors may use different standards. This may generate quality problems in the connection. The appropriateness of such links should be considered carefully, especially if an interpreter is involved in the proceeding.

Furthermore, the number and position of equipment items is key for effective VC communication. The number of VC participants in different settings can vary considerably, from one-to-one sessions, such as lawyer-client consultations, to much larger proceedings. The distribution of participants is also highly variable. Generalisations are therefore difficult but the following points should be considered.

First, several points arise with regard to the cameras. The general purpose of VC cameras is to offer a view of all speakers to the participants in the proceedings. The number and position of the cameras therefore needs to be determined in relation to the number and location of the expected participants. Rotating cameras present a more flexible resource than fixed cameras but they require operation during a VC session. In either case, different camera positions can normally be saved as pre-sets in the VC system and quickly retrieved. This is particularly useful in court proceedings, where different participants speak in turn. One important point for bilingual VCs is that a pre-set position should be created for the place the interpreter occupies. This will ensure that the interpreter can be made visible to the remote side promptly as soon as s/he takes the floor. This handbook strongly advises that interpreters should be visible on screen. Seeing the interpreter is crucial for accessing his/her non-verbal communication (which may indicate uncertainty, doubt etc). It also helps understand more quickly when their delivery is completed and someone else may take the floor again.

A separate document camera should be used to show documents, images and other material relevant to the proceedings. Given that it may be used to show minute details, this camera should have a particularly high resolution. Importantly, the interpreter needs to have access to images from the document camera.

VC rooms designed for remote participants (e. g. prison VC rooms or witness VC rooms) are normally much smaller than a court, and normally require only one camera. However, it is important to select a camera with a wide angle to facilitate showing more than one person simultaneously, i. e. a remote party or witness together with the interpreter and possibly a lawyer. Furthermore, a zoom function at the remote side is important to enable a witness or defendant to demonstrate physical actions to a court (e. g. to indicate how they were hit during an aggression). Similar points about camera choice also apply to other small rooms used for VC in legal settings, e. g. police interview rooms and VC rooms in court that are used by lawyers to communicate with clients in prison before or after a hearing.

Second, the number of screens required also depends on the number of participants. Rooms designed for small groups may be equipped with one VC screen, so long as this is clearly visible to all participants. As mentioned above, the interpreter in particular requires a very good view of all speakers to carry out their task. Therefore, extra care should be taken in positioning the interpreter with respect to the screen. If the number of participants means that it is impossible to share a single screen without compromising good visibility for all parties, multiple screens should be installed. Text, diagrams and images displayed by the document camera should be clearly visible to the interpreter, especially if these need to be orally translated during the proceedings.

Third, it is important that all participants who are expected to speak in the proccedings are provided with individual microphones (unidirectional microphones are recommended to limit background noise). This applies especially to interpreters. The task of linguistic mediation requires high levels of focus and attention to communicative details. Sharing a microphone with one or more participants would require interpreters to divert part of their attention to microphone management, reducing their ability to focus on interpreting. Interpreters also need to be able to mute their microphone.

Whenever possible, the interpreter should also be offered the use of headphones. Good quality headphones help with background noise cancellation and improve the interpreter's ability to listen carefully to the current speaker. Furthermore, interpreters should be provided with volume control.

When remote interpreting is used, particular attention should be paid to the preparation of the remote interpreting facilities (e. g. in an interpreting hub). Especially the acoustics and sound quality in the location of the remote interpreter need to be considered thoroughly (including volume control for the interpreter and headsets where appropriate, as explained above). However, the use of appropriate screens, the interpreter's distance from the screen and other factors such as lighting and ventilation are important as well. It is crucial to involve interpreters in the planning and set-up of facilities for remote interpreting.

Unless a video link is used frequently and its functioning is monitored on a regular basis, VCs should be set up and tested by a technician beforehand. This is especially important for video links with remote sites that are "new" to an institution's network and/or whose technical specifications are unknown. In such cases, the link should be tested in the presence of the interpreter to check that audio and video quality meet the interpreter's needs. In addition, technical assistance should also be available during a VC. Procedures for dealing with technological failure should be set up by the managing authorities.

After the initial installation, VC equipment should be kept up to date. VC administrators should periodically investigate the possibility of upgrading the equipment to maintain the highest standards. Where an upgrade to the existing system is considered necessary, this should be piloted and then progressively rolled out to the entire network to achieve the highest possible level of consistency.

An audio feature which may require consideration in the mid-term is the inclusion of multiple, independent sound channels in the system to support simultaneous interpretation remotely. This can remove the need for the interpreter to be co-located with any of the main participants, leading to a three-point VC. Alternatively it would enable an interpreter who is located in court to deliver a simultaneous rendition to a remote witness or defendant. (At present, this is only possible in the form of whispered interpreting when

the interpreter is co-located with the remote witness or defendant.)
However, the use of simultaneous interpretation in legal proceedings requires
further discussion; many stakeholders feel that it is not suitable for all types
of proceedings. For example, highly interactive parts of legal proceedings
such as investigative interviews and witness examination are traditionally
rendered in consecutive mode. Furthermore, if the law of a country
determines that the interpretation needs to be recorded as well as the original
speech, a system designed for consecutive interpretation only may be more
suitable. However, additional audio channels may be useful for cases that
require interpretation into/out of multiple languages.

Summary

- Policy makers: VC equipment that is used in conjunction with
  interpreters must provide high sound and video quality and connection
  stability at all times. As your system is likely to be used with VMI,
  make sure that you take into account the presence of an interpreter in
  the technical specifications. The use of interpreting services requires
  adjustments to a monolingual set-up and additional peripheral
  equipment to ensure that the interpreter has appropriate access to
  sound and images, and can be heard and seen by all participants.
  Consult with technicians to make sure the technical specifications are
  adequate to your needs. The appropriate level of technical assistance
  will need to be considered as well.

- **Technicians**: You may be asked to help draft VC requirements for
  procurement, or help with the installation of equipment. In either
  case, you should ensure that interpreter-specific technical
  requirements are covered. Equipment should be state-of-the-art and
  installed on a network that supports synchronised audio and video
  transmission without loss of information. Peripherals are also
  important: In the process of room design, consider how many VC
  screens and cameras you will need and where to position them—all
  participants including the interpreter should be able to see and hear
  clearly (see also Ch. 8 VC Management). Participants who are

expected to speak should have individual microphones. The interpreter's place requires special attention. It should have its own microphone and a very good view of the VC screen. In some settings, headphones will be useful.

5 Participant Distribution Highlights

- The physical location of some of the participants in VC-based proceedings is normally pre-determined (e. g. in court—in prison). However, there are often options for the location of other participants and that of the interpreter.
- There are advantages and drawbacks to all possible interpreter locations. The options should be carefully considered in the context of the situation.
- Strong asymmetries in the participants' distribution should be avoided, where possible. Where applicable, the other-language speaker should be co-located with at least one other participant, e. g. a representative of the authority or a lawyer, and the interpreter.
- When a defendant and his/her lawyer are in different locations, a video link should be made available for a lawyer-client consultation before and after the proceeding. If an interpreter is required for this, s/he must be part of the video link.
- A three-way video link should be considered as a way of integrating the interpreter into VC-based proceedings in which the main participants themselves are distributed.
- When the interpreter is separated from all of the main participants ("remote interpreting"), due attention needs to be paid to ensuring that the interpreter can carry out his/her task satisfactorily.

In the various VC settings in which the main participants themselves are distributed (see section 1. 3), the location of the main participants is normally pre-determined. In court proceedings, for example, the judge and the legal representatives will normally be in court, while one of the parties or a witness will appear by video link to the court. The interpreter may attend from either location, or from a third site. Each of these configurations has advantages and drawbacks, which are outlined below. Similarly, in investigative interviews with remote witnesses or suspects and in probation or custody reviews with remote suspects, the legal authority (e. g. a police officer or prosecutor) will be linked to the remote other-language speaker from his/her office. Again, the interpreter can be co-located with either side or work from a third location. Only the setting of "remote interpreting" is different in that in it the main participants are together on site, whilst the interpreter works from a remote location.

Interpreter co-located with the other-language speaker: Among the advantages is the opportunity to talk to the client prior to the video link, e. g. to carry out a language check without taking up time allocated to the hearing. Furthermore, this configuration gives the interpreter direct access to' the other-language speaker's facial expressions and other non-verbal behaviour, which is crucial for the comprehension and contextualisation of their utterances. The physical closeness makes it is easier to build a relationship with the other-language speaker, clarify potential misunderstandings and also to provide some emotional support (often merely by the presence of a person understanding and speaking the minority speaker's language). This is especially important if the other-language speaker is a particularly vulnerable person. Furthermore, the interpreter can use whispered simultaneous interpreting in this configuration to deliver the interpretation to the other-language speaker, which helps to speed up the proceedings.

Drawbacks of this configuration mainly relate to settings in which the other-language speaker is a defendant in prison. First, the interpreter needs to travel to the prison and submit themselves to security checks, increasing the time they spend on the interpreting assignment. Also, rooms in prison are perceived as undesirable working environments by interpreters. The physical closeness to an inmate may be intimidating for an interpreter, even if a prison guard is present, and may undermine the legal professional's perception of the interpreter's impartiality. There is furthermore a possibility that the interpreter takes on other roles such as explaining legal concepts to an inmate. The latter happens especially when the defence lawyer attends from court rather than from prison. This points to the fact that the location of the interpreter in this setting is closely linked to the location of the defence lawyer.

If the defence lawyer attends in court, another problem can arise from the nature of hearings with remote defendants. Given that the defence lawyer tends to talk on the defendant's behalf, while the defendant often says little, the interpreter needs to make sure that everything that is said in court (by the defence lawyer and the others) is interpreted. It will be important to give the interpreter enough time to do so. By contrast, if the defence lawyer attends the hearing from prison, it is more practicable for the interpreter to attend from prison as well. Otherwise, it will be difficult to interpret any confidential communication between the lawyer and the client during the hearing.

The interpreter is co-located with the authorities speaking the official language: In this configuration legal professionals can control the amount of interaction between the interpreter and the witness/defendant. However, the distance from the remote participant reduces the interpreter's relationship with the other-language speaker and removes the possibility for an introduction and language check prior to the VC session. The interpreter cannot use whispered simultaneous interpreting to deliver the rendition of utterances in court to the remote participant. The use of consecutive interpreting throughout a long hearing is time-consuming. In asylum hearings it has also been pointed out that a remote asylum applicant may perceive an interpreter who is in court as a "collaborator" of the authorities.

In small-group settings such as investigate interviews, probation and custody reviews, and lawyer-client consultations conducted via video link it will often be more practicable for the interpreter to be co-located with the person speaking the official language (e. g. in the prosecutor's, police officer's or defence lawyer's office). Given the small size of the group, any drawbacks arising from this can be compensated more easily.

The multi-faceted nature of each configuration makes it difficult to provide general guidance on the "best" place for the interpreter. One possible solution to mitigate the problems and disadvantages of each setting are to

integrate the interpreter from a separate third location, which requires a three-way video link. At first sight, a three-way video link may lead to a more equal distribution of opportunities to contribute to the communication for all participants including the interpreter. However, research shows that this setting comes with its own challenges. Removing the interpreter from all main participants makes this configuration more similar to "remote interpreting", which is generally considered to be more difficult than interpreting while being co-located with one or some of the participants. It increases the interpreter's distance to the participants and the co-ordination effort required on the part of the interpreter. It may push the interpreter into a moderator role. Furthermore, a three-way video link is likely to work more smoothly when additional sound channels are available to enable simultaneous interpretation, which presents other practical problems in legal settings (see Chapter 7 Mode of Interpreting). Given the potential benefits of three-way video links, however, their use should be explored further from the point of view of technological implementation and communicative dynamics. In any case, it is important to include the interpreter in the decision of whether to use a three-way video link it a specific situation.

Another solution to resolve problems with configurations in which the interpreter is co-located with one of two sites is to appoint two interpreters, one on each site, which is advisable for longer proceedings, especially witness examinations. When two interpreters are appointed, it is important that they can liaise with each other prior to the video link to coordinate their co-operation.

Summary

- Policy makers: In order to enable maximum flexibility in the organisation of video links, the provisions you prepare need to make it explicit that the location of some participants is not pre-determined, and should be discussed on a case-by-case basis to achieve the optimal participant distribution. In your provisions, encourage legal professionals to consider that strongly imbalanced configurations can create a feeling of isolation in the other-language speaker. When you prepare local guidelines for the use of your VC system, you may wish to mention explicitly all the available options regarding the location of the interpreter. The introduction to this handbook can be helpful in drafting this part of your guidelines. With regard to court-prison video links, encourage legal professionals to think about where the defence lawyer and the interpreter will be located. Point out possible options—but make sure that you include provisions for separate lawyer-client consultation links for cases in which the lawyer attends the hearing from the main site. Consider the use of three-way video links to integrate an interpreter into the proceedings.

- **Legal professionals**: You will need to think about where the participants in the VC proceeding are located. Some of them may have to attend the hearing from a specific site (the judge, the prosecutor), while the position of others can be negotiated (the lawyer, the interpreter). In organising your proceeding, make sure that you avoid strongly unbalanced situations. The other-language speaker should always be co-located with someone else. Consult with interpreters to determine their optimal location. If it is not highly impractical, encourage lawyers to attend the hearing from the remote site. That way, their client may be able to ask them questions about the proceedings. If the lawyer is attending the proceeding from the main site, make sure that you can set up a separate video link for a lawyer-client consultation before and after the proceeding.

- **Interpreters**: Consider carefully your location during a VC, as each configuration will come with advantages and challenges. Depending on the circumstances of a proceeding, it may be more appropriate for you to attend from the main or the remote site, and there is often no configuration that is objectively "better" than others. If you are asked where you would like to attend the hearing from, do not dismiss the importance of the question. Ask about details regarding the VC. Is there any particular reason why the legal professional thinks you should attend from one or the other side? Is it a witness or a defendant requiring your services? If you are asked to go to a prison, who else will be there? If you have any concerns about the location you have been assigned, warn the authority as soon as possible and explain why you think the chosen configuration is not adequate.

6 Pre-VC/Post-VC Highlights

- Thorough preparation of all VCs is essential, both from a technical and a communicative point of view.
- Each institution should clarify the procedure for setting up and booking a VC, both in general and with additional provisions for the presence of an interpreter. All participants should know in advance that a video link will be used.
- Interpreters working in legal VC settings should be provided with documents outlining at least the basic elements of the communicative situation—briefing an interpreter does not reduce their ability to be impartial.
- Allowing the interpreter some contact with the other-language speaker prior to the hearing, e. g. to perform a language check, is important, regardless of whether the two are co-located or not.
- If possible and appropriate, it would be beneficial to have a short debriefing with the interpreter after the VC session to obtain their feedback.
- Any reported problems should be dealt with as soon as possible, and discussed with legal professionals, interpreters and technology providers as appropriate.

Thorough preparation of all VCs is essential, both from the technical and the communicative point of view. VC equipment should be tested regularly to check that the system and all its peripherals are operating correctly and that nothing needs to be replaced. Other than the general equipment check-ups, it is also important to test the VC connection with the remote site. While most sites in a judicial network have remote sites they often connect to (e. g. vulnerable witness rooms in the same building or local police stations/ prisons), VC systems are also used connect to a variety of remote sites, with different levels of VC technology and broadband capacity. Therefore, in particular for remote sites that are "new", tests should take place in advance of the main VC. This is even more important if the technological setup of the remote site is not fully known. If an interpreter is brought in from a third site using a three-way connection, this should also be tested thoroughly ahead of the proceeding.

Each institution should clarify the procedure for setting up and booking a VC, both in general and with additional provisions for the presence of an interpreter. All participants should know in advance that a video link will be used. The organisers should make sure that participants have received appropriate VC training before the proceeding takes place. It is particularly important for interpreters to know whether a video link will be used, as this can influence their location. Interpreters should be given the opportunity to liaise with the legal professional organising the VC to discuss their potential location and agree on the configuration to be used in the proceeding. Interpreters should also discuss formal procedures for the hearing with the legal professional conducting the session. These should include introductions, communication procedures, management of turn taking (e. g. length of speech turns, signals to request clarifications or pauses) and other topics which are mutually agreed to be relevant for the communicative management of the VC event.

Interpreters need to be fully briefed. This applies both at a general level (i. e. they should be informed that they will be interpreting via video link and they should have received VC training) and specifically as regards the proceeding during which they will be interpreting. At present there is still little consensus over whether interpreters should be briefed and what this briefing should include. Briefing interpreters is seen by many legal professionals as an unnecessary process which may jeopardise confidentiality and the interpreters' impartiality. However, interpreters should receive at least a minimal briefing on the purpose and content of the communicative situation, in order for them to prepare effectively for the topic to be discussed. This process of interpreter preparation is all the more important for interpreters working in legal settings, where mistakes can have a negative impact on the outcome of the proceedings. For this reason, interpreters working in legal VC settings should be provided with all relevant information covering at least the basic elements of the case and the communicative situation (i. e. number and location of participants, regional variety for the speaker for whom they will be interpreting, their age range and gender, any issues regarding speaker vulnerability, basic facts of the case, including the legal charge). In court proceedings, the type and number of documents and the nature of the information to be provided to interpreters is in principle a matter to be resolved between interpreter associations and the legal system. While the agreed quantity and nature of information may vary in different countries, it is important to come to an agreement outlining minimum standards of information interpreters can rely on for their work.

When there is no opportunity to brief the interpreter in advance or when additional information needs to be given to the interpreter prior to the start of the VC, this needs to be arranged regardless of whether the legal professional responsible for the briefing is co-located with the interpreter or not. In settings of remote interpreting, it is advisable for the legal professional to interact briefly with the interpreter before the proceedings start.

Professional interpreters are aware of confidentiality requirements, and it is part of their professionalism to maintain secrecy on the content of documentation and information which is entrusted to them for the purpose of their work. Therefore, if courts work with professional interpreters, issues of confidentiality should not arise. Language professionals (or the contracted company providing interpreting services) may enter in an agreement with the court that legally binds them to maintaining confidentiality regarding the documents received.

It is also important to emphasise that impartiality is not at risk when briefing an interpreter. Interpreters do not need to be given a full picture of the details of a proceeding, and need only factual information for their preparation outlining the basic elements of a proceeding.

For the same reason, interpreters should be given the opportunity of a brief interaction with the other-language speaker before the beginning of a VC to perform a language check. This needs to be arranged regardless of whether the interpreter is co-located with the other-language speaker or not. This enables the interpreter to ascertain the level of linguistic proficiency of the witness/defendant and get used to their accent/variety/tone of voice. Allowing the interpreter some contact with the other-language speaker also means that the interpreter can be used by the authority to deliver a brief VC induction to the witness/defendant. This enables the other-language speaker to understand how to communicate through the video link and get basic information on the organisation of the proceedings. It is the responsibility of the authority in charge of the proceedings to provide this induction, whose importance should not be overlooked.

If possible and appropriate, it would be beneficial to have a short de-briefing with the interpreter after the VC session to discuss any technological, organisational or interactional issues arising from the hearing. Other forms of feedback, which are potentially less time-consuming, are evaluation questionnaires open not only to interpreters, but to all participants. These can be completed in order to offer comments on the quality of the service and make suggestions for its improvement. This is particularly important during the first pilot project and/or the first phase of the full project. Any reported problems should be dealt with as soon as possible, and discussed with legal professionals, interpreters and technology providers as appropriate.

Summary

- Policy makers: An important part of a VC policy is the establishment of clear procedures for setting up and booking a VC. These should cover who is responsible for what actions, from the decision to use a VC to the booking of the required facilities/services, their delivery and management. It is fundamental to identify participants with the required knowledge and abilities, and make sure they are aware of their responsibilities. Additional provisions need to be outlined for VMI. Who will book the interpreter? What kind of briefing will the interpreter receive? What documents are they entitled to consult beforehand, and how are they going to be delivered? It is important to not underestimate the need to brief the interpreter, and to outline clear guidelines for legal professionals in this respect. Indeed, legal professionals often view briefing an interpreter as unnecessary and potentially harmful for their objectivity. However, interpreters need to be provided with basic information on the proceeding in order to prepare efficiently. A lack of preparation may lead to mistakes which can have serious consequences on the proceeding. Therefore, the interpreter's right to be briefed should be stated clearly in the procedural documents provided to judicial authorities, along with the documents that interpreters have a right to consult. In order to negotiate a list of such documents, you should consult both judicial authorities and interpreters' professional associations.

- **Legal professionals**: If your institution has produced procedural guidelines for VC, you should consult them to help you understand your duties and responsibilities in a VC. If you are organising the link, you may have to book facilities and services. Among them, you may have to request an interpreter. If you do, make sure the interpreter is fully briefed before attending the proceeding. It will be very helpful for the interpreter to receive basic information on the proceeding (e. g. the charge and other factual information) some days before the event or as much in advance as possible. The interpreter may also ask to see relevant documents, which should be provided. Professional interpreters are trained to maintain confidentiality. When the interpreter arrives on the day, make sure they get a few minutes for a language check. This is to ensure that the interpreter and the witness/ defendant can understand each other. If you want to make sure that the interpreter and the other-language speaker do not get into personal topics during the language check, direct their conversations. You can use this stage of the proceedings to brief the other-language speaker through the interpreter. During the briefing the interpreter will be able to notice any potential problems, and both the interpreter and the other-language speaker will get used to each other's accent, linguistic variety and tone of voice. If any problems arise at this stage, make sure they are resolved before the proceedings start. After the VC, ask the interpreter for feedback on the VC communication. If necessary, feed back any problems to those responsible for the VC system.

- **Interpreters**: As with any interpreting task, you will need to prepare for a VC. Make sure you know at least the basic subject of the hearing and some factual information. Ask for relevant documentation. If you find it is problematic to access the required information, make sure you bring this to the attention of the professional association you are part of. It is important to reach an agreement between interpreters and justice sector authorities on the minimum information you are entitled to. On the day, make sure you perform a language check with the other-language speaker regardless of whether you are co-located with him/her or not. If the authorities do not wish you to have any form of contact with the other-language speaker prior to the VC, explain to them why this is necessary. If they are concerned that this may skew your impartiality, propose that they direct the conversation. Encourage the authority to offer some basic information about the video link to the other language speaker. If there are any problems at this stage, ask for these to be resolved before the proceeding starts. After a VC, mention to the legal professional in charge of the VC any issues you may have experienced. Your feedback is important to improve the way video links are carried out.

7 Mode of Interpreting Highlights

- The decision on which mode of interpreting to use is related to (a) the equipment available, (b) the location of the interpreter, (c) legal provisions for recording legal proceeding and (d) the authority's own preferences.
- In most jurisdictions, proceedings that involve an interpreter use consecutive interpreting.
- The consecutive mode is advisable when the interpreter is located with the authority.
- When the interpreter is located with the other-language speaker,

whispered simultaneous interpreting can be used to render the utterances from the official language of the proceedings into the other-language speaker's language.

- If the interpreter work from a third location, the choice between modes is mostly dependent on whether the VC system enables simultaneous delivery.

- If the local legislation requires proceedings to be recorded, consecutive interpreting is a more appropriate choice to suit the legal requirements.

The decision on which mode of interpreting to use is closely related to the equipment available (specifically, to the presence of separate audio channels) and the location of the interpreter, as well as legal provisions on the recording of legal proceeding and the authority's own preferences.

In most jurisdictions, legal proceedings that involve an interpreter traditionally use consecutive interpreting (in which the interpreter's rendition follows the end of the speaker's turn). Simultaneous interpreting (in which the interpreter delivers their rendition at the same time as the speaker using special equipment such as a soundproof booth or a tour guide system) is a less frequent solution, mostly because the technical equipment is not available in courts and other justice sector institutions. However, whispered simultaneous interpreting is used in many countries to render the utterances of those speaking the official language into the language of the litigant, suspect, defendant or witness. At present, VC systems do not normally offer additional sound channels to enable remote simultaneous interpretation. However, this may be an option for the future (see also Ch. 4 VC Connection & Equipment).

At present, the location of the interpreter is an important factor in the choice of the interpreting mode in VCs. When the interpreter is co-located with the authority, normally their interpretation is delivered consecutively for both sites. A (whispered) simultaneous interpretation for the remotely located other-language speaker would create an undesirable overlap between the officials' speech delivery and the interpreter's rendition. In turn, this would result in unclear communication and the impossibility to hear/record the words of participants independent of the interpreter's voice. Therefore, the consecutive mode is the advisable standard in a setting where the interpreter is located with the authority.

By contrast, when located with the other-language speaker, it is possible for the interpreter to deliver the interpretation into that speaker's language using whispered simultaneous interpreting. However, the sound of whispering or speaking with a low voice is amplified when it is fed back through the microphone to the other site and can be disruptive. It is therefore advisable for the interpreter to mute his/her microphone while s/he is interpreting in order to prevent sound overlap at the main site. Using whispered simultaneous interpreting in this setting is advisable, as it speeds up the proceedings. However, the interpreter needs to have control over the muting function of their microphone. The other-language speaker's delivery is interpreted consecutively into the official language in this setting.

When the interpreter works from a separate location, the use of the simultaneous mode would require the addition of sound channels to the VC system. As pointed out in Ch. 4 VC Connection & Equipment, this is an option for the future, although it will require further testing and evaluation.

In all settings, legal provisions regarding the recording of the proceedings should be borne in mind. If the local legislation requires proceedings to be recorded, it is important that the recorded audio does not present significant overlaps. Consecutive interpreting is a more appropriate choice to suit the legal requirements.

Finally, individual justice sector institutions have different preferences on the mode of interpreting. Some prioritise the speed of proceedings, and therefore try to enable the interpreter to deliver simultaneously whenever possible. Others prefer to use the consecutive mode to allow their speakers to deliver without background noise and to maintain closer control over the communication. Ultimately, the most appropriate solution for a particular setting or case should be discussed and agreed with the interpreter prior to the VC session.

Summary

- Policy makers: In making arrangements for procurement and

implementation, you should find out which interpreting mode is more suitable for the requirements of your institution. You may find that legal professionals and interpreters prefer the flexibility of a VC system which enables both solutions, but you need to be aware that simultaneous interpreting is not possible in all configurations. Building a flexible system will require specialised equipment, such as additional audio channels. Also, bear in mind any legislative limitations to the use of the simultaneous mode—if your system requires hearings to be recorded, simultaneous interpreting may not be the solution for you.

- **Legal professionals**: The choice of interpreting mode is related to the available equipment and the distribution of the VC participants. Refer to this section for details on which configuration enables the consecutive and/or simultaneous modes. Involve the interpreter in the decision—it is possible that they may advise you to use a combination of interpreting modes, interpreting simultaneously in one direction and consecutively in the other. Each mode has advantages and drawbacks, so the choice will also depend on the factors you wish to prioritise. Whatever mode you settle on, make sure this is technically feasible and does not disturb communication among participants.

- **Interpreters**: Agree the interpreting mode with the legal professional in charge of the VC before the beginning of the hearing. The minimum agreed standard is usually the consecutive mode, but you may be required to deliver simultaneously as well. Offer your expertise as appropriate, taking into account your location during the hearing. You may wish to liaise with technicians to understand how the VC system can support you in your delivery.

- **Technicians**: Before the start of a VC-based proceeding, make sure you know how the interpreter intends to deliver his/her rendition. This will influence the equipment you need to make available, and you need to have this ready for a prompt start. If you think the intended interpreting solution cannot be adequately supported by the system, offer your expert opinion on this matter. It is better to have a clear approach from the start than having to rearrange equipment and settings during a proceeding.

8 VC Management Highlights

- VCs generally do not support the same level of contact and interaction between the participants as face-to-face communication, especially when the communication is mediated by an interpreter.
- Care should be taken to ensure that those involved in a VC as a party or witness feel that they are part of the proceedings and are able to clearly identify speakers and their roles.
- VCs should be set up so as to allow mutual visibility of all participants.
- The interpreter's location and visibility should be carefully considered. The interpreter should be visible regardless of the setting, unless this presents a risk for his/her security or that of the other-language speaker.
- VC cameras should be set up so as to capture the communicative dynamics of the proceedings and show at least the current speaker.
- Justice section institutions should assign a member of staff to the management of the VC equipment and instruct them to ensure the visibility of participants.

The management of a VC has several dimensions, i. e. spatial, technical and organisational, but it mainly refers to the layout of the rooms in which VC equipment is implemented and the participants' seating arrangements, which should both be carefully considered. The position of the screens and cameras, and the participants' positioning in relation to the equipment, will strongly influence the view of participants and the perception of the space. The pivotal criterion for implementing VC facilities should be mutual visibility of participant including the interpreter. In practice, this means that, when considering the design of a VC room, it is necessary to bear in mind three key points.

（1）As a general principle, all speakers including the interpreter should be made visible in turn, with the current speaker always being on camera. As the seating positions of the main participants are normally fixed (e. g. criminal courts have allocated spaces for judges, lawyers, prosecutors, defendants and witnesses), it is advisable to use pre-set camera positions in order to focus clearly on the different speakers as soon as they start talking. A pre-set should also be defined for the interpreter to ensure s/he can be made visible as soon as s/he takes the floor. Rotating cameras with a zoom function can be particularly helpful as they reduce the number of peripherals needed while still maintaining the ability to show different speakers. In addition to the various camera positions for individual speakers, a pre-set view should also show an overall picture of each VC site to give participants a general understanding of the environment.

Exceptions to the principle of being visible are cases where showing a participant or the interpreter would constitute a threat to their safety and security (e. g. where a witness's identity needs to be protected or where an interpreter belonging to a small minority-language community would potentially be recognisable by other members of the same community).

(2) As a complementary principle, participants at all sites should see the current speaker, with the exception of cases where being visible would pose a safety or security risk.

(3) All participants need to know what the participants at the other VC site(s) see. Therefore, it will be useful for the VC participants to have a self-view image (normally provided as a so-called picture-in-picture) during the VC to monitor how their own position with respect to the camera.

One particular aspect to consider in the spatial arrangements in bilingual VCs is that the position of the interpreter is not necessarily fixed. The following should be borne in mind for each configuration.

The interpreter is located at the main site: In this configuration, problems are likely to arise when there is no pre-defined location for the interpreter who, using the example of a court setting, may stand next to the judge, or share space with the lawyer/prosecutor in an ad hoc approach. This is likely to distort the perceptions of the interpreter's role and neutrality, and can therefore not be considered appropriate VC practice. It will be useful for the interpreter to occupy the place which would otherwise be assigned to the other-language speaker. This place should be equipped with all necessary VC peripherals. As pointed out above, the interpreter's place should also be included in the pre-set camera positions so that the interpreter can be shown to the remote participants when s/he is interpreting (consecutively). The interpreter's visibility for the remote participants is important as it is likely to improve the understanding of the interpreted content.

The interpreter is co-located with the other-language speaker: The seating arrangement at the remote site is often governed by what seems practicable. Especially when the remote site is a prison or police station, where the VC room is normally fairly small, the interpreter sits very close to the defendant, and all participants gathered at that site sit in a row facing the camera and the VC screen. However, this arrangement is unsuitable as it results in defendants being more inclined to turn their head towards the interpreter during the delivery of the interpreted turn, while authorities at the main site will normally want to have a clear view of the defendant's face at all times. Moreover, the seating arrangement in a row may give the impression that those present speak "with one voice". Therefore, it is more advisable to position the chairs for participants to sit at an angle. In rooms where the seating arrangement is pre-determined by the presence of chairs bolted to the floor, the angled position should be considered at the stage of implementation.

Although a court may require a close-up of the other-language speaker in order to see the detail of their facial expressions (e. g. when they are being asked questions or they are providing answers), this guide recommends that both the other-language speaker and the interpreter should be shown in the same shot. The camera in such small rooms should therefore be a wide-angle camera and should be equipped with a zoom function. In addition, the ability to rotate and show other parts of the room would also be useful to show further participants who are also present at the remote site (e. g. the defendant's lawyer).

The interpreter works from a third location and the main parties are also in separate locations (three-way video link): In this setting it is important for the interpreter to get a clear view of the two other sites in order to grasp quickly who is talking, observe possible reactions from the recipient(s) and maintain a rapport with all participants. All participants should be able to see the interpreter, who can be displayed as a picture-in-picture within the image of the other VC site.

The interpreter is the only participant working from a remote site ("remote interpreting"): In this setting the interpreter can be displayed on the screen and receive a either a general view of all participants or an individual view of each speaker at the other site. In this configuration, it is advisable that the speakers at the main site sit at an angle, in order for the interpreter to be able to see their faces (at least partly) while they interact with each other.

In all VMI settings the image displayed on the screen needs to focus on the current speaker and on following the evolution of the proceeding. Changing the camera view through the camera pre-sets for different speakers can be a complex task for proceedings with many participants, and it may not be undertaken effectively by participants tasked with other duties (e. g. the presiding judge or the interpreter). Courts should assign a member of staff to the management of the camera work. This staff member should be thoroughly briefed about the implications of camera choices on the communicative dynamics before undertaking this task. It is important to point out, however, that despite efforts to move cameras and select "optimal" images, VCs are still not normally perceived by participants to enable the same level of contact between the participants as traditional proceedings, especially when an interpreter is involved. Therefore, decisions should be made on a case-by-case basis to ensure that those participating in the proceedings as a remote party or witness feel that they are part of the proceedings as much as possible, and that they can clearly identify speakers and their roles.

For this purpose, the impression of eye contact should be created as far as possible with camera work. Apart from seeing the remote site, participants should also have access to a self-view image (also known as "picture-in-picture"), which can help them monitor their own position (especially at the beginning of the proceeding) and use the VC effectively. The self-view image is particularly important for the interpreter, who needs to be certain that their visual signals can be seen by those at the other VC site(s).

Summary

- Policy makers: It is important to consider that VCs do not currently support the same level of contact between the participants as face-to-face communication. This is particularly true in bilingual proceedings involving an interpreter. In light of this, it is important to consider what uses will be made of VC in your legal system, and carefully prepare appropriate legislation and guidelines which regulate the applicability of video links to different cases. These should outline minimum standards and specific criteria that need to be met if a proceeding is to take place via VC, and include specific provisions for the exclusion of proceedings or cases for which VC is considered inadequate.

- **Legal professionals**: If you consider using a video link, you should assure yourself that the type of communication your case entails. Consider the number of active participants, the appropriateness of the VC spaces and the available technology, the expected duration of the VC, the need for interpreting and any concerns that may make VC inappropriate. If the use of VC is appropriate for your case, make sure that the proceeding can support a good level of interaction between participants. Consider the interpreter's presence and liaise with them to make decisions on their location. From where will they attend the hearing? Is there any reason why it may be more appropriate for them to be with the remote participant(s)? Where will they be sitting? If you are chairing the hearing (but also if you are a lawyer/prosecutor), consider carefully the possible repercussions of the use of a VC on the quality of the evidence you will receive. You will not be able to interact with the person being heard as you would normally. The drawbacks of this may be magnified in interpreter-mediated proceedings, as the technological dimension adds distance to the linguistic barrier. In all VCs, make sure that the remote participant(s) can clearly identify speakers, and get a view of the current speaker at all times. Also, make sure that other-language speaker(s) get a view of the interpreter if they are not co-located. If needed, the interpreter can be shown in a picture-in-picture. You will need to assign a staff member to the management of cameras and to monitor the picture-in-picture. This person may be a court clerk or a technician. In either case, it is important for them to be trained in the use of VC equipment.

- **Interpreters**: If you are invited to interpret in a VC, make sure you know from which side you will attend, as this will impact on your ability to interact with other participants. If you believe that the arrangements that have been made for your attendance are not suitable for the case you have been asked to interpret for, notify the legal professional chairing the proceeding of your concerns as soon as possible, if you can. It is unprofessional to provide an interpreting service if you are not confident that the level of interaction you will get from the VC is sufficient for you to carry out your task to a high standard. When you are interpreting, make sure you maintain contact with the other-language speaker if you are not located with them. This helps build a better rapport, and it is very important as you are the only person the other-language speaker can directly relate to.

- **Technicians**: If you are tasked with setting up a room for VC purposes, take visibility as your main criterion for placing the equipment. The cameras you install need to show all potential speakers, and the screens need to be visible by all participants. If you have rotating cameras, ensure that the system is equipped with pre-sets covering the position of all potential speakers. Check with legal professionals where the interpreter usually sits, so you can store their location in the pre-sets, too.

9 Communication Management Highlights

- VC is useful for short proceedings involving a small number of participants.

- The responsibility for managing the flow of communication and interaction between participants in VC-based proceedings lies with the legal professional who is responsible for the proceedings.

- The interpreter is responsible for coordinating the communication and interaction only to the extent that this is necessary to ensure there is no loss of information.

- The legal professional in charge should agree communication procedures with the interpreter before the VC session starts.

- At the beginning of the VC the legal professional responsible for the proceedings should check that all participants can see/be seen and hear/be heard clearly, and should introduce all participants.

- All participants should be instructed to speak clearly, using clear and unambiguous language as far as possible.

- During the VC the legal professional in charge should take due care that all participants can contribute appropriately, irrespective of their location.

- Particular attention should be paid to the remote participant(s), who may also need guidance in the use of the video link.

- The interpreter should be given space and time to interpret and to carry out his/her task effectively.

The present chapter focuses on the management of the flow of communication and interaction between the participants in a VC. This includes actions to coordinate the turn-taking between the different speakers, to resolve overlapping speech and to mitigate the feeling of distance between the participants in different locations. Effective communication management is important in bilingual VCs to ensure that all participants, and especially the remote participants, have the opportunity to contribute appropriately to the proceedings and that the interpreter is given adequate time and space to perform his/her role effectively.

As a general point it should be noted that VC is useful for communication of a short duration and involving a small group of participants. In the case of longer proceedings (e. g. a witness hearing that is expected to last for several hours), it will normally more effective to gather all participants in the same place, as long VCs can be tiring. Moreover, VCs involving larger groups of participants (e. g. several defendants) are more complex in terms of communication management, and this may result in communication difficulties. This applies especially to bilingual VCs, where the linguistic mediation through an interpreter adds a further layer of complexity.

Given the communicative challenges inherent in VCs in bilingual legal proceedings, it is crucial that a legal professional is in charge of managing the communicative flow and the interaction between the participants in the VC session at all times. This should normally be the legal professional who is in charge of the proceedings, i. e. in court the presiding judge, and at the police the officer in charge of an interview or a custody review. The different aspects of VC communication management are outlined below.

At the beginning of the VC, the legal professional in charge should check that all participants can see/be seen and hear/be heard clearly. This can be done through a microphone test or by carrying out preliminary introductions. The legal professional in charge of the communication is also responsible for introducing the participants at the different sites, making sure that the identity of those attending is clear to all people involved in the VC. In court hearings involving a remote participant, for example, it is important that the remote participant understands who is present in court and in what capacity. Participants may be introduced directly by the judge or officer in charge or may be invited to identify themselves. The camera management should match the introduction, so that the people who are being introduced can be clearly seen at the other site(s).

Another important aspect to check at the beginning of the VC and to monitor continuously is that all participants can contribute appropriately, irrespective of their location. Particular attention should be paid to the remote participant and to the interpreter. The physical separation of the participants in a VC can make it difficult to assess a remote participant's behaviour. For example, a remote participant's signal indicating that s/he wishes to ask a question or further elaborate on his/her answer may not be picked up easily at the main site. Similarly, a remote interpreter's request to intervene, e. g. to ask for clarification, may not be obvious. Remote participants and interpreters therefore need to be monitored closely. For example, it is important to monitor the other VC site(s) visually and to ensure that the sound from the remote site(s) is loud enough to pick up all the details even in a situation of background noise.

Participants may require guidance in the use of the video link: Legal professionals and legal interpreters working in VCs should receive systematic training in bilingual VC communication. Individuals who participate in legal proceedings as litigant, accused, suspect, defendant or witness and who are not used to communicating via video link require careful management and help during the VC to mitigate a potentially stressful situation. If the proceedings involve VMI, this is likely to present an additional source of stress and vulnerability, especially for participants who are not used to communicating through an interpreter. They may find it difficult to be coherent in their speech, to adapt to speaking in short "chunks" and to pause for the interpreter as appropriate. It is therefore recommended that other-language speakers are carefully briefed on the use of a video link involving an interpreter. The person in charge of the communication should agree with them appropriate signals (e. g. start, stop, required intervention) and monitor their behaviour closely. If necessary, other-language speakers should be explicitly allocated the floor to make sure they can contribute or directed to pause to make sure their utterances can be rendered by the interpreter.

Communication procedures should be agreed with the interpreter before the VC session starts: These procedures should clarify, for example, how long speech turns should normally be, how the interpreter will intervene for clarification, how they will ask speakers to pause and if/when there will be breaks for the interpreter. The level of involvement of the interpreter in the management of communication should also be discussed. The interpreter should be responsible for coordinating the communicative flow only to the extent that this is necessary to ensure that there is no loss of information or distortion. The interpreter may therefore need to ask for repetition or clarification. However, the interpreter should not be in charge of the overall communication flow, as this task is not compatible with their role of linguistic mediation. It is the legal professional in charge of the VC who should try to prevent or quickly resolve overlapping speech, and who should remember to pause—and encourage others to pause—regularly for the interpreter. Furthermore, the interpreter may need to have breaks during long proceedings (i. e. over 2 hours). The interpreter's request for a break should be respected to ensure that the quality of the interpretation is maintained to a high standard and does not suffer from the interpreter's fatigue.

All participants should be instructed to speak clearly, but without raising their voice unduly, using unambiguous language as far as possible. Disturbing noises, such as tapping the desk near a microphone, should also be avoided, and any such disturbances should be brought to the attention of the person in charge at the earliest opportunity. The legal professional presiding over the proceedings should take charge of explaining any problem arising to the participants.

Summary

- Legal professionals: In any proceeding in which you use a VC, make sure that it is clear to all who is in charge of managing the communicative flow. Ideally, this should be the person of highest authority in the room. Managing the communicative flow means making sure that all participants can hear/be heard and see/be seen, and that they have adequate space to intervene in the proceeding as appropriate to their role. Therefore, if you are in charge of the proceedings and hence the communication flow, you should check that the audio and video quality is appropriate for the event, and you should make sure that participants are aware of each other's position and role in the proceeding. Carry out introductions as appropriate—this will help you perform the audio/video check and provide participants with important information at the same time. Brief the remote participant (s) on how the VC session will proceed including how the floor will be allocated to the participants. Individuals involved in legal proceedings are unlikely to be expert users of VC technology, and any information you can give them on how to use the equipment and what they can expect of a VC will be useful to them. Remember that you will need to impose a certain communicative order on the event，so that overlapping speech is avoided and everyone at both sites has a clear understanding of what is being said. While this also applies to a traditional proceeding，the importance of clear speech with no overlaps is increased by the physical separation involved in a VC. Also，make sure the interpreter gets adequate space for intervention，and that the turns they need to render into the other language are not too long. You should coordinate with the interpreter for this purpose，and agree signals you can use to interact with each other prior to the beginning of the VC. If you expect the proceeding to be longer than two hours，discuss with the interpreter the possibility of a break，and remember to provide it at the right time.

• Interpreters：Before the beginning of a VC，discuss with the person in charge of the proceeding how you will interact with them and the other participants during the proceeding. You should agree signals to indicate that a speaker should pause or repeat their utterance，or that you need to clarify parts of the message. Based on the expected length of the proceeding，discuss whether you think you will need a break and how you will request it. Remember that you are not in charge of the overall communication flow，and that your interventions should be limited to those required to perform your task in the VC situation.

10　Further Support and Training

All professionals taking part in VCs should receive an induction to VC. Given the increase in legal proceedings requiring the services of an interpreter，such training should also cover bilingual videoconferencing. The training will increase their understanding of VC as a tool for communication and will help them to evaluate the appropriateness (or otherwise) of using VC in a particular proceeding. Professionals should be trained to develop an understanding of：

　　—the key concepts relating to VC as a tool for distance communication；

—the different configurations of participant distribution;

—the rationale for using VC (in different configurations) in legal proceedings;

—the scope of application of VC in their legal system;

—the legal provisions that apply to the use of video links;

—the (current) differences between the uses of VC at national and cross-border level;

—the affordances and limitations of (bilingual) VC communication;

—the basic principles of (bilingual) communication in a VC.

This training can be conducted face-to-face, or—as we have shown in several training pilots in AVIDICUS3—the medium of VC itself can be used for delivery.

Regardless of how the training is delivered, training sessions should encourage the active participation of those attending through hands-on tasks. Participants should be made to interact with others through the VC equipment in simulations, i. e. with practical activities such as role plays. In order to organise realistic role plays, different groups of stakeholders should be trained together in their respective roles. If possible, technical staff should also attend joint training sessions in order to familiarise themselves with the legal professionals' and interpreters' needs while developing confidence in the use of the equipment. Joint training allows potential VC participants to increase awareness of their respective professional needs and will enable them to develop common approaches to the resolution of difficulties and conflicting needs.

Apart from covering the different configurations of VC outlined in this handbook, the training should also include different modes of interpreting to enable the participants, for example, to compare the affordances and limitations of consecutive and simultaneous delivery, and to learn how to pace their speech to cooperate efficiently with the interpreter. At the end of a training session, actual performance should be discussed against expected standards, thus encouraging discussion of the difficulties encountered, the techniques that can be used to overcome them and opportunities for further improvement. Participants should be encouraged to reflect upon their performance in the simulation, seek feedback from others and discuss the strengths and weaknesses of different configurations. The discussion should be based on observations from the role-plays, but moderators/trainers should also encourage participants to discuss other aspects that may arise.

A summary of the group discussion, along with general guidelines for the use of VC, should be circulated to all participants after each session as material for their own personal reflection. The guidance provided in this handbook is intended to be both a starting point for training and material for further self-study.